I0806784

Time Will Tell

Collected Poems

David Middleton

Printed in the United States of America

FIRST EDITION, 2025

Cover design by Cody Gates, Happenstance Type-O-Rama

Cover art painting, "North Louisiana Country Scene" (1977) by David V. Middleton Jr. (1922-1996), oil on panel, photographed by Deborah Lillie, Department of Art, Nicholls State University, Thibodaux, Louisiana

Library of Congress Cataloging-in-Publication Data

Names: Middleton, David, 1949- author.
Title: Time will tell : the collected poems of David Middleton / David Middleton.
Other titles: Sabine series in literature.
Description: First edition. | Huntsville, Texas : TRP: The University Press of SHSU, [2025] | Series: The Sabine series in literature
Identifiers: LCCN 2024027007 (print) | LCCN 2024027008 (ebook) | ISBN 9781680033700 (cloth) | ISBN 9781680033687 (trade paperback) | ISBN 9781680033694 (ebook)
Subjects: LCGFT: Poetry.
Classification: LCC PS3563.I362 T56 2025 (print) | LCC PS3563.I362 (ebook) | DDC 811/.54--dc23/eng/20240624
LC record available at https://lccn.loc.gov/2024027007
LC ebook record available at https://lccn.loc.gov/2024027008

Praise for David Middleton

"What has long intrigued me about Middleton's work as a poet is how humble it is regarding its own authority. The poems make their agrarian indictments of modernity. They look with reverence on the South's past, even as they confess its sins and know the resultant condition has proven tragic. They relish the possibility of verse to speak clearly and in an elevated but natural diction in iambic measures . . . Now, as that work approaches its end, it is time to discover the major poet who has lived among us, surveying the natural and spiritual terrain of the cosmos within the sacramental, flowering figure of Louisiana."

—James Matthew Wilson, *The Catholic World Report*

"David Middleton provides a novice with an excellent means of learning to read contemporary poetry. The meaning of his verse is not obscured by tortuous syntax, esoteric diction, or erudite allusion. He does not dazzle his reader with figurative pyrotechnics or lavishly contrived labyrinths of imagery. As a result, his work may appear deceptively simple . . . But read again, and yet again, and the rhythm and the verbal music of the verse will reveal more and more the beauty and subtlety of his carefully modulated language."

—R. V. Young, *Touchstone: A Journal of Mere Christianity*

Praise for *Outside the Gates of Eden*

"For several decades early in the last century, the writers of the American South published some of our most important literature—works of religious seriousness, historical scope, traditional reverence, moral reckoning, and formal dexterity. The heirs to such achievements have been few. David Middleton is one of the best among them. In his few but distinguished books, he has again and again brought us poems where the profound beauty of meter joins with the high themes of human life, where rootedness in place is joined with metaphysical vision. He is surely one of the finest living poets of the American South and a poet destined long to be read by everyone with an ear for music and an eye for classical precision."

—James Matthew Wilson

"David Middleton develops in this new volume major panels of his vision. Announced by his title, the Judeo-Christian tradition underpins the whole. Among other sources of inspiration are the classics, nature, great Southern figures, and twentieth-century rural and small-town South, treated with deep reverence and sentiment. Graphic art, one of Middleton's longtime concerns, provides material for many fine poems, generally ekphrastic and based on work by Poussin, Constable, and Millet. Fittingly, death must occupy a place. "The Potter's Epitaph" joins the two themes, death and art, strikingly. The poet's moving word-pictures illustrate his sweeping vision, pastoral but, of necessity, reflecting the flawed human condition, broken after Eden."

—Catharine Savage Brosman

"In the time and distance between Grecian lindens and Louisiana oaks, there are few gates that David Middleton cannot peer through in his search for meaning in the poetry of earthly life, with its mythologies, histories, paintings, fellow poets, and landscapes. His observations in *Outside the Gates of Eden* are told and revealed with the highest poetic craft and art."

—John P. Doucet

"These beautifully structured poems show . . . contrasts between life now and that of the once-perfect Eden. All are elegant, stately, and carefully constructed. Middleton's well-chiseled poetry, centered on what 'Eden' means, captures brilliantly many elements of life—its challenges, loves, austerities, and wisdom—in such a way that clearly elevates Middleton to the position of one of the most important American poets alive today."

—Olivia Pass

"Vibrating with the fathomless question of human being, these poems pay homage to all that mends our minds and souls as we wander the world, exiles of an ever-remembered Eden. Erudite without being oblique, written in measures and yet bursting with primordial verve, Middleton's verse partakes of the great, centuries-old conversation while wrestling new yields from its words and the Word."

—Joshua Hren

"At once quietly perceptive and cosmically directed, Middleton's poems unfold the ontologic mystery of existence, even as they remind us of God's immediacy in our revealed creation."

—Emma Mason, *Dappled Things*

Praise for *The Fiddler of Driskill Hill*

"'To be national in literature,' wrote William Gilmore Simms, 'one must needs be sectional.' Middleton's finely crafted, almost classical poems, grounded in the English poetic tradition, allow him to 'defend and illustrate' the genius loci of Louisiana in its human and topographical variety and its deep historical and cultural meaning. Through this close attention to people, locales, and seasons, his writing underlines broad truths and demonstrates that what the collection calls 'the rhythms of poiesis and this place' are those of human life in general. Middleton's contributions to American poetry cannot be doubted."

—Catharine Savage Brosman

"David Middleton commands contemporary poetry with a Proustian imagination, and he is surely one of Mnemosyne's brightest descendants making poems in the world today. In *The Fiddler of Driskill Hill* this master poet reminds us that remembering still can be a sacred act, that each thing we call a poem is a sacred vessel, and that the poet descended into mindful remembering acquires a voice that is itself descended from the sacred. *The Fiddler of Driskill Hill* expands history and love poem and hymn to include the experiences and the memories of a poet who knows the music of the line and the song of the poem as few other working poets do."

—Darrell Bourque

Praise for *The Habitual Peacefulness of Gruchy*

"A powerful representation, in the music of vowels and consonants, of Millet's work . . . A major and memorable accomplishment."

—George Garrett

"A highly original and beautiful poetic sequence that translates into verbal terms not merely Millet's nineteenth-century world but the art itself, its lighting and shaping, its vision."

—Catharine Savage Brosman

"Middleton's empathies seem almost commensurate with those of the great painter and this book of poems, read alone or in companionship with the art, sounds a music that seems to rise from the earth that Millet embraced."

—Fred Chappell

"Both Millet's art and Middleton's poetry are immensely enriched by the intermingling of the two sensibilities. It is a remarkable experience to share this deliberate immersion in the sensibility of another, and a masterly achievement of Middleton's art."

—Helen Pinkerton Trimpi

"My favorite ekphrastic poems . . . Middleton usually begins with descriptions of [Jean-François Millet's] paintings, moving from foreground to background or from background to foreground, drawing our attention to significant yet easily missed details. From there he proceeds, often in the third or fourth stanzas, to possible allusions and to thematic reflections. . . . Middleton's poems helped me not only think about these paintings . . . in a deeper way. They helped me think *feelingly* about them. They drew me into a contemplative mood."

—Steven Knepper, *Dappled Things*

"Except for David Middleton, I can name no other contemporary poet whose work I would choose to describe as stately. In his case, this rare quality is achieved through technical mastery, devoted labor, judicious sympathy, and loving contemplation. *The Fiddler of Driskill Hill* is the best work to date, a splendid achievement in its every aspect. There is variety in plenty in the pages—speakers and stories from times past and present, folktales, tributes to personages who do not often receive tributes—but this variety is made harmonious by the power of a vision both equable and passionate. Here is poetry for the ages."

—Fred Chappell

Praise for *Beyond the Chandeleurs*

"Pervaded by a profound Christian sensibility and controlled by a highly disciplined respect for the poetic craft, the poems in *Beyond the Chandeleurs* are a series of remarkably evocative meditations on the mystery of God revealed to the poet in his relationships with persons, contemporary and historical—his parents, his grandparents, a Sunday school teacher, the yeoman farmers of north Louisiana; in his experience of places and events—visiting Oak Alley Plantation, studying the battle of Franklin, Tennessee, in 1864, making a journey to appear at a literary conference; and in his experience of the natural world and its creatures as they exist in his native Louisiana—"Azaleas in Epiphany," "Blue Herons," "Beyond the Chandeleurs." A celebration of the reality of the mystery of God in the face of the amorality of the "post-Christian age," *Beyond the Chandeleurs* may appropriately be called the work of a latter-day psalmist."

—Lewis P. Simpson

"David Middleton's powerful poetic imagination, rooted in Louisiana's history and its soils and waters—small towns, tilled fields, piney woods, hardwood forests, swamps, bayous—evokes familiar, circumscribed human dramas of love, joy, illness, and death in their social and natural settings, and at the same time reaches out to read the eloquent testimony of the stars, as they bear witness to the divine, universal Presence. His broad, sympathetic vision and the sense of order it implies are supported throughout by his seasoned command of formal verse. This new collection makes it clear that Middleton is among the most accomplished of southern poets now writing and the preeminent voice of Louisiana in verse today."

—Catharine Savage Brosman

"Bravely and independently, David Middleton walks his own way, making poems of great clarity and distinction, poems rooted in his faith, his sense of history, and his love for people and the natural world. *Beyond the Chandeleurs* proves him a poet of increasing depth and heightening stature. Readers will cherish his work, provided they care for tradition, accomplished music, and formal excellence."

—X. J. Kennedy

"David Middleton's densely wrought poetry demands the kind of close attention that most poets of our time do not ask. He rewards such attention with an original perspective and a searching meditative exploration of contemporary experience. He has sought to be among the 'seekers who would bring to what they find / A loving objectivity of mind.' His loving objectivity makes his poetry a unique and compelling achievement."

—Helen Trimpi

Praise for *The Burning Fields*

"*The Burning Fields* has recovered for us the unfailing poetic theme, God and the mysteries of his creation. Fire destroys, but burning sugarcane stalks makes way for another crop and life. There is little abstract language here. Middleton's muse repeats in high clarity and blood feeling those cooperating opposites by means of which we display God's secret intentions. Quite properly this poet's Christian world is placed not in the Copernican but in the Ptolemaic order. David Middleton's poetry is a fresh and authoritative southern voice."

—Andrew Lytle

"I have known and admired the poetry of David Middleton for close to fifteen years. His theme is the recovery from the subjective mind. The recovery takes the form of orthodoxy in religion and traditional forms in literature, but these forms are not mere repetitions of the past. They are means by which Middleton can sharpen and illuminate his experience. Middleton does not believe in formalism for the sake of formalism. He adds a new edge to the leaf. He is one of the most important poets to come out of the South, or anywhere else for that matter."

—John Finlay

Time Will Tell

Collected Poems

In Gratitude for Encouragement, Guidance, and Support Over Many Years

My late parents, David V. Middleton, Jr., educator and artist, and Anna Sudduth Middleton, homemaker

Francine Anne Kerne Middleton, wife, mother, companion, friend, librarian, artist, scholar

My daughter Anna Middleton Conrad, art historian, and my son-in-law, Dr. Joseph Locke Conrad, professor of forestry

Donald E. Stanford, Lewis P. Simpson, Andrew Lytle, and George Core, editors of *The Southern Review* and *The Sewanee Review*, literary quarterlies in which many of my poems appeared as well as William Thompson, editor of *Alabama Literary Review*, a literary annual, and the supporter not only of my own poetry but of the poetry and prose of Alabama writer John Martin Finlay (1941-1991) for whom I have served as literary executor since 1990

The publishers of my books and chapbooks: Robert L Barth, Louisiana State University Press, The Cummington Press [Harry Duncan], Blue Heron Press, Louisiana Literature Press, Measure Press, and TRP: The University Press of SHSU

Fellow poets and lifelong friends Lindon Stall and John Finlay

and

John P. Doucet, colleague, poet, playwright, scientist, administrator, and invaluable assistant in literary matters

There is neither speech nor language; but their voices are heard among them.

Ps. 19:3

He telleth the number of the stars; he calleth them all by their names.

Ps. 147:4

The Wonder Clock involves this cyclical, recurring experience of the old, familiar things day in and day out, from the preparation of breakfast to the tucking of children in bed—a repetition of daily activities that never results in boredom, jadedness, or world-weariness. These old things that intoxicate and nourish are the permanent, lasting sources of joy and wonder that inhere in work and play which honor nature's laws and God's design. . . . There is the poetry of the home in *The Wonder Clock* that elevates humble work and domestic life, transforming the honest toil and simple, innocent pleasures of the home into glimpses of heavenly peace and reminders of Eden.

Mitchell Kalpakgian (2006)

We are still in Eden; the wall that shuts us out of the garden is our own ignorance and folly.

Thomas Cole, "Essay on American Scenery" (1836)

TABLE OF CONTENTS

THE FIDDLER OF DRISKILL HILL (2013)

THE DWELLING PLACE (2003-2013; 2022)

OUTSIDE THE GATES OF EDEN (2023)

SELECTED NEW, UNCOLLECTED, AND PREVIOUSLY UNPUBLISHED POEMS (1973-2023)

FOREWORD

The Striking of the Lyre: Demodokos in Modernity

A Statement on Poetics

When, in *The Odyssey*, we first behold Odysseus, he is weeping on the shore of Kalypso's isle, gazing over the waves toward Penelope and home and thus toward his intended human place and fate—not as divine consort to a goddess nor yet as a shade in Hades, nor as one of Circe's herd—but as ruler of far-off Ithaca, an island realm in the middle world washed by the middle sea.

But then, set free by the will of Zeus, Odysseus with Kalypso's own strong olive-handled ax, fashions a raft out of the felled black poplar and alder trunks, a raft that takes him over the turbulent waters until it breaks apart—and floating for two long days upon a single beam, at last from atop a rising wave he has an "unexpected glimpse of wooded land" and then is swept away onto the rocky shores of remote Phaiakia to whose untroubled people the gods still show themselves without disguise.

Guarding his identity, Odysseus comes as a nameless stranger to the palace of Alkinoos near which lie perfect gardens with their "orderly rows of greens, all kinds . . . lush through the seasons" and orchards of pomegranates, apples, figs, and pears whose fruit is exhausted or spoiled "neither in wintertime nor summer." And in this pastoral kingdom Odysseus hears the bard Demodokos sing twice to his fine "clear lyre" of Odysseus' own role in the Trojan War, including the final ruse of the wooden horse.

In response to the powerful singing, this "stranger"—whose own great exploits have been thus traumatically revealed in the rhythms and in the words of measured verse—first seeks privacy by hiding his head under his purple mantle, yet then uncovers, and, by pure compulsion, publicly weeps: "tears running down his face before the Phaiakians." And when Demodokos pauses, Odysseus—who soon after such singing will at last risk revealing his identity to his host—once again "would take the mantle away from his head, and wipe the tears off, and taking up a two-handed goblet would pour a libation to the gods." And so this crafty hero, who wept for the return to his full humanity on the sands of Kalypso's isle, now weeps from the depths of his being at poetry's shattering revelation of who he is.

This profound effect of poetry on a hero both modern and archaic is among the most compelling evidence we have that our greatest verse and the mystery of human existence are at one. And there are other clues. Keats, for instance, in his search for ideal disinterestedness, named Socrates and Jesus as the only persons in history who attained to such a state, though their teachings were taken down—perhaps in necessary accordance with this ideal—only by others. Yet what do we find when we examine the final acts of these two figures who so readily stand as symbols of the two great strains in the Western tradition—the Greco-Roman and the Judeo-Christian?

Awaiting death in his cell, Socrates turned Aesop's *Fables* and the *Prelude to Apollo* into verse because his daimon had said for him to "practice and cultivate the arts," and fearing now that not philosophy but poiesis was intended, Socrates says: "I thought it would be safer not to take my departure before I had cleared my conscience by writing poetry and so obeying the dream." Likewise, on the cross, before the final cry that escapes him with his spirit, Christ, according to Matthew, utters his last words in the poetry of the Psalms: ("*Eli, Eli, lama sabachthani?*" Psalm 22:1). Even Plato, whose life and thought link Socrates and Jesus, declared on his deathbed, by the slightest gesture, the *differentia specifica* of verse: "Plato died at the age of eighty-one. On the evening of his death he had a Thracian girl play the flute to him. The girl could not find the beat of the *nomos*. With a movement of his finger, Plato indicated to her the Measure" (Eric Voegelin).

The origin of measured verse is lost in prehistory. But it seems reasonable to suppose that, in some long defining moment, primitive man awoke from animal sleep and so was struck with wonder and with terror at the beauty and the mystery of a world in which he seemed fated to dwell as a being on the verge, placed in a middle station somewhere above the flora and the fauna and the elements, yet well below divine powers obscurely apprehended. The cycling of the seasons, the progress of the stars, the rhythms of the body and the stages of human life—such things must have drawn forth from out of the depths a first measured response to consciousness both in music and in words. Perhaps at last man recognized a strange power in language that led him to think of the Maker's power as a language in itself, an attribute of deity, as in the Book of Genesis, where, in God's own mind, the *word* "light" somehow came before and helped to give existence to the *thing* called "light": "And God *said*, 'Let there be light'; and there *was* light" (Genesis 1:3).

The story of Adam the Namer, who spoke to the answering beasts before the Fall, and the story of the Fall itself as involving disruption—not only between human beings and the other creatures and between language and things but even between words and the very Word itself—may be archaic indicators that poetry lies at the center of human life and remains the one power by which man might still return from his long sojourn through history to a realm where Edenic innocence and conscious existence, both in time and beyond time, are reconciled at last.

Such reconciliation may be symbolized by Homer's bard Demodokos, who sang of the fall of Troy amid the gardens and the orchards of Alkinoos' pastoral kingdom. And indeed, it is King Alkinoos himself, who, in one of the most remarkable passages in *The Odyssey*, encourages Odysseus, so profoundly stirred by Demodokos' song, to transform himself from listener into poet not only to tell his own story but also to say why he weeps at tragic history, for such history, says the king, is not the final end but rather a godly gift for a further, sublime purpose: "Explain to us also what secret sorrow makes you weep as you listen to the tragic story of the Argives and the fall of Troy. Were not the gods responsible for that, weaving catastrophe into the pattern of events to make a song for future generations?"

And to this may we not add that as long as human beings continue to ask those two primary philosophical questions—Why is there a universe instead of nothing and Why is that universe as it is and not otherwise?—poets will try to write what Wallace Stevens called the "central poem," a poem in which the poet attempts the great return from the fallen world to the Bible's *peaceable kingdom* (Isaiah 11: 1-9). Such poets will glimpse what Jacques Maritain calls "the radiance of the ontological mystery," and, like Caedmon, the cowherd poet and symbolic initiator of the English poetic tradition, they will "Sing about the Creation." And should the authors of these poems ever close the circle of being—if such an act be possible and allowed—then, like Adam the Namer, they and we may commune once more with all those things which, even now, as the Psalmist says, mysteriously converse among themselves: "Day to day pours forth speech, and night to night declares knowledge . . . There is no speech . . . yet their voice goes out through all the earth and their words to the end of the world" (Psalm 19: 2-4).

To all such poets who attempt the "central poem" should go the praise Odysseus himself bestows upon the Phaiakian: "No one on earth can help honoring and respecting the bards, for the Muse has taught them the art of song and she loves the minstrel fraternity."

So the doer of great deeds pays homage to one of those through whom such deeds live on, Demodokos, whose measured verse was chanted to the striking of the lyre.

David Middleton

Time Will Tell

THE BURNING FIELDS

(1991)

Provincial Letter

No question unresolved at the Sorbonne
Is alien to a small-town southern lawn.
Eyes bleared with reading Plato and Plotinus
Grow sharp as I edge around the dunged hibiscus
Whose sifted scents drift downward from the sun.
As much as Eden, Kew, or Babylon,
This tended place engages with a Mind
Whose processes play over it as a blind
Man traces a face he cannot guess,
Detecting fleshless form within the flesh.

Though natural life and death could be enough,
Oxalis springing pink, wild mustard tufts,
Summer's onionflowers, the autumn buttonweed,
Yews greening as the winter sleeps in seed,
These generated grains, the source's spores,
Are counters to the Mind they play before:
Mute origin of all, superlative degree,
The cause of cause whose end these ends decree.
O may a mind immured in bone and brain
Find end as meet as this Your world contains.

I. THE SOUTH

The Vision

for my maternal grandmother, d. 1962, Saline, Louisiana

It had been far too long since you had said
"Remember me," the southern covenant,
When in a troubled sleep I stood again
Before the lonely house in which you died
Some twenty years ago, your weak heart broken
By the relentless heat of sixty green Julys.
Beyond fine sands blowing their ghostly roads
Through North Louisiana's pinewood hills,
I saw the pale boards brighten in the sun,
The white and pink oxalis lining the walk
Where bold moss-roses welcomed back the day
And long melancholy summer afternoons
Woke up the four-o'clocks to watch them fade
Into the primrose evening. There, where you lay
With pills and pistol ready by the bed
Listening to sweetgums whisper in the fields

And bobwhites call aloud their human name,
One night, as you had prayed, you died in sleep
And took your place among the Sudduth graves
Made fragrant by your dignity and grace.
Now you had come: no dream within a dream
But luminous and true, radiant as a source,
Shelling your purple peas, rocking on the porch,
Letting the perfect knowledge of your face
Release me in the calmest depths of love.
You dressed in cotton lavender, of course,
But in a modern style, your spirit's mild
Contempt for time, so quietly expressed.
We did not go inside the darkened rooms
Whose figures moved through half-remembered scenes,
But with your softly wrinkled arm about me
We slowly circled round the house and yard
Seeing each thing as what it fully was,
The old pecan cocooned in dry June skies,
Crepe myrtle great with bees and dragonflies—
Measureless wells, pellucid in their noons!
No fantasy's compensatory lie
Or image drawn at random from the flow,
You were the angel summoned up in pain
That innocence might walk upon the earth's
Envisioned ground, by memory sustained.
At last our circle closed, but as you stopped
And I awoke to consciousness and tears,
You said, "It'll be all right," words whose truth
Is all we crave, the voice of providence.
You sat back down beside your peas and flowers,
Smiling, talking, laughing, singing aloud
But to yourself alone, there, where you wait
And think of me until I too can go
Into the only world the heart would ever know.

The Patriarch

for my grandfather, H.E.S., d. 1959, Saline, Louisiana

So near the unscreened porch's rotted edge
You stood alone, as always, unafraid.
Breathless, speechless, trembling on your cane
You stared ahead at nothing as the rain
Slashed across exhausted winter fields. But though
Your country sense and self-wrought classic mind
Told you one more stroke would be the end,
Like the yard's half-frozen asters you held on

Beyond the private self's demise, sustained
By public forms your life had realized.

Like you, the land was old, rugged bluffs
Whose rivers drained the wrinkled pinewood hills.
Blue clay, limestone, silt, the fossiled marl
Printed with whalebones, figs, and mastodons—
These weighed on sandy gravels of the Drift.
Even further down, an ancient basin lay,
Floor of the inland sea. Below it all,
Dead echoes of Jehovah's virgin word
Heard when you woke to taste in nightmare sweat
Its prehistoric salt, the Gulf's archaic bed.

Born between the Old South and the New,
You fought against the elegiac life.
But on an April evening when the wind drew
The bruised magnolias' fetid-fragrant scent
Over your slave-made desk, in Freeman's *Lee*
You'd feel it all again: the early victories,
Too easy, incomplete, the West ignored,
And then a smoky dusk through which there rode
As softly as the heartbeat's softest thud
The ghost of Stonewall slumping in his blood.

That was your native ground: for when you "saved
Democracy" in the greater world's Great War,
You met each German charge as though you held
Cold Harbor, your pounded doughboys not Yanks
But Hill's Third Corps at Petersburg, entrenched
Along the Marne. Later, as an ace, you saw
The blackened parishes of France, statues
Of the Virgin burning in No-Man's-Land
As in the Wilderness whose wounded spoke
In cindered limbs the long dead tongues of flame.

Back home you tried to live the civic life.
Yet even when as mayor you spoke each fall
Your ode on Flanders Field, below the drying
Courthouse oaks an orange-poppied fire
Spreading from Troy to Columbia, in your mind,
Troubled the busts of Jefferson and Lee.
At night you read *The Georgics* and you dreamed
Of that established land. But you were here,
A Trojan ghost plowing through Priam's dust,
The salted plots Aeneas left behind.

Warden, deacon, lector—on Sundays you knelt
By the clear window. Outside, a rare bloodroot

And common roadside mallows stained the glass.
Here eighty years ago, stabled in the nave,
Union horses stamped in dung when brevet
Majors testing new repeaters and their nerve,
Pane by pane shot out The Kneeling Kings.
Shattered by that light, you read the lesson
Telling of a prince estranged from God by wealth
And foreign wives—poppies of Solomon!

Beyond the narthex-porch on which the sun
Still rose and set as it had always done,
You seemed a steward of the middle world.
Tomatoes, melons, beans, potatoes, corn
Raised by the posted roads of time and space—
These grew up to the house, familiar forms
To those raised eyes that found in the planted night
Appearances created and prepared,
Things in place, the flowering roots of light,
The constellations that were truly there.

That was your South, a many-layered tract
Of mind and soil, its tragic past made whole
By providential guilt and true defeat.
But with the last wild dogwoods rooted out
From cash-crop pine, you knew you'd lived too long,
A pastoral patriarch who winced
At sonic booms and heard B-52s
Droning over the Drift in lethal dreams
Of Eden as a paradise of power,
The massive Appomattox of the earth.

The house you built and died in long since sold,
Today across the acres kept so well
Lie oily guts of disassembled cars
Disfiguring that domain. And yet between
The morning-glory vines and thistle-weeds
That hold the loam poured out from God's own palms
Uncultivated melons for a time
Will ripen in July, the cracked rinds
Opening up their sweetness to the fields,
The great red hearts riddled with darkened seed.

The Shepherd

a Christmas play, 1954, Saline, Louisiana

Outside the country church's open door
Closed on the growing cold of Christmas Eve
I waited—the other shepherds gone before—
Till summoned by an angel-child to leave
Those early stars peeking sheepishly from night
I swung my golden crozier over them
And entered into a world of warmth and light
Walking the pinewood aisle to Bethlehem.
First grandson of the town's first family,
I heard "the city of David" as I came
To stand beside the manger, and to me
The psalms and gospels mingled in my name.
Behind us in the dark I just could see
The painted Jordan sliding on its tide
Into the waters of the baptistry
Where a thirsty lamb had curled away and died.
The pageant quickly ended though we prayed
Before the baby Jesus' doll-like face—
Candy-canes, mint tea, and lemonade
Luring even Mary from her place.
Then running out to play among the dead
I saw our family plot through ghostly breaths,
The long low wall enclosing at its head
An infant son—there were no other deaths.
Yet like a shepherd boy whose single sheep
Is lost as prey, I sat on that low wall
As on a sheepfold fighting off a sleep
In which I still could hear the slain lamb's call.
"David! David!" the stiff grass made me shake
As my grandfather nudging me with his cane
Slung me over his shoulder half-awake
And took me limply home to bed again.
That was long ago. And now alone above
The Sudduth graves so silent in the grass
Where once a boyish shepherd, out of love,
Tried not to fall asleep and let death pass,
I tear green blades from epitaphs grown old
Wearing out the night whose Herdsman searches on
Till each lost star is gathered in the fold:
"The Lord is my shepherd." "Thy will be done."

The Planters

for the Agrarians

a bayou plantation, near the Gulf, Louisiana, the 1980s

i.

Where sodden bottomlands give way to swamp
And brackish bayous widen into the Gulf
Two hundred years ago we banked and drained
These marshy arpents of our first estate.
Once slashes of sweet-acacia, cypress slews,
And cat-tail brakes were cleared by naked slaves,
Sloping back from the frontlands' breezy crest
Rice and cane hissed in the tropic sun,
Grasses of Adam's voice and Adam's curse.
Raised in such a place, generations came
Repeating evil yet somewhat restrained
By things whose presence qualified the earth.
Vesper-sparrows perched on old-field corn,
Secretive bitterns stalking deep in reeds,
Wild shrikes impaling lizards on the thorn,
Quiet mouse-eyed owls, and mockingbirds who'd greet
The fragrant nights in moonlit summer blooms—
These led to lower terraces whose shores
Let out the broad fresh waters flowing toward
The barrier isles of oak and indigo.

ii.

In time, bayou-captains, landing at our docks
With whiskey, ice, and papers from the North
Saw rise beyond the old unpainted cabins
Tall columns white with sun, the warm verandas
Drenched by coastal showers and the shade
Of planted oaks whose limbs swayed like punkahs
Over the cooling rooms and favored slaves.
Meanwhile, in the fields, through noon's ceaseless heat
Others picked cotton, black gold yielding white,
Returns of a backward Christendom, a late
Anomaly of Eden and of time,
A dream we kept on willing ourselves to dream.
And so they appeared, compensating demons,
Furious justice set against maddest pride:
Ironclads with near-invulnerable guns,
Sliding quiet as gators in the stream,
On flimsiest pretense shelling the galleries

Glass shattering across the study floor
To show unlettered slaves a high contempt
For mildewed texts of Scott and Cicero.

iii.

Then, just at harvest time, those people came,
Obtusest slaves to Luciferic dreams,
Deniers both of history and guilt
Who seized on present evil to postpone
Awareness of their own millennial sins.
We called them Satan's angels, the crude recruits
Of Sherman and his kind, sorry little Fausts
Groping after silver deep in cedar chests,
Fingering lingerie in the dark armoires,
Then taking slave-girls between the family tombs.
Some few, we later heard, went further still
Beyond the expected ruthlessness of war
Slaughtering calves in winter on the altar
Of St. John's, incited by wild tunes
Banged on the organ to disinter the dead
Relieving them of wedding rings and fingers,
A fleshy resurrection! At last, they left
To kill the buffalo and starve the Sioux
While we merely subsisted, eating seed crop,
Purged by the grim provisions of our need.

iv.

To assess the situation and regroup
A hundred years in earthly purgatory
Were endured, counting the dead and wounded,
Still mired in that long war between the spirit
And the letter of the constituted law
That promised us all impossibilities.
Now, once again, we seem to be invaded
By carpetbaggers, scalawags, and yuppies,
Atlanta flanked, invested, sapped from within,
Our generals scribbling dispatches under siege
Across the metaphysic battleground
On which the war continues to this hour.
And here by the Mississippi's ancient bed,
The Lafourche, where Bishop Polk once made his home,
Skeletal rigs still pump up for consumption
The new black gold, a wasting plague whose signs
Are not the blazing casements torched by Yanks
But marsh crosshatched by canals, oak-salting tides,

Night's fiery river plants, and flooded mansions
Through whose Ionic shafts the moccasin glides.

v.

So this is General Order No. 10:
To fight along the old interior lines
Of Christendom, crossing all departments
(*Pace*, Jeff!), arts, letters, economics,
Theology restored, recalling Stark Young
Who said that of the South what matters most
Is that to which the South itself belongs
However distantly—the universe
Of Dante, Aquinas, Aristotle,
With Mary at the center of the Rose,
The flowering womb of all things ever made.
Through these in some humility we'll grow
True stewards of the world our fathers left
Inhabited by powers, devoting lives
To regimental memoirs, re-enactments,
Parish histories, family trees, extracting
Universals from the local and the known,
Shoring the barrier isles, reclaiming thus
From highest tides of Chaos and the Gulf
The unsurrendered ground, our proper home.

The Abandoned Manor

With Olive trees and oile-trees overgrown
Chapman, Od. V. 647

Its salted fields dissolved in marsh, reclaimed
By deep repeated incursions of the tides,
The house these great dead oaks once cooled and framed
Half-sunk in pooled reflections still abides.

I knew it as a boy. My mother's aunt,
Late child of the antebellum patriarchs
Who saw their world become the mind of Grant,
Preserved her fathers' manor and its parks.

She leased the sugarfields as tenant farms
Keeping her shares and titles well in hand
And tough beneath her genteel ways and charms
Held on to the richest portion of the land.

Year after year her kinsmen gathered there,
Branches high and alive in the family tree,
I and my cousins play-fighting everywhere,
Rebs winning the war, creating history.

In time reunions ended as the dead
Or life in northern cities claimed them all
Though I, who was the closest, in their stead
Now came alone and often to the hall.

In winter I shot ducks in the stinging air
And heard the storm-winds crying on the coast;
Summers I played my war games solitaire
Turning Sherman's numberless blue host.

Each spring I thought of causes lost and won
Deep in the old magnolia's moonlit shade
And saw in fall's dark apples ripe with sun
Some fallen thing of which all things are made.

Then having lived past all her other kin
My maiden aunt bequeathed her land to me
Directing me to college to begin
Mastering classic tongues and husbandry.

Returning full of science and design
I made my aunt small profits till she died,
Then laid her in the earth that now was mine
And found myself unchecked, unsatisfied.

Old tenants soon bought out, delusions grew
As dense cane sweetened in the late fall chill
And blacks sweated salt until the sun withdrew
Cutting the crop then trucking it to the mill.

And yet, in spite of nearly record yields,
Wage-slaves of the southern islands' torrid zone
Working longer days in hotter fields
Raised crops whose prices undercut my own.

Weak lordling of a pastoral citadel,
Held by no estate, I let myself be paid,
Leasing to those who sucked from every well
Oil of the blackened creatures long decayed.

Soon rich, I took *Cold Harbor* out to sea,
My sailboat where the bankers partied nights
Toasting lucky winds that blew us steadily
The momentary gold of waterlights.

To ward off deep ennui I learned to prize
Coins of a phantom Caesar's briefest reign,
Old folios of brazen profiled eyes
Dreaming of eastern tribute once again.

Then lost in late Latinity I'd stand
To read on vellum hung from golden rods
Redactions of Phaeacia's heightened land
And feel a southern cousin of the gods.

At last, the payments ended and the wells
Were left with half the marshes breached and slashed
By long canals through which the tidal swells
Threatened the Doric porch toward which they splashed.

My holdings were consumed securing loans
Spent to recover ground once drained by slaves,
Yet, in the end, beneath their foamy stones,
Even the dead were moved from family graves.

The manor was abandoned though I found
The overseer's cabin, set back, could be a cell
From which to watch the mansion as it drowned
Gazing into a shared reflected hell.

Now I, the brutal steward left behind,
Must live content with what the sportsmen pay
Crouched in dying marshes firing from a blind
Until they take their limit for the day.

Still on afternoons when storm-winds blow mild
I dream of No-man stirring in the shades
Of cultivated olive and the wild
Waking from the sea to find Phaeacian glades.

October Oaks

Blown clean of summer heat,
The exhausted oaks remain:
Roots wrapped in wizzled peat
Disturb the buried rain.

Beneath a blackened mass
Of sunlit evergreen
The bladed shadows pass
Through dead St. Augustine.

By twilight crisp with sound
Old crickets pitch bare cries
From the darkened mating-ground
To where the high boughs rise,

And where the high boughs sway
With fireflies' dying lights,
The stars' long tenebrae
Marks out far colder nights.

Epiphany in Baca

> And being warned of God in a dream that they should not return to Herod,
> they departed into their own country another way.
> Matt. 2:12

Flowing over the window's spectral crèche
Of wire-mesh papered forms—the wise men, sheep,
And angels washed in gold—a deep light glows
From the elevated wafer of the moon.
Rising to walk the dog, I gulp strong coffee,
Fumble with the collar and the leash, then
Follow my eager mixed-breed into the dark.
Half poodle, half terrier, she's a natural
Burrower into accidence and substance—
Whiffs of a tomcat drifting from a culvert,
Then the jaded eyes unblinking at her bark.
In and out she breathes her doggy breath
Snuffing the essences of mongrel studs
Alive within a world her senses find
Unending but which her master must complete,
His stick tapping the slabs like thirsty Moses
Till well-struck verses saturate the mind.
Ahead, the abandoned icehouse. Above its roof
Where broken starlight gathers in the glass
Of shattered bottles and where the pigeons coo
Their dumb annunciation of our stroll,
Fixed in the deep-gorged bolgias of the cold
The stars, like Dante's field of burning tombs,
Turn on the ontic axis of the pole.
Below, on the long north road watchdogs growl
Between barbed wire and the fluted tin garage
Whose spent gladiolas' rotted olive heads
Bow to a MIDAS sign's plastic gold mirage.
Darkness gathering west against the day,
We pass the KC Hall, absurdly new

At the alley-end's two hundred years of oaks
Once the approach to torn-down Desiré.
A land-grant plantation chopped up into lots,
Its few spared trees, the offspring of giants
That lived and died for ages undisturbed,
Rest on trunk-thick lichen-covered limbs.
These lie by frosted anthills where a boy
Has stirred awake whole armies with a stick
Watching them swarm like Yanks attacked by Jackson
Or by those Rebel dead whose flesh was laid
In earth beside the church where once they prayed
For Christendom and where their scion-heirs
Now pray as slaves to Janus-facing dreams
Of antebellum mansions lit all night
By river plants refining gas and crude.
Above the tended graves unblighted elms
Bright in the powdery marrow of the moon
Cast across worn tombs their netted shade
Held by the blades that guard the dank remains,
The deadened grass still living in its roots.
Circling the church, we take the old way back
Where Desiré once looked out on its fields
Rounding on ourselves as morning light
Guiding us down our block and safely home
Climbs the weatherboards to touch the sill
By which the delicate crèche's wise men kneel.
Made of papier-mâché and brittle gilt,
Antique in decoration, gesture, dress,
They bring to us their timeless attitude
Bearing the gift of their epiphany
Forever through a world of desert snow.
And though we seldom hearken to the voice
Murmuring under the surd, contingent world
Those echoes of creation that were heard
When Moses wrote and Christ became the Word,
At least we gaze on those who gaze on Him
Till rapt by manger-light and Cherubim
We come to take our places in the crèche
Of things so made and postured by their God
That each one bound by its own plenitude
Rises deprived to flourish in a love
Whose roots clutch the ground of matter, nothing, doom,
A burning bush still burning unconsumed.

The Burning Fields

South Louisiana

Turned back upon themselves at the levee's edge,
Under a sky more ancient than the stars
Bare sugarfields declined toward virgin swamp.
Machetes flashing in the early night,
The migrant cutters, bending remnant cane,
Chopped off dry stalks from elevated roots,
The failing earth, once more to be endured,
Dark harvesters across the martyred land.
Along the rows of stubble where the mold
Of tie vines and the false poinsettia froze,
Cupped matches struck by the older men
Kindled in undergrowth a steady flame
And the empyrean crossed cremated ground.
Like gods in the choking sweetness of the air,
They watched the holocaust their need compelled,
The burning eggs of insects, radiant webs
Of starlight strung from the spider's mire,
Crazed field mice flushed from incandescent nests,
Shot at by pellet guns of the younger boys,
Squealing between the double lines of fire.
When the scorched tinder ended and the blaze
Sank back before the stark bank of the break,
Drawn up from the sullen Gulf, faint tangs of salt
Spread out through smoke translucent in the blue.
Alive in the burning fields of foreign light,
The moon was matter bared, a glowing crust
Of cold between oblivion and the One,
Creation of the waste whose winds blow on before
Those twinkling fields that blacken toward the core.

II. COMMEMORATIONS

Elegy for a Father

Francis L. Kerne, 1911–1979

So fluent in the language of your pain,
Your breath grown short as winter passed away,
We clutched at every word you barely spoke
And read the withering parchment of your hand.
With agony of body, wretched and aware,
A shrunken corpse in labor to be gone,
You lived beyond endurance till you died,

The hero of our fears. By gentleness
Defied, your end could only claim the brute
Inhuman body, dwindling into pain.

Alive with cancer, you did not betray
The origin of grace, or how a death
Could will mere fate into a human thing.
No body of the Christ or simple flesh,
That part of you which flickered into dark
To shed at once the burden of its earth
Endures in us as what you really are.
The anguish that you faced has died away
But what you shared remains: the private witness
Of a nameless faith, human, complete.

The Stoic

On ramparts tough as stone
Devised of cranial bone
Alone I face the strife
That is my life.

But under fortress mind
Within the heart I find
Emotions insecure
I must immure.

For out there is the dark
In which the brainless bark
Of dreaming beasts inane
Drives me insane.

No order can be found
Within or nigh around
And endless is the fight
In reason's night.

So when I die cremate
My flesh to dissipate
Pure mind who came too late
To this estate.

And let the ashes burn
Till soul alone discern
The quintessential fire
That I desire.

Leave nothing for the ghost
Of what I fear the most
Within us or above,
Redeeming love.

On the Suicide of the Chairman of the Math Department

Divided from your wife,
Life added up to ought,
Grim integer whose rife
Tautology you taught.
How long the problem lingered.
So pressed, how long you fingered
Solutions, only to balk.
Then answer's pure occasion
Became, beyond erasion,
Irrational numbers figured
In blackness white with chalk,
Until explosion triggered
A final train of thought,
Your brain reduced to naught.
Factored out, beyond persuasion,
You balanced the equation,
Finding the terms you sought
In the barrel's double-ought.

The Gentleman Scholar

for John Hazard Wildman

Enlightened by traditions we had lost,
At first you seemed benighted and we joked,
Hearing the obliquer ramblings of your thought—
Self-deprecating "don't-you-know's," verbosity
That seemed to leave the text uncriticized.
But as we mused, linguistic odysseys
Whose ship was civil mind, whose oars
The adverbs that you spoke lugubriously,
Would steer us toward the heartland of your faith:
Christian *humanitas*, of Marian catholicity.

Last of the gentleman scholars of your day,
Refusing to abandon ancient truths
In robe or gown, of Academe, or Rome,
Or New Jerusalem, you scorned "mere fact"

Of secular church or corporate university,
And made us judge the text by human life.
The books you wrote and taught assumed a world
Whose virtue public manners bodied forth
Though rude autonomies have brutalized
The nurturing life, withdrawn to solitude.

Unlike the rest, you knew the critic's task
Could not be done alone, his discipline
Dependent on the artist and a faith,
In word of God or man, not self-contained.
These values you entrusted to the souls
Who lived within your city through the years
And grew in love to understand your kind
And generous concern.
                                        Tonight, within that light
Of the polis, gravely dimmed, we kindle
Into life the public honor of your name.

The Buried Life

in memory of H. J. Sachs (1904-1983)

Almost to the last
You ridiculed the past–
Patriarchs, prophets, kings,
The Covenant–all those things
That haunted you and defined
A Chicago left behind
Some fifty years ago
When you moved south. I know
The good you did here, the fight
Brought to the far right
In your English class: racists
And the rubes, Southern Baptists
Who snarled below your thunder
Till guilt would draw them under.
Attacking our taboos–
Religion, sex, the Jews–
You dreamed a human race
Homogenous and free
From guilt and history
And reason was the plague
You called down on the vague
Prejudices of that school
Whose students called you fool.
You were northern, liberal, Jew,

Humanist, atheist too,
For whom our old beliefs
Were sources of the griefs
You relished to defeat
With a logic too neat
In time even for you.
For Time and Age who drew
You nearer that disease
No medicine could ease
Awoke the sleeping fears
Of Yahweh and the years
Of exile from the Law
Whose ruthless truth you saw.

Retired to rooms beside
The hospital where you died,
For years on holidays
You watched me from a haze—
Five packs a day you'd smoke!—
Until stroke followed stroke,
And mind, your god innate,
Began to dissipate,
The last diaspora
Of that apocrypha
Which hid your buried life.
Though you kept up the strife
In monologues for two,
You were the Wandering Jew
Until the very end
And you would still defend
A life that had to seem
Lost in the animal dream,
A physical ideal
Adrift in the unreal.
But that last time I came,
Though the bombast was the same,
Where Russell used to lie
To delight your doubting eye
On a cleared desk I saw
The Sacred Books of Law
And the firmest evidence
Of two Old Testaments,
Hebrew and the English,
No more could you distinguish
What you were from what you knew,
The humanist, the Jew.
And so at last you tired
Of all you had desired—
The secular Messiah

Become his own pariah,
Whose earthly Canaan faded
From eyes the one god shaded–
And when your breath was strong
You sang a Heine song,
But if the pain grew worse
You whispered David's verse,
Escaping in a psalm
The flesh's Babylon.

So on the day you died
And the long-denied heart cried,
At last a rabbi came
And spoke the ancient name
That you could not disown:
The god of desert stone,
So imageless and hard,
Remote from your regard.
To final things come late,
Your love embraced its fate,
A covenant upheld
Before the night compelled
An end to moral choice
And the defeated voice.
Utopias of the flesh
Entangled in their mesh
Exhaled with your last breath
So eloquent in death,
Freeing the immortal soul
From the bitter mind's control.
A posthumous bequest,
You publicly confessed
When bright, releasing chains
Slick with November rains
Lowered the metal box
To words pure Orthodox.
Then silence. You were gone.
Buried in the dawn.

For a Needlewoman

to Francine

Her yellow hair held tight by a golden bow,
Though here and there gray curls already fray,
She bends above the linen's bare expanse,
A radiant place not fully shaped or found,

A tangled skein of blankness undefined.
And there she plans her sampler of the world:
A line of numbers, black and underived,
White letters where the ciphered hyle thrives,
Its seasons incandescent at the edge,
The April fire-pinks burning in their field
And honeysuckle sipped by summer bees,
The autumn goldenrod, mock bishop's-weed,
October's rare clematis, then winter stars
Alive in skies of uncreated space.
She soaks her strands in colors of the South
And Old-World tinctures such as Pliny praised—
The saffron asphodel, bayberry gray,
The yellow weld, blue woad and indigo,
Dog-hobble brown, brown cutch, the rosy sloe—
Cultivated natives, the foreign, and the wild,
Stains of the very plants whose forms she mends
With numbers, letters, colors, textured names
Till things become as real as they can be,
Needled awake in the thread's quintessent flesh.
But though she loves the creatured silk, the sampler's
Burnished plane, she knows her work undone,
Her woven world's frayed ends and frayed beginnings
Unraveling on the darkened underside.
Yet while her started tears still wet the twist,
She sews in gold the words of Genesis:
"And God saw everything that He had made
And it was good." So, too, her nimble skill
Might please Him best who brooded on the waste
And made her from the clay He strove to make,
Brute matter and His mind drawn tight in seamless weave,
Her threaded leaves dyed green with leafy blood.

The Maker in Lent

to Anna

As new to me as you
This walking through dark halls
From twelve o'clock till two
I hold you as you squall
Your artless, garbled cry
When colic monsters growl
And pull your legs up high
Wrestling you in your towel.
Then softly as you drowse
Below the hardwood shelves

Whose classic texts arouse
Some few to know themselves,
I hum bright songs in place
Of poems I'll not recite
Until you too must pace
These lonely rooms of night.
But now, how great the good
We share in wordlessness,
This Lenten fatherhood
When love may quietly bless
As much as those hard texts
Where wifeless, childless, deep
In their profound and sterile rest
Cold Paul and Plato sleep.

The Journeying Moon

At two o'clock I scooped you from your bed,
A tangle of blanket, doll, and teddy bear,
Then rolled you into the car seat and said,
"Just stay asleep. I'll wake you when we're there."

It was a crazy notion, I confess,
To take you by myself and have to face
Driving the state in half a night no less
Through swamps and hills to reach my parents' place.

At times we went dead slow in blinding fog
Up winding bayou roads I couldn't see,
But when it cleared I noticed you agog
At something still invisible to me.

It was a humpbacked moon abroad in dark,
A swelling yellow crescence bared by the sun,
Abstract in cold remotion, vivid, stark,
The waxing bright detritus of the One.

That's what I saw. But then I watched your eyes,
Dilate in primal wonder, almost round,
Drinking in creation where the skies
Receded bleakly into the black profound.

"Moon!" you cried. I nodded as I steered,
For word and thing to you were nearly one
As in the dim beginning they appeared,
An imaged act of God both said and done.

At daybreak you gave in at last to sleep,
The moon absorbed within a greater light
It hurts to look upon, and yet as deep
As memory can be you'll keep this night,

A night in which the mystery, last and first,
That anything should be and as it is
Journeying toward the source from which it burst
Woke up a child who crossed that vast abyss.

The Quiet Garden

You held me in your womb and in your arms,
Nine months, nine years, a lifetime, in a world
As simple and mysterious as the child
Whose unborn heart first beat with human blood
Between the milk and honey of your flesh.
Watching me as I toddled in the garden
With unsure step, the fall certain to come,
You sat among your flowers, your skin white as mine,
And would have washed away the very earth
From hands that brought you crickets, worms, and spiders.
I hurt you with the truth of common things:
The loud baby squirming in its filth,
The half-wild boy so righteous and afraid,
The ruthless teen, marriage, divorce, ill health,
But through it all love kept its steady course.
Then, in my son, I gave you back myself.
And though we could have lived on there forever,
In memory's redemption set apart,
By seventy the cancer had returned
Eating behind your nipples to the heart.
Beside an open window, propped up in bed to stay,
You cradled my gray head in yellow arms
Until our tears became a single stream
Finding in wrinkled breasts familiar ways.
Outside, the quiet garden, still in scented sleep,
Let in the night that led you past your pain,
The long-closed morning-glories, far from dawn,
Four-o'clocks folding before the cankered shade
In which you said "please hold me" and were gone.

The Miscarriage

2.22.86

Dear Lord, take back that which you would not give,
Soul of our little baby, that could not live.

III. THE MIDDLE WORLD

The Middle World

Eric Voegelin, i.m.

1. The Craft of Noah

In clearest day, in clearest blue of noon,
Out of the brightest clarity of the sky,
As I rested there beside the olive fields
I heard my name repeated by the Lord
In an almond's cloud-white bough, and I awoke,
As if from sleep, beneath the leafless tree.
He spoke to His own reason, fixed in me,
Of mysteries beyond the reason's end,
Enabling thus by my contracted craft
A hidden revelation of His means.
So, in cloudless spring, amid the withered dill,
I built of driest cypress caulked with tar
An ark some fifty cubits straight across,
Three hundred cubits long and thirty deep
Raised up on bracing stands, as He decreed.
And there, when men made brutish by their vice
Hooted my work of curious design
Fashioned by tools from Adam handed down,
I pitched my voice across a fading sky
Calling from night by names they hardly knew
The beings of creation, two by two.
They came aboard as raindrops splattered the planks,
The wrinkled elephants ponderous and slow
And darted dragonflies so quickly still,
Mammals, amphibians, reptiles, insects, birds,
The animal kingdom ordered by His will!
And where the closest breeds remained discrete,
The godwit and the whimbrel well defined,
I saw the ghostly species take their place,

Those unmade shapes who prove the world divine.
Then, when my sons and daughters entered the ship
And looked down on the damned wading hard at last
To clutch at the holy thing I made of wood,
There poured from the broken heavens and the land
Foam of Chaos lifting us up over
The surfacing depths out of the world of man.
Thus I, the chosen witness of the scene,
Watched the rain of justice cover the earth,
A saltless sea where salt tears shed too late
By those long sunk in gluttony and lust
Embittered the tide that swept them from the peaks
And flooded the ruins of Eden with their blood,
While guided by my craft, this starward ark,
I rose on the trembling image of the dark.

2. Elegy of the Ploughmen of the Stars

They shone for us as they had shone before
Each night in the barest centers of the sky,
Appearing still in their appointed course
As stellar terraces and torchlit porticos
Gathering in their depths the heightened fires
Out of the pregnant essence of the core.
There in the dim extensions of the surd
They kept the primal covenant of God
With every hind who wondered at the stars
And feared the blue savannahs of the dark.
The Shaper's dateless calendars of light,
They marked untimely waters that would coil
To hiss against His walls of glowing stone,
Profoundest of foundations, citadels,
The burning halls of aether where He dwells.
For centuries we lived in His desmene
Ploughing by night so near the moated gate
That when He made a song of all He made
Scattered in drafts across the palisades,
We heard His music fill the upper fields
With grace notes so canonic and restrained
The angels sang in silence when they sang.
With tempered blades that brightened in the ground
We tilled the mellowed acres of the waste,
And when the crops stood high in golden rows
We pitied our restless brother, tired Orion,
Chasing his prey forever through the cold.
But though we sowed the heavens and the earth
With milted seed of Pisces and the corn,
Now we only cast our shadows on the land,

For in a strange disaster of the stars
A nightmare rose to enter into the forms:
A cankered angel curling to the root
While the Shaper, shaken from dreams of keener scythes,
Saw His walled dominions smoking in the char,
The exudate grown wild with native strains,
The rotted stalks of Nox, the headless grain,
The embered gods of Plato in their cars.

3. Dominion: A Pastoral

> Humanity's task from creation is . . . to join in God's will for order.
> from a commentary on Gen. 1:26

Between the bleak extremes of night and day,
Cerulean noons, the depthless ebon dells,
We stood alone concentered in spheres
Reflected in the mind, appearances
Whose euphonies so swayed the absonate
With roundelays of violence and love
That when the heavens spun they voiced as one
The blood-cries of the eagle and its dove.
Stationed between the angels and the orders
Of the waste, we knew our place, ourselves,
Walking like creators across the settled shelves.
Once hunters whom the migratory beasts
Had made to follow their own compulsive ways,
We came to be the shepherds of these hills
Driving our flocks by twilight to a crest
Of scented rhododendrons thick with bay
From which we saw beyond the highest pines
Those torrid zones of Chaos and the gods.
Along such ghostly outposts of the One
We sensed what we were given to possess,
The borderlands of skin and bark and star
Beyond whose surfaces we probed and guessed.
And when our flocks would wander from the fold
Calling loud for their shepherd's crook and pipe
To charm the old dominion of the cold,
We seemed the fallen angels of their trust
Playing the songs of evening with a grace
That blessed them as the Seraphim blessed us,
In radiant unawareness, from their place.

4. Advents of Evening

Who is this god?
Plato

Beneath the shady fig, the storax, and the gourd,
The son of Jesse knew that music well.
His gold hair flowing crimson as the sun
Died on a distant hill far from Bethlehem,
Above the drowsy flocks that bleat and feed
The shepherd felt by twilight as he played
Amid the bitter aloes of the rock
Along a brow old Samuel's thorny hands
That very day anointed with strange touch
The drops of oil grown red like beaded blood.
How long his fellow shepherds held those fields
Watching the solemn progress of the night
In wonder, till there came a foreign star
Leading them to a stable where they gazed
On flesh that glowed so brightly in the cold
The angels who descended to behold
Saw love and nature cradled in His grace.
Yet in this late foreshadowing of time
Whose bleak concretions flowered in their signs,
What shepherd could foretell a later day
When Seraphim themselves would turn away
In terror from the darkened face of God
And look down on a starlit afternoon
To hear Him sing above the ringing nails
Prime angelus and last of all the psalms,
The King of Heaven yet King David's son,
His pastoral song embittered by the sponge
Speared on a double-plant He twined as one,
Hyssop of dura-stalk and of white marjoram.

5. The Covenant

Look at a rainbow.
Owen Barfield

Such music fled forever, leaving behind
A partial mind impartially distended,
According to itself, by earthen light,
Dominions dimmed, diminished, atomized,
Stripped of the Shaper's beauty and His sign.
And yet for those within the middle world
His stars will shine as they have shone before
Each night in the barest centers of the sky,

Accreted gleams of being, set apart,
Checking the void with presence, mark, and name
Declaring the blatant waste. They are, we pray,
Effectual effigies of some most distant advent
Toward which their farthest flarings bear our hearts
Beyond the rotted quadrants of the Nox,
Beyond the ends of energy in process,
Beyond the fourfold centuries of Lent,
Our one hope that the lesser cannot shape
The greater, nor may clay the human mind
That holds all souls are novas of His love.
Till then, the unbarred heavens in full flood
May wash the nights with fire where Noah rode
Over the blossomed waters of the stars,
The last to go with God and know the whole,
Who saw, as the dove winged freely from his hand
Returning as a native to its own returning land,
A rainbow made at last, the last thing made,
God's memory emblazoned in a haze
Through which the light refracted, in each act,
The colored world dependent on His gaze.
This is the sign devised by Him alone
Who still so loves the creatures that He made
From being uncreate and undeprived,
Sustained by their affections, not our own,
In exactest right relation, proper worth,
That from them may emerge, and we behold,
Beyond the end of everything on earth,
Old Plato's ghostly orders of the soul.

IV. THE CLASSICAL PAST

The Naming of the Trees: Odysseus to Laertes

Od. XXIV

Old man, whoever you are, serf or king,
Who wrested out of nature this orchard
Kept by labor and the favor of the gods,
Dust off your knees, get up out of the soil,
And sit by this tall tree you surely planted:
I am a royal stranger, hear my tale!

I fought with Agamemnon ten long years
Before the holy citadel of Troy.
I was the first to grasp Odysseus' mind

And gladly hacked down firs to rib that horse
The pious Trojans thought no hollow gift
Though Zeus by then had given them to us.

That night they got a bellyful of Greeks
And woke to armies entering opened gates
Butchering the royals in their sleep,
Aeneas alone eluding us through flames
In which restrained Apollo, looking on, saw
The blood of Priam bubbling on the stones.

For ten years after that I wandered toward home
Strangely tangled in woodcraft, herbs, and trees—
Gardens of Alcinous, the poplar raft,
White moly and the Cyclops's shafted eye—
Still haunted by the image of a horse
Made to seem a thing it could not be.

At last I happened to land upon this isle—
Ithaca, is it not?—and saw in these
Green terraces and fields the vast plantations
Of an absent king. I found his palace
Held by feculent men. I slaughtered them all,
Then came to give you proof of who I am.

Here in this tended orchard grow trees
Whose names the young Odysseus learned to say
Numbering each kind planted in its row.
Over there stand ten apples whose round rough trunks
Brushed by the soft spring leaves and pinkish blooms
Are weighed down in fall by reddened pomes.

Then spaced out in the open forty figs
With broad leaves deeply lobed take the full sun
Bronzing their oblong globes of sweetest flesh.
Near them, in well-drained soil, thirteen pears
On limbs of scaled black bark and finest grain
Put forth white blossoms, toothed leaves, gritty fruit.

Last, over this rise that blocks my sight
Are set out fifty rows of various stock
Whose swelling grapes grow heavy through the year,
Each reaching its maturity in time,
The early purple yielding rich red wine,
The whites plucked late from dry Corinthian vines.

I drank from every row to celebrate
The death of Priam and his fifty sons,
And yet from that old man's blood-encrusted face

So like my father's, I knew that even Zeus
Would find in a dead king's countenance his own
Gazing on Fate that brings all sons back home.

Yes, I am Odysseus! I alone survived
Poseidon, the Sirens, Circe, and the dead
And yet to be the man beyond my fame
Required me to return to name these trees
That mark the place you, father, kept for me,
This middle world beside the Middle Sea.

Four Poems from *Hesiod in Old Age*

> The deathless gods are never far away.
> *Works and Days*
>
> In my time one tower and nothing more was left of Askra.
> Pausanias
>
> . . . his name rang loudest
> On the stone of Wisdom: Hesiod lies here.
> an epitaph

Contest

Dreams edge upon the day. Night and the past
Expand to an eternal equinox.
Excluding the provisional at last,
Austere in Dorian tone, my syrinx
Pipes no Delian fantasia's high pretense.
Old fingers, charred with cold, still modulate
Dank exhalations, trills weaving in silence
Windless on the precipice I know too late
To know. Those gods the blind Ionian
Conceived—elusive, distant progeny,
Wintry analogues, brightening from oblivion
To haunt a human face. Hypostasy
Begot Theogony. Who made it so?
Arch postulate my discipline would know!

Catalogue

Omphalos; Boeotian fens; hordes; eolithic Ur;
Ilium's cindered calm; pharoahs laved in myrrh;

Wife-sisters in swathes of balm; amphoras charred
In Knossos' crackling agoras; torches tarred
By Night, fires swamping Mycenaean rooms;
Femurs of kings strewn in the rifled tombs;
Weeds teemed on altar stones, spindling in Cadmus'
Grove, spiders strung over moldered temenos;
Leaf-blown by alder boughs, by Asian scrolls,
Tiresias' templum, ruined in starry boles;
Agamemnon's heartblood stunning greasy tiles;
Minos' pain effaced on Rhadamanthan isles;
Blackened remains of half-burnt daidalons:
The catalogue of iron, lone threne of Kithairon.

The Visitation

Hollows Zephyros sounds on Helicon
Issue faint tangs above Narcissus' Spring.
Cauling in sense, lambs wake in Homer's world.
Bogs swell with irises where Boreas whirled
On floelights. Within—a distance, echoing,
No pregnant voice too truly whole to share
But slight, evasive clues, a silence fraying
Into sound, a trace of presence lingering
Whose residue abstracts essential air.
Enchanted Amphion, we have become Night's
Rival iconographers, arch emanants
Who track in quiet skies paled icy prints
From Chaos' origin. Look. Untainted heights'
Narcissus sprays trill down on Helicon.

Genealogy

Oblivion. Rupture. Dolloped ooze.
Chaos stirs. Breeding against the dark, gods bear
The Demiurge. Night foals her progeny.
Kronos scythes. The bloody drops of sperm
Seethe on the tipping breasts of Aphrodite
Philomedes, hips traced with spawning foam.
Kronos spews rock. Politic Zeus struts forth
From Titanic sprees. Though Prometheus yellows,
A tenuous flare crackles in fennel-stalk.
These strains were the world I had to sing, not
Homer's shameless pantheon—high-mannered,
Cleansed of fetish, the stunning, bleak ideal—
But lines unjustified, newborn bastard mind
Writhing from blood to wile its oblivious sire.

Chiron the Headmaster

They squirmed on a long clean stone within the glade,
Vexed wrigglers slumped before my lectern-stump.
Restless when I praised the mere idea of things,
They craved the nightlong hunt, a garish kill
To smear their crudded flesh with umbles-blood.
Scratched on linden bast, the gnomic formulae
Sang to the silver bridgings of my lyre,
And as we drew the gods from random stars
I tried to spark their hearts with stellar fire.
Bombastic, cruel, reductive, how soon they all
Slipped backward into nature's weakening dream.

Now, where the boys sat, lichen stains the stone.
Wind sifts their dust from the cooled ash of Troy.
Retired to this high cave, I see far off
The harbor where I met them, ruined Iolcos,
Ancient Cretan piers rushed by relentless seas.
What brutes they proved in Pergamum! a nightmare
Haunting my sleep for twenty years. But worse
Than oozing livers slivering over the bronze
Is the image of a horse, profane with life,
Dark matter disemboweling from its form,
Blade-glints swarming down the quiet colonnades.

Chiron on Asclepius

I. Nativity

Brown in grasses curling on the mount,
Exposed by shadows pulled back under the bays,
In Ossa's minted winds, heavy with ligustrum,
Coronis slept in heat. Red irises,
Coppered in full day, opened over her
Spreading sunburned arms. Atop a poplar,
Shivered by lightning, a white crow stared and flew.
Impressions of Apollo in the flesh
Swelled from her belly, heady with his power,
Hung with the ripening beads of sweat and dew.
Detached from its own divinity and name,
Gliding under a moon not quite paled out
In dawn, the cult-abandoned bird teased the god.
He whispered of an Ischys as her lover,
Knowing it only a breeze that stirred her nipples,
Only the young blades stabbing at the air

That roused her from an older dispensation.

Leaned back against the sheepfold's moldered stone,
Serene Apollo raged, almost moving. In time,
He slew them both. Sleek arrows tipped with hellebore
Slid through a throat still purple with his kiss
As she eased her rounded womb upon the water.
Under a boulder rolled down Pelion,
Ischys smeared the schist. Forked flailing on a pyre,
They burned in innocence. Scrying the fires,
Apollo knew, charring the crow with their ashes,
And tugged from the womb, splitting aflame,
a ruddy son.

II. A School of Medicine

Years after he would bring to me a boy
Hiding behind him, squeezing his two fingers
In two hands, naked as an animal,
A god. With him a school of medicine was born.
He rode upon my back through oleanders,
Pressing smooth cheeks against my hairy shoulders.
The tiny thighs pinching when I galloped,
A tightened body sliding on my foam,
His quiet fear could master me like love.
I washed him in the effervescent springs,
Or let him mount behind me in the pool,
Reflecting on my form, embracing me.
Together we picked the simples of the gorge,
And I would gently guide his nervous hand
To pull, from kindred poisons, curative herbs.
At evening, he would make a linden tea,
Restorative of flowers, and tell me
Of hygienic days of sport and curious lore,
And we would kiss when poppy leaves entwined.
Later, he took the daughters of the Lapiths
Deep in the flowering hollow, where they lay,
Though I would have him stay, Uranian, and pure.
Physical, hard, contained, and unaware,
His body browned against its dark pubescence.
The irises of his eyes, coppered by the sun,
Were dank caves worming under a limestone brow.
My knowledge made his own, he kept from me,
Cold to a rare affection tense with mind,
Remote in self-regard as I had been
The day his father watched me from the grove.

III. Memoir

The boy Asclepius is far away.
Machaon, Podalirius—his children—
Served at Troy, physicians to Achilles
When he struck against Aeneas—each my charge—
Once playmates in the meadows of the vale.
But standing in his shrines, the carven god
Asclepius remains: statued like the dead,
Stone dogs asleep forever under his chair,
The snake twined like a garland round my staff,
Old skin sloughed off his sleekness like my life.
Near death, I seldom sleep, and never dream,
Yet if I could, my dream would be of him,
Not in the finished marble, crumbling out of time,
Or high in darkening temples, emptied of prayer,
But on that day Hippolytus was thrown,
And he, as I would him, brought one to life
To share the virgin days with Artemis
And love his own reflection in the pool.
Zeus killed him for that action, with a bolt,
So he became a power of the earth,
Olympian and Chthonian in one,
Eager to descend, though solar born,
Nurturing the dead who haunt these upper shades
Till the cold Huntress comes to Helios—
Her blood aflow at last and great with light—
Shining over the lost and moonlit ground
Where long ago he knew an ancient love.

The Death of Chiron

Glossed by the fluent winds their essence scents,
Black clumps of berried laurel fringe the cave.
Their blown tangs ruffle in the mouth's blind damp,
Strains babbling back from pools in the subterrene.
There, branching sprays sound out the deeper faults,
Murmuring in the foam where the frothy tongue
And rippled lips enthrall a hovering song.

Easing from the night, stars brighten into dream,
Blank analogues of light above the gore,
Echoes heightened from the cavern's floor
Where stealth has made them signs of weightless sheen.
These images, that I abandon here,
My musings vivified, the sleeping forms
A eulogy may waken into love.

Disconsolate Achilles, my twin fists
Hold bitter sprigs of wormwood, centaury.
But when I come, to comfort you alone,
With shadow tears upon a shadow face
My shade will spread to you in depthless space
As Hermes rises from the unwrought stone
Guiding me toward your livid eidolon.

The Cliffs of Epidauros

Hippolytus on Theseus

When the epicene granddaughter of the sun,
Tiny-breasted Phaedra, sick of grizzled thighs,
Teased Theseus with a rape she only dreamed,
Stroking my hidden flesh with naked eyes
Till the old king, smelling her sex, blurted
A curse to end my cold white life: I drove
Through the slitted cliffs of Epidauros,
Up bloody ruts he thrust through crime and mud,
To virgin wood, the brown and fallow rise
Perigone kept till a young man's hardened stare
Fell on her legs in the parted underbrush,
On her who that green night, like other girls—
Child-women, wet with lust—gave my father
One more son among the wild asparagus.

To the Platonic One

Though you would still exist
Before the primal cause
And past all ends persist,
Transcendent of the laws,

When Chaos came to sift
From beauty, truth, and good
Night's matter, pure in drift,
Old Ocean's foaming wood,

Your name is all you'd hear,
A faint, repeated word,
Remote within the sheer
And uncreate absurd.

V. VISTAS

Emerson at Belsen

> Our word is our bond.
> Geoffrey Hill

Yes, I have come to see them, even I,
Sifting through these pits of lime and bone
To find that utmost evil I deny:
This is the Old World's doing, not my own.

Original sin transcended was such bliss
(Brave Nature's healthy language my true bond!)
That even now I hear, through some faint hiss,
Clean showers fall on Concord and the pond.

"Evil the Unreal," my German masters said.
(See the blossomed wire, each daisy in the sun!)
So if they died en masse and what is said
Was done, I say the All received them, one by one.

Blue Essences: The 1890s

Rich cigarettes
Drawn away
From dry lips wet
With absinthe set
In the dim cafe.

Before the glass
The vellum sheet
Where shadows pass
The wordless mass
Of hell's aesthete.

The exquisite pen's
Indelible taint
Could stain again
Had you still been
The muse's saint.

But that is past.
And so you sink
Into the last
Hermetic fast
Of smoke and drink.

Mallarmé Over Hiroshima

I glowed in saffron robes, a mystic of the East,
Epiphany's technician, poet-priest,
A hothouse rose unfolding from its name,
Pure in science and art and pure in flame.

The Conversion of Wallace Stevens

There must be more.
Beyond this life, beyond this death,
Something, which, for the mind
Would be enough.
All this is not enough.
Not life, not death,
Not what we fix with the hardest
Most unevaded gaze,
Nor anything of God we can conceive.
What we want is everything,
From those remotest poles
To these most fragrant faces,
Yet everything itself is not enough.
What we want,
And what could be enough,
Is one green queen in one green heaven
Singing in deepest light, far
Beyond the brightest
Most distant skies of noon.
This queen
Who, to the heart, and to the
Vastest imagination of the heart
Is everything,
To the mind, and to the mind alone,
Is nothing.
Yet this nothing,
This nothing of the mind
That can never be enough
Hearkens. She says,

The mind itself can never be enough.

The Old Guard's Coronach

for R. L. Barth

I could not recall hearing of works celebrative of victory
but only of relentless resistance culminating in defeat.
David Jones

"Situation grim"—the annals closing terse
After the death of Arthur on the Somme,
Bayonets fixed we waited for the worst
Driven trench by trench the way we'd come
Over the works of time firing as we strode
Out of the open grave of the Sunken Road
Across the long north wall so thinly manned
To the chapel where we made a desperate stand
Then on toward Buellt in whose December frost
We harried the borderland Llewelyn lost
Chased from Alfred's fort, wary of the net,
Deep in the marshy heart of Somerset
Torching Camelot before we left
Its blackened court to raven, chough, and elf
Flushed from all positions but the last:
The closing gates of Troy through which we passed.
Now time and Troy are gone and we defend
This timeless place of origin and end
Climbing God's holy mountain in retreat,
Regulars turned guerrilla by defeat.
From smoky slopes of aether near the top
Pressed on every front, we scatter our shot,
Skirmishers in melee on the heights
Who, hand-to-hand, hold off the final night.
Never reinforced, always under siege,
We are the Old Guard massed between our liege
And the enemy below whose spirits rise
In columns of defectors switching sides
For power, comfort, greed, and those abhorred
New weapons so advanced the art of war
Becomes a savage science of pure technique
Aesthetic and obscene.
The day grown bleak
We cede the rubbled crest and disappear
In unmarked country ambushing flank and rear
Disrupting grandest strategies with delays,
Partisans of the bedrock's hidden face
Drinking from ancient springs whose fountainheads
Nourish the roots that feed us as we spread
To fight on in bands too small to be dispersed
Or all alone until the last reverse.

Two for Taliessen

1. Taliessen's Apostrophe to Arthur

Fire's vassal, sun prince, green man, ice-eyed scarecrow
Of the twilight moon, glade's column, lightning's thane,
The harvest pumpkin's crenellated glow, Queen
Night's ultimatum, regent of dawn, prime heir
Of the springing blade, the untoward sacrifice,
Virtue's brutal icon, the winter child of Troy,
Shuffling adept, hagiographer's despair,
Cuckqueaned, the light's façade, sin's outcast kinsman,
Calix of dust, the uncut glossary
Of charm, horse soldier, Roman provincial,
Celts' wanton paragon, the proselyte
Of God, wax dummy, airy illusion,
The consort of the blood, ciborium of dream,
Christ's factotum, fairy knight, my lord and king.

II. Taliessen on the Embarkation of Arthur

Steadied against the flesh my broken harp
Constrained, slipping in icy grasses' warm
Slicks of viscera, he staggered into the sea.
His brainblood tallowing down a single string
Tautening in cold, scored the unmeasured wind.
Green brine effaced the crossgrains of the greaves.
Then, the barge was there. Clearing the dead it came,
White faces streaked with time, leaning back to pain.
Pitted by spears, split paint on iconic gold,
Pridwen's underside glanced off the unfigured prow:
Mary's leavened eyes flaked blue from blinded iron.
Choughs huddled in elms, deaf to the keening screes.
Blown twilight rains extinguished Candlemas.
I laid him on hazel-wood before the queens.

Lines for the Dormition of the Virgin

Mother of love who felt in None's full moon
The Passion of your flesh so long ago,
To starlit Chartres, Cistercian Clairvaux
You bore the thousand years of summer noon.
Then dark Cartesian dreams, disturbed at birth,
Made knowledge pure as will in pure release,
Which, in the single kingdom of your peace,

Severed the realms of heaven and the earth.
Now, power, wealth, and sex, detached, discrete,
Inside their telic hells, guilty with hate
Declare themselves an uncreated state
Too whole for you to enter or complete–
You, who woke in us a love you were denied
And rose above the flesh you glorified.

Thomas Tallis to William Byrd

on the dissolution of the English abbeys

spem in alium

for Lindon Stall

i.

Late dawns of an early winter chasten the day,
Breaking in shattered windows where the glass
Was prized by pikes, then shivered from its arch,
Blue slivers of the Virgin scattered on slabs
Scrubbed clean of the shaken frankincense and myrrh,
Blank stone beneath blank panes of fallen light.
And so the mass was ended, my dear friend,
A pitiless miserere faded away
In the desecrating silence of the air.
Enflamed by Henry's pride, these darkened archways
Blazed great traceries of clerestory fires,
Charred arcs of the gutted heavens cindered spheres
Whose gloried smoke still glitters in the sky.
Defender of the Faith, Regent of God,
Maker, patron of makers, friend of More–
These were the fragrant titles he debased
With a lust for human sons–till in the end
Submerged inside the atavistic flesh
His florid brain seemed eaten up with sex.
Sad master of the fantasy of power,
He sank into a rage of blind commands,
Perplexed and apoplectic as the world
Became a zodiac of vagrant forms,
Unspeakable excrescences of earth,
Viscid isles of matter drifting near
His tired and clotted kingdom of the will.
Keen twinklings from remotest ends of night
Possessed his severed mind that had denied them:

Those molded shoals of diamonds, roses, lions,
Ranked planes between the angels and inane,
Old Homer's feignless chain of golden light
And Dante's lifted terraces of stars,
The graded range of being and of love.

ii.

The night from which they came had made them cold,
Grave agents of the king, the useful tools,
Mounted apparitions beating darkened ground,
Condensed from the solid fog through which they rode.
Their cramping hands held tight the royal words
Whose faint refrains and soundless countersongs
Still pulled hard hearts toward England's catholic god,
Children turned away from the hated face of love.
Such minions are the creatures of their day,
Distracted by the sycophantic task,
The happy factors of the passing chance
Whose axes cracked the chains of our jeweled
And leathered volumes lettered in pure gold.
The things within they touched, then left behind—
Fragments of Plotinus scattered on the downs,
Plato, Proclus, Porphyry—old presences
Once gathered here from European dark
When Roman will burned out in blackest ash
And Greece enclosed itself a thousand years
In far Constantinople's inmost walls.
I tell you, William, that the time will come
When Beauty in itself will be destroyed,
Its imaged world stark nature to the mind
For whom the soul is nothing but a light
Phantasmal spray diaphanous on the sea's
Eternal bursts of foam, a sheer consistence
Set adrift in the mere and shapeless waste.

iii.

How can our music live in such a dark?
Upon what vivid parchment shall we score
These gnomic prayers, these coded lamentations,
Recusant litanies, these cryptic hymns?
What catholic response, here in this drifted isle,
But to heighten, from within, diminished forms,
Those shining signs inside the native *res*,
To find rose-windows in the wayside rose
Or Mary in the bluebells of the fall,
To sense real presence in the dogwood's

Reddened bracts, in scarlet cardinal-flowers
Blazing over the frost, or to brood on
A Roman hyacinth asleep within its seed,
Or the spermy fruit of winter mistletoe
Bared on the pagan oak, even to dream
Saint-Peter's-wort spread wide on the moulded floors
Of autumn woodlands, golden in the hoar.
These common signs of earth, the unappointed feasts,
Are exiles in a Douai of the heart,
Plain names of the hidden matter that we praise
Until a holy physics of the world
Declares itself inside the starlight mind,
A sacred ordination of the made,
True unities of Seraphim and stone,
From the atoms of Lucretius to the sphere
Where the fixed stars stray westward into night,
Those ancient harmonies of silent sound
Toward which our anthems flame like abbey fires.

The Old Man's Flowers

At evening we'd glimpse him through the trees
Before the stars appeared, his hands and knees
Deep in humus, turning up his garden,
A quiet old man, humming now and then,
A watchman long retired who still preferred
To work at night and not be overheard.
He'd toil for hours spading out tough clots
Of monkey grass and clay that clogged his plots,
Almost in despair to find so many weeds
Unplanted by his hands that crushed their seeds.
He raised his flowers for beauty, not for gain,
Delighting to call in season each new strain
Out of the mottled blossoms of the rocks—
Oxalis, fire-pink, aster, purple phlox—
The budded loam and tongue become the same
Unfolding from the night as from their name.
Then, tired and content, he'd rest in his own bed
While high in the flowering heavens overhead
Star-gardens would emerge as by design
Rooted in the dark blue humus where they shine
As whorled escapes or radiant bouquets
Dotting the blackened meadows set ablaze
By a gardener burning off as he extends
His stands of aster to their cindered ends.
And though we haven't heard him sing in years
His work-song that became the music of the spheres
Descending when he tilled the fertile rows

Of maiden space in which his seed still glows,
Sometimes at evening in silence as profound
We hear a tune well hummed above this minded ground,
This patch of starry bloom and blossomed star
By some old man who tells us what we are.

The Family Tree

for my "country grandmother," d. 1962

It always brought the fall to you off guard,
This old pecan, its brown husks clustered hard,
While on the lawn's high grass leaves crisp and bent
Touched nuts and newborn moths with bitter scent.
More quickly then, as if you'd been delayed,
You'd gather cabbage in the evening shade
And dig up late potatoes with your spade
In a garden that you planted near the end
From pride and need. Just there is where I sinned,
Though still a city boy who could not read
The seasons' book of hours and took no heed,
For once in bright July, in my Sunday suit
I climbed the pecan and plucked unready fruit
Smushing the pulp inside each pliant hull,
Eating rubbery nuts until so sick and full
I ran to you as you read your Bible verses
On the long front porch, your innocent curses
Holding me as you turned to where time weaves
Births and deaths and weddings in the leaves.
Then, distracting me from a stomach so torn
You traced the family tree till I was born
Once more. "Don't pick too soon" was all you said
As distant winds blew faintly overhead,
Yet only now, so far from summer calm,
The hard brown hulls held tight in my hard palm,
Can I suspect how soon you saw the end
To which all family trees and world-trees tend
In an old pecan, which, when the fall winds cry,
Shreds its dead cocoons against the sky.

BEYOND THE CHANDELEURS

(1999)

Louisiana Passage: The Whippoorwill

for Jack Wise

A night or two in April, then no more
They call in latest twilight from the skies,
Migrants who fly between the stars and foam
Now come to this hard ground where dark abides.
And when the moon illumines each chill bloom
Of dandelion and violet and flag
Still trembling in a latent winter gloom,
The birds sing their own name so clean and clear
Whip-poor-will, whip-poor-will, whip-poor-will—then
Swooping to scoop up insects on the wing,
Mayflies and ladybugs in those wide mouths,
They feed and fly away to nesting-grounds
Remote from those the Caddo once had known
Deep in the virgin stands of silent pine.

And yet in gold October they return
Ghostly over the uplands' folded wolds,
Riding the ancient flyway as they climb
Into a dawn where centuries ago
Their ancestors had crossed without a cry
Green kingdoms of the oak and tupelo
Unbroken from the Ozarks to the coast.
And pausing there upon the last chenier,
Made voiceless as they gaze beyond the Gulf
Toward some most catholic South their flight implies,
They listen with intent for one who calls
Each creature in the language of its name,
And when they hear they pass through silent skies
Toward Adam and the earthly paradise.

The Sunday School Lesson

north Louisiana

The room was full of thirteen-year-old boys
Unhappily constrained by polished shoes,
Bow ties, oiled hair, orders against all noise,
And one eternal hour of Good News.

I joined the class each summer in July
When visiting my kin in that small town,

Lazing away the weeks till by and by
The signs of autumn brought my parents down.

Distracted like the rest, I, too, was bored
Though not a friend who shared the cycling year's
High rites of church, school, fair, and sports that stored
A common mind with common loves and fears.

Long-legged and ungainly in my chair,
I'd lean on the shoved-up window while the fan
Would spin a weightless haze of heated air
Around the sullen room as class began.

Jack Hopkins was our teacher though I doubt
He ever saw himself as any more
Than someone who could see an hour out
With tall tales of his catch the night before.

I'd watch his bulbous nose and long-drawn face
Both reddened in a steady heart's decline
As once more he would tell, with skill and grace,
Of nine-pound bass caught on a two-pound line.

One day, though, he seemed different, hardly there,
Gazing over the graves with restless eyes,
Searching for something distant and yet near,
Unfixable in cloudless summer skies.

At last, he slowly read, then half-recited
In a strong drawl which measured out King James,
Those passages in Matthew where affrighted
Disciples cried to Jesus as He came

Walking across night's foam upon the water
To grasp weakening Peter who'd looked down,
Distracted by the winds that made him totter,
Now mastered by the fear that he would drown.

Fumbling with his glasses, Mr. Jack then tried
With chuckles and an animated glance
Around a room from which all sound had died
To end the solemn calm and his own trance.

Those verses always moved him, he confessed,
Because of that strange evening on the lake
When a sudden storm caught him and he pressed
Against its wind to reach a cypress brake.

Perhaps it was the play of dark and light
Or just his tiredness vivified with fear,
And yet he swore that at the torrent's height
He saw the Christ by lightning drawing near.

With that, the lesson ended and the class
Rose awkwardly one by one and left the room
Embarrassed, even scared to have to pass
This man who'd gazed beyond the body's doom.

And though time brought him soon to what he saw,
It took me over thirty years to know
How soul's redeemed by wonder, lost in awe
Before those depths through which I, too, must go

With doubt and faith like Peter on the sea
Sinking in fear and chaos of the foam
Yet looking up toward one who has to be
There before the winds to take us home.

Toward North Louisiana

for the Literary Forum of Bastrop, Louisiana

Driving along the bayou through Lafourche
Then up the River Road past Baton Rouge,
Going to read my poetry once more
In those small north Louisiana towns
So like the one in which this life began
Some thirty years ago—my Eden-place,
Saline—addressing those arch arbiters
Of taste, the women's reading clubs, all named
The Literary Circle, Friends of Books,
The Sunday Afternoon Association
Or some such like, so seldom deeply moved
By those whose books their members often scorn
As merely modern, rootless, crude, untrue:
I take the interstate outside of Bunkie
Under an unrelenting puritan sun—
Now westering, remote, yet still intense—
Leaving behind the boggy coastal arpents
Gone back to goldenrod and indigo
For those plain farms of pole beans, squash, and corn
Beside whose lonely houses lately placed

Satellite dishes whiten toward Orion.

I make good time and so in time I turn
Onto a slower road the state maintains
And then a sand-and-gravel parish lane
To see the ghostly groves of old pecans
Grown on the soul's home ground. And there
Where fall's gold twilight holds them in one fire
Of sun and moon and stars, the holy boles
Whose limbs hang thick with clustered hulls take flame
Above an earth the matted shadows claim.
I stop and walk among them for a spell–
The past brought back by elegiac mind–
Trespassing there as here because compelled
By love toward sacred acres undisplaced,
Seedbeds of the weathered essences we sense
When a great horned owl, its feathers widely spread,
Dropping in quiet through curled and bitter leaves
Claws the stunned mouse, then quickly reascends
Gliding under the moon to take its prey
Into the blue seclusion of the trees.

Such literal appearances remain
Hard verses in the Bible of the things,
Jehovah's old and fatal delegations
Interspersed among those palmy psalms
Whose gladder affirmations we would sing,
Whispers risen from red clay to the bluffs
Where dogwood bracts grow rusty in the sun,
Interpretable words ever kept in trust
Both spoken of and from this native place
Coming to us whose tongues become their own.

So when I'm called to read to seasoned souls
For whom the Word still echoes in the hills
They hear no single voice or slanted line,
But if we all are stewards of the gifts
We join as one in praising what is made–
Anthems of river sand and hymns of limbs
Sagging with apples, blazoning roulades
Of redbirds blessed with Pentecostal song–
And even in those oaks whose heavy arms,
Glutted with nuts, owls grip with dripping claws
We hear not just the dreaded designata,
The clammy lamentations of the blood,
But fluent *whoos* proclaiming Adam's names
Here in the bleaker reaches of the north
Whose winters grace the pines with riming glaze.

Azaleas in Epiphany

for Father Robert Cooper

Delicate hot-pink bloom,
The first chill hint of spring,
Aflame outside my room,
What message do you bring?

Some think you self-sufficient,
Spontaneously there,
Mute matter's co-efficient,
Unfolding unaware.

But I can only deem
As holy petioles
And pedicels that teem,
Leaf-tongues and petal-scrolls.

Thus taken, in their stations,
All things are angels sent
Blazing into creation,
The Word's embodiment.

For an Artist with Parkinson's

in memory of my father, David V Middleton, Jr. (1922-1996)

So still beside the window in a chair
Whose wheels you cannot move and barely clutch,
You scan with eyes harsh medicine has blurred
A winter world once rendered by your touch.
Black seed-pods and a last few orange leaves
Crackling in dwarf crape myrtles, stark pecans
Mistletoed and bared of leaf and nut, grackles
Cracking berries in the frosted holly groves–
All these you stained in ink, the pot's baked glaze,
Or brought alive in oils–those earthen shades
Made from the very things whose shapes they made.

When you were in your prime I was a child
Held tight in the softened muscles of your hug
Riding on your shoulders while the spring
Grew wild with buttercups and ladybugs.
On summer days, heat pouring from above

Beat strong on your hard arm that hammered down
Long boards to roof a workshop where you wrought—
Absorbed in the timeless habitude of craft—
God's objects set aflame with human love.
And though your gift was modest, still in kind
You knew the joy of Buonarroti's mind.

One day in fall now forty years ago
You took me to a sloping melon field
That crested in an oak whose thickest limb
I straddled as you sketched me from below.
Evasive of your gaze grown so intense
I stared down at the dried and shriveled vines,
Dreaming of greenest rinds in late July
And heard in the still green needles of the pine
Faint windblown strains refining to a quiet
In which a newborn gift delayed by grace
First stirred as you shaded-in my gazing face.

Now you are old and ill beyond all art
Yet just as when you sketched me on the day
My head of curls was wreathed in curling leaves
And I was drawn and chosen we still serve
The Giver of our gifts: for when I draft
Quiet poems upon this table whose thick top,
Split with hard use, you covered up at last
With plastic sheets held taut by roofing nails
My pen moves where you painted, stained, and glazed
Giving for years to beauty and the muse
Those hands a child had thought would never fail.

A Quiet Reply

for my mother, Anna Sudduth Middleton,
who became a housewife and mother in the 1940s
in north Louisiana

The house is silent now, yet through the rooms
Once filled with laughter, music, talk, and tears
I hear the sounds of children who will play
As long as love still draws their spirits near.
And there beside a window what remains
Of my good husband stares across the yard
At that locked greenhouse he cannot recall
Ever having built or even seen before.

His pension, savings, what the children send
Will do until he dies and I move in
With one of them to live in that last room
With pictures and the pictures in my mind.
A housewife and a mother who performed
The common sacraments of daily life
On stove and tabletop and ironing board,
I thought my work a calling, nothing less.
My sons' wives seem to think me incomplete
Yet there they are, outraged by their own tears
When toddlers left at day-care cling and scream
Torn from their mothers' arms before the dawn
And not picked up till dusk by those who gave
Their best at work and now crave rest alone.
I hold my tongue and let its quiet reply
Be answer to their barely hidden guilt
That would in me have cried out from the heart
Where deepest things can never be denied.
But still I pause and try to understand
The kind of lives they say they have to live
And wonder whether I am one of those
Whose bent was taken late from ancient ways
Now passing with the world I used to know.

And yet I still remember and remain
In that sweet peace I entered long ago
Trusting in those old customs love sustains
By sacrifice till truth is realized.
Our wedding night on which we gave ourselves
As virgins to the ways of man and wife,
Those early months before the children came,
That small garage apartment where we lived
On what a navy seaman was allowed,
Then parenthood that bonded us in joy
And duty to the family and to God—
Such blessings were the laws that set me free
Through all those years the children were at home—
Nursing them with milk from my own heavy breasts,
Coming to calm their night fears with a hug,
Watching them sleep and wake, helping them walk,
Reading them Bible stories, Mother Goose,
Teaching them colors, numbers, shapes, and words,
And showing them the games I used to play,
Ring-around-the-roses, hopscotch, hide-and-seek.
And for my love of them, my husband, too,
I made a home for us as best I could
And welcomed every task I had to do,

Washing the breakfast dishes, folding clothes,
Cleaning the house or going to the store,
Gardening and sewing, working at church,
Absorbed in the sacred making of the day.
Thanksgiving, Christmas, Easter, summertime,
The births and birthdays, marriages and deaths—
These were the greater and the lesser feasts
That filled life's calendar with poignancies.

The children now of course are grown and gone,
My husband only waiting, tired of life,
My days with him but disciplined routines
Of food and drugs, of silences and naps,
Then bed in which each struggling breath sustains
A body all but ready for its death.

I know he soon will pass away and I
Will leave this house in which for fifty years
We found our place within a settled world
Where God permits us all to apprehend
The nature of creation and its end.
And what will I remember when I go
To live my final years in that last room
One of my children must prepare for me?
The night I showed my husband our firstborn
Was kicking in the womb I made him press,
The first warm cup of tea those autumn dawns
I relished in the coolness on the porch
Before my family woke, or that quiet day
I told my youngest child about the time
The sun stood still for Joshua while outside
That very sun at noon shone down again
On irises that seemed to bloom and bloom
Forever in those lingering full beams
Until our eyes grew bright with selfless love.
Such moments stay alive within my heart
And in this private journal where for years
I've filled so many pages, not with rage,
But love preserved in memory's glad tears.

Ancien Régime

South Lafourche

for John Doucet

The night spreads out along its native plain
Whose lights still shine as they have always shone
Inside the burning manors that remain
So long as souls respond with love alone

As they do here where salty floods subside
Before the old plantations' lower fields
And bulging trucks rumble through Christmastide
Strewing tall stalks of cane from record yields.

Stray offerings made to harvest gods that die,
The stalks are crushed to splinters under cars
While overhead where heaven binds the sky
The Dippers pour forth darkness from their stars.

And though we have been told the time has come
To know the earth unhallowed, merely here,
It is a creed too bleak for Christendom
In which a child drew kings and shepherds near:

And so we hold these fields of sweetest dust
Like Mary, who submitted to the Lord,
The Father and the Son, in utmost trust,
Freely compelled by all her soul adored

For then alone do constellations sing
Of God's collations underneath the moon,
A primal rhyme of image, thought, and thing
Still moving to an unprecluded noon.

Ex Nihilo

darkness is not darkness until light
has made the concept of darkness possible.
Dorothy Sayers, *The Mind of the Maker*

He left the cave, drawn by a winter moon
That bared the only world its light could find,
An unimagined land of gradeless shades

Transfigured in a random pantomime
Of some black pastoral that had to be.
On distant holy hills the shadow-swains
Piping the wordless dirges of the *res*
Ravished his heart until its maiden cries,
Melodic in the somber minor keys,
Soared toward untransposable refrains.
A frosty spirit chastened by its breath,
He burned in cold remoteness as the stars
Blazing against the night they hate and crave
Soon twinkled out and fell so far away
They reached a place no place could realize.
Fearful of desire, the given, happenstance,
He sifted finest particles of dark
Dug from the moonlit claypools of the cave,
Grinding the dust of nothing to create
The bleak Matter of Matter—his romance.

*

After the vows, the tossed bouquet, champagne,
He sought in the moaning flesh his tongue aroused
Articulate embodiment, a vital
Dialogue with the substance of his craft.
Yet, in the rhythmed heaves of breath and sex,
He sensed only a rude, mocking, inadept
Variation on his own unmetrical text.
Objectified and used, thus truly loved
As cold young poets love, when words failed
She left those rooms where he stayed on alone
That rich and bitter spring, seeing no one,
Losing himself in notebooks, cheap red wine,
Lonely acts of lust, and drunken sleep.
To free himself from chaos and despair
He wrote Shelleyan sonnets to the moon,
Courting the muse with floral catalogues,
Bright likenesses all heightened from the life,
Bouquets of white narcissi, passionflowers,
Names of the imaged things once bred from love,
Gifts of the one who comes but never weds.

*

Midsummer's green domain grown stark and hard,
The modulated planes of dark and light—
Split in the cryptic prism of his verse—
Were strained through screens of Christendom and Greece.

Yet drenched in the viscid tissues of the brain
His mind became its own dread messenger
Telling not of a god whose silence
Lets us speak but a mumbling demiurge.
Meanwhile, in time, a needlewoman came
Who only asked to love him as he was.
At night, when he had suffered long enough
Drafting a verse to gloss the utmost crux,
She made him close his book of Genesis
Then took him deep inside her till they cried,
Dependent creatures helpless in their joy,
Sharing to the full the things they fully craved,
The gifts of love and personhood and sex,
Content with their set portion of the good.
Thereafter, when they wove their words and threads
They were each other's muse and truly wed.

*

He waited for the mystery to fade
As Wordsworth said it would, yet on the Gulf—
Their voices sweetening deep into the fall—
The mockingbirds had never ceased to sing.
Late summer had alerted him: cool pre-dawns,
The paling light of shortened afternoons,
And evenings when the crickets' scattered cries
Proclaim desire itself desires an end.
Somehow, within, the old and simple wonder
Had survived, and, by its vital power,
He strove to learn the native tongue of God,
Those seminal declensions of the *res*,
Thing-words to which our word-things correspond.
Sometimes his daughter sought her father-god
To sing away night's goblins, ghosts, and elves,
Though like a greater maker's, it may be,
His lyrics seemed to blossom from the dark
Like autumn's Indian pipes, those nodding white
And solitary blooms, erect in fruit,
That blackened when he plucked them from the ground.

*

And yet, at last, nurtured by faith and grace,
He came to understand and then rejoice
That darkness could not be without the light,
Each defining each as twin contingencies
Divided from the undivided One.

The countless stars, all counted, named, and known,
Migrations of the geese and galaxies
Out of the nesting-grounds of ice and fire,
Physics-in-metaphysics—the blooming root!—
Fruitions and transcendences of the fall,
All types and antitypes in the metaphors'
Confluencies of spirit, heart, and mind:
Such elements make up the measured text
Satan would break apart, opening the forms.
And so from the winter heavens it appears
That all things here are never merely here
But called and spoken into place by God
Who whispers out of the deep, His *privité*,
Sweet nothings that persuade us as we praise
Old Arcadies of darkness and the stars.

In Acadie

A gibbous moon made full this autumn night
Shines down through chilling windows to a bed
Where lost within its pale archaic light
We only know what silent tongues have said.

No novices too eager to possess
Phantasms who elude their rude desire,
We wait till blood grown flush with each caress
Is slowly roused to climax in the fire.

Your hair's soft strands falling across my chest
As you ride me high in rhythms willed and random,
My warm lips sucking gently on your breasts,
My firm control sustaining your abandon—

This is the sweet confessional of flesh
Where words both raw and tender will be said
Which, when we wake to innocence afresh,
Remain behind in silence and the bed.

And though in darkened windows darker skies
Proclaim the stark contingency of light
In stars that burn and die in bright reprise
Of some prime cause which moved against the night,

Here in a world reproved by constant love,
In bodies we possess but for a time,

Live wedded souls made one by One above
Who came to earth that love might be sublime.

The Heron at the Weir

on Bayou Lafourche,
between Canal and Jackson Street,
Thibodaux, Louisiana

for Don Stanford (1913-1998)

So still amid the foam that plays
About his legs the heron stays
Atop a rock below the weir
That brings the silver minnows near.

He knows that what the weir provides
The darkly flowing bayou hides
Until the spray breaks at his feet
And offers up bright fish to eat.

His gaze seems fixed and icon-like
Till beak and eye by instinct strike
Taking a prey that never heeds
The reedy legs it sees as reeds.

And there amid the things that change
The heron stays so still and strange
Within a quiet he all but hears,
An earthly music of the spheres.

Stars at Noon

for Father George Walker, rector,
St. John's Episcopal Church,
Thibodaux, Louisiana

Throughout the dawn they vanish one by one,
Those stars that still proclaim the ancient night,
Screened off by blinding rays of our own sun
Which brings the day's blue dome of air and light.

And in that dome the mind has come to know

Each creature made and stationed in its place
By Him who left us shepherds long ago
Of all His meadowlands of time and space.

Magnolias holding huge white blooming moons,
Pelicans scooping minnows from the tides,
Sunflowers climbing high in cloudless noons
Or bowing while the twilight still abides:

Such palpable abstractions as they fare—
The gleaming things, the brazen shapes ablaze—
Grow holy and beholden unaware
Of those galactic pastures where they graze.

And when, beyond the darkness and the stars—
Those primal givens riven from the One—
We find the great foundation nothing mars
In that First Cause who willed each brilliant sun

Then deep within the heavens' stellar wells
We sense a love whose overflowing glow
Still claims us when we gaze toward where it dwells
And matter seems no longer all we know

Just as the stars at noon are ever there,
Remembered and expected, though unseen,
Flaring against the darkness they declare
As like themselves, a part of what they mean.

Night Fears: A Lullaby

for my daughter, Anna, at two

Shaken from a dream
Of dark and starry lands
I waken to your scream
And feel the tiny hand
By which you made your way
Along the shadowed hall
Searching for the day
With teddy bear and doll.
And as you hug so tight
This father whom you love
I know you fear the night
Within us and above.

And so I come to place
Beside your rumpled bed
A night light with the face
Of some bright star that sheds
Its glowing painted smile
On gloomy walls and shelves
To keep you safe awhile
From bogies, ghosts, and elves.
All tucked in now between
The new bed's guard-rail bars
You sleep again and dream
Of fathers and the stars.

Then kissing you good night
I sit in dark alone
And wonder if you might
Recall when I am gone
And it is you instead
Whose own night-frightened child
Stands crying by your bed
With eyes so wide and wild
How you too sobbed in fright
For one no longer here
Who brought a little light
And held you warm and near.

For where no teddy bear,
No talisman of stone,
Or faintest breath of air
Can go we go alone
Far down that blackest hall
Of echoes dead and hollow
Through which no toddler's calls
Or footsteps can follow.
Yet even in that place
A Father from afar
Bestows His love and grace,
The night lights of the stars.

Walking the Roots

to Anna

Your once uncertain toddling being strengthened
Into the steady rhythm of a walk,
Your seed-words sprouting out in sentences,

In your own early spring you gazed on spring
And knew the word-things God, in saying, made.
Purple maple leaves as tender as your hand,
Green stalks of pussy willow tall as you,
Tasseling oaks and rampant dandelions–
Such things, in the beginning, you construed
From taintless names, the grammar of creation,
And there you found, in soundings of the One,
Identity, the true similitude.

Then clambering onto my shoulders you would sing
Into the wordless voicings of the wind,
And when I heard the blending, like a child
I felt my heart beat fast with love again.
You pointed everywhere at everything
Demanding names–"What's *that?*"–then tried them out
On cardinals and robins, dragonflies,
Periwinkles, marigolds and slugs,
But most on slinky caterpillars creeping
In shadowed grass, massing on the great pecan
To climb and spin cocoons that butterflies
Might lose themselves in blossom-scent and light.

And swinging you up there overhead and down,
I showed you how to step from root to root,
Each one sinking deep in mind and ground.
Your stiff left arm bracing against rough bark,
You giggled gingerly–caught off guard
By anthills, thorny bramble, unraked leaves,
And quick green lizards–yet made it back around
To where we'd packed and smoothed the hauled-in dirt.
"Write ANNA!" you cried, and so, with a stick,
I wrote the stick-like letters in the dust
That held you as you watched your symboled self
Emerge from earth and essence as it must.

And asking those old questions born of wonder–
"What is night?" "Where do the stars come from?"
"What's behind the sky?" "Why is the moon the moon?"–
You started to probe the surfaces of things.
And though you walked on roots clutched at some black depth
By matter's shapeless hell–you looked beyond
Topmost boughs leafing out toward heaven and saw
Bright clouds condensing under the aether-fields
Marking as home this designated place
Prepared by One who speaks unceasingly
Through every plant and animal and star
And every child who names the things that are.

Embertide in Advent

for J. R. W.

They waited beneath the cold December snows,
Late flowers of the fall, the folded rose,
The angels'-trumpet crumpled in the mold,
Daisies of Michaelmas, the hidden lily curled
In dust of goldenrod and marigold,
Old matter's liturgy, a pregnant world
Out of whose star-of-Bethlehem arose
A Roman hyacinth, sweet-olive of the snows.

Dinner on the Ground

When Moses sent them to explore Canaan, he said,
"Go up . . . into the hill country. See what the land is like."
Numbers 13:17

Caroll Eubanks (1919-1997), i.m.

You drove us there at twilight last July
Up roads that ran through memory's summer realm
Leading into a deep primeval green
Where memory itself is overwhelmed.
Then just one slope below the weathered crest
We paused where a sleeping meadow made its bed
Over the Old Spring Church's flowering graves
Whose headstones nod forever toward the dead.
And there a sign's blunt letters raised in bronze
Before a house of God no souls possess
Told stories of a congregation's fate,
"Part of our state's rich history" . . . nothing more . . .
This church whose firm believers lie so still
Below the unfilled soil their plows once turned
Like pages of a faith's inerrant text.

The slabs preserved brief annals of their lives,
A birth and death date, Bible verse or rhyme
For Enloe, Weaver, Evans, Hopkins, Toms,
Descended souls whose own descendants filled
A vanished world in which you had been born
Near eighty years ago in these same hills.
You called the common things by proper names—
Hardscrabble Point, Owl's Hollow, Choctaw Creek—
And going on for hours down bramble-paths

Would seek out churchless graveyards long reclaimed
By overgrowth, then prop up marking-stones
On which you read a culture's epitaph.
And while the twilight shaded into night
Whose stars provoke the dark with spoken light
You begged us just to listen for a spell
As winds blew through the cedars in reprise
Of all you now felt so compelled to tell.

Your heart gave up its deep most urgent words
And as we looked around we almost saw
Emerging from the greenwood's waking glades
Some Sabbath dawn a hundred years ago
On foot, horse, mule, or clackety wagon-seat
Folk set to spend their day of rest with God,
The gaunt tall men in black, the women prim
Yet comely in their hand-sewn Sunday clothes—
The clinging blooms of gingham, calico—
And children running in homespun till all hushed
And waiting on the cushionless straightback pews.

Beyond those souls, the Table of the Lord,
White pine stained dark as though with Christ's own blood,
Above which rose a pulpit where the sun
Reached down until a single finger-beam
Fell on the burning words the pastor read
With Jacobean accents clearly heard
In Holy Writ and backwoods southern speech.
He preached to them of Canaan and the spies
Who, in the Valley of Clusters, gathered up
From midnight groves Jehovah's starlight marked
The scattered pomegranates, grapes, and figs,
Bringing them back to Moses as a sign
His fathers' earth still held its Hebrew seed.

And when the sermon finished with a prayer,
The yeomen closed their eyes and saw their farms
Hard wrested from the wilderness—rugged slopes
Well-watered by the salt of sweat and tears
That raised up from a thin resistant soil
Spring shallots and the summer butter beans
And corn to feed the beasts that fed their flesh
After the fall's dark harvest of the blood.
And with their longings now made manifest
In tales of turning home toward Eden's fields
An older hunger drew them from the cross
Toward rows of tables laden in the pines

With floured chicken fried up to a crisp,
Deep bowls of steaming okra, squash, and greens,
Potatoes with their fluffy butter-wells,
And pots of bubbling salt-pork seasoned peas.

Then through the long slow-moving afternoon
On bedspreads dyed with native muscadine
Stern elders breathed the scented woodland air
Till drowsy, dozing, they gave in to sleep,
Dreaming a dream more ancient than their faith,
Inhalers of the fragrant pagan day.
Meanwhile late mating cries of mockingbirds
Would draw stray couples down old hunting trails
In silence to the virgin kissing-trees,
And there, while fingers played with ribbon ends,
Young Southern Baptist tongues found maiden mouths
So open to the firm wet searching tips
That passion drove off guilt, their chaperone,
Till blushing and reluctant they returned
To hear an evening message, then depart.

The preacher with his Bible stood alone
Beside the spring that gave the church its name,
Declaring how God made the dark and light,
The waters of the heavens and the stars,
While overhead the congregated fires
Of southern constellations held their course
Flaring out of the Lord's imperative,
Spinning the endless sentence of His will.

And so with God's two books become as one—
Pages of Genesis blazoned in the sky—
The service closed and all the farmers turned
By foot, horse, mule, and wagon toward the roads
Laid over trails first cut by buffalo
Grazing these hills twelve thousand years ago.
And as they neared their lonely homes they saw
Against the primal outline of the corn
A hay-stuffed scarecrow crucified in light
Descended from a distant quarter-moon,
His painted face so bright and unaware,
His voice a wind that rises in the maize,
Old ragged Adam working all his days
There in the very place where Michael's blade
To keep God's holy ground from mortal eyes
Swung blazing from the gates of paradise.

Of Lunar History

Born of the cataclysms of the core
Or captured by a weighty sway of air,
The moon stared down on earth's erupted shores,
Unnamed, unapprehended, unaware.

Then marking time so time might come to be,
Its changing light awoke inchoate mind
Which gathered from the dusty lunar seas
The Huntress and the Witch and Pluto's Bride.

And in those days when time grew great with child
Through Mary's blood whose cycles mimed its course
The moon shone on the stable and the hill
Made bright with light drawn down toward light's own source.

Yet no less bright and fair through starkest nights
It glared on Nagasaki's glowing tomb
And on those souls that suffered holocaust
In showers and the ovens and the womb.

No wonder then when in that dust and stone
Where astronauts plant flags and breathe earth's air
We see a face whose gaze contains our own
Transfixed by history's brooding lunar stare.

From the Journal of Branwell Brontë

the Black Bull Inn, Haworth, January, 1848

In this dark place where visions fail
Between black pints of Yorkshire ale
While hard against shut tavern doors
Snow blows from godforsaken moors

I think of when our father came
With soldier-toys we made a game
And then a world for which I grieve,
Play's Eden place I'll never leave.

Now Charlotte, Emily, and Anne
Write secretly apart and plan
To make the sprites of fairy tales
Gruff Yorkshiremen in Yorkshire dales.

But nothing of their novel art

Can capture Glasstown or a heart
That only some most potent brew
Or drugs console now play is through.

And though my life has been a waste
By pain, disease, and failure graced,
That life seems richer than the prose
Ambitious sisters still compose.

Yet if at last they earn their fame
Biographers will learn the name
Of one who roamed on darker moors
Than those outside the Black Bull's doors.

The Enclosed Order

His parchment legal sheets,
A flare-tip pen his brush,
On brief internal retreats
He finds within the rush
Of ringing hours that pass
In conference and class
Eternity-in-time,
The closure of a rhyme.

Those public places sought
Across the altar rail
Or lectern where he taught
Grow private as they fail
The herbalist of words
Who knows his verse engirds
The ground he has to fill
With garlic, hyssop, dill.

Devoted to the names
Of those who kept the Word—
Tyndale, Cranmer, James—
(Grave cadences unheard)
He serves the old estate:
Incising fine and late
By Ptolemaic globe
The copper scrolls of Job.

Along the Banks of Pishon

A river flowed out of Eden . . .
Genesis 2:10

We saw it first and only when we raised
Eyes dazed by the primal blinding of its sheen
Flowing cold and golden as it blazed
Along the flawless fault of its ravine.

Then come from the living waters vivified
We lay on tangled banks of marigold
Sighing in scented winds that now replied
With all the holy silence had foretold.

The pomegranate, apricot, and palm
Heavy with fruit that hung forever there
Ripened in time while deep in timeless calm
The healing leaves dripped balm in balmy air.

Then one still summer noon the sun would come
To lave with light the river's cloven flow
Till shades of onyx-stone and bdellium
Shone in the golden bed that glowed below.

And there we swam within the current's surge
Then drifted as it thrilled us with our fear
Of being drowned where dark and light converge
Or so we sang as Noah's clouds drew near.

So, too, in these drained fields we find no rest
Scything the grain or pruning back the vine
While loam crumbles and foams on the river's crest
Yet still we long to taste the bread and wine

For Pishon flows from Eden like a fountain
Washing the Dead Sea clean of all its salt
Then turning round beside God's Holy Mountain
Goes flowing back again along a fault

To paradise where Adam named each thing
Under the twining boughs on either shore
Whose leaf and fruit and bloom together cling
Upon the Tree of Life forevermore.

Junior Warden

> In an Episcopal church, "the junior warden is responsible for the maintenance of buildings and grounds."
>
> *A New Dictionary for Episcopalians* (1985)

for Millicent

My charge might seem to be the lesser thing
Like Martha's sweat to Mary's scented hair
For neither grounds nor buildings make a church
But people—as repeatedly we're told
By those whose faith may nonetheless increase
When graves are graced by lilies and the palm
And stained-glass angels fill with Easter light
That thrills me like a love-hug at the Peace.

I'm God's odd-jobber of the common task—
Blocked drains, frayed wiring, beetle-eaten trees,
The playground's rusted slides and glider-pipes,
Leached water in the floorboards, belfry bats,
And termite-rafters cracking wild in storms
That drench our sanctuary's fresco-dome
Till stars drip down behind the altar rail
On church mice munching dry unleavened crumbs.

Workdays, it seems, the parish is my own,
The priest and people mostly self-excused,
Yet those few hearty souls who come at dawn
To pull up poison ivy from the shrubs,
Scrub lichen off the sunlight whitened tombs
And paint the children's swings bright red and blue
Bond deeply in exhaustion's sweet release,
Our bodies' salt their shared mortality.

And though I still find idols in the minds
Of some who pine for worn-out things and ways—
Staid vestries, deacons, priests, and fusty rites,
A church turned inward, dreaming of its past
And all those golden shields of Solomon—
I know my womanhood's essential good
In every Adam's longing for his Eve
And in each child their soulful loving brings.

So, too, at parish dinners and the Mass
In due and just proportions we receive
A foretaste of the Lamb's great wedding feast

And almost glimpse the New Jerusalem
In heaven's grounds and buildings raised by love,
God's temple of the body and the stars
Where Jesus washed the dust from Peter's feet
And made mere bread and wine His flesh and blood.

The Deep South, the 1840s

1 Frost in August

Humid light tinges the late predawn
In black skies faintly fading deep slate blue.
Stars glint in iron heavens soon withdrawn
Beyond a pastel azure's placid hue.
Smooth limbs of the bloomed mimosas barely sway
Against the prior stillness they declare.
Short nights stay far too warm to take away
Heat poured from the brightest heights of midday air.
Along a stream the dark's departing moon
Casts down into the grass that now grows slow
Pale beams that seem more lucid than the noon
In reaching through the shades toward things below.
Mature black crickets, rubbing wing on wing,
Detect the slightest cooling in the breeze.
Later, mated females filled by what they sing
Will lay thick globs of eggs before the freeze.

2 Song of the Stunted Oak

Born of a seed that fell
Into the dark I dwell
Under an ancient spell
Here where I grew.

All through the spring I urge
Summer's green leaves to emerge
Yet the first cricket's dirge
Calls me to you.

Stunted and young I rot
Into my birthing spot,
Mother, your womb my lot,
Hail and adieu.

The Wargamer

Bending the mapboard back
Unfolding Waterloo,
His fingers sift the stack
Of counters pink and blue
Into opposing groups
Of abstract cardboard troops.

Each corps, each division,
As the rules plainly state,
Must with great precision
Be placed to emulate
A history without gore,
Art of the art of war.

Wholly absorbed in play,
Indifferent to the end,
A master either way
To attack or to defend,
He doesn't have to care,
Playing solitaire.

At Quatre Bras to start
Ney battles on the heights,
Dice and the combat chart
Decide the bloodless fights
In cipher-sayings grim:
"A-back-2." "D-elim."

The dead pile grows all day,
A pink hill flecked with blue,
As Wellington gives way
And the Old Guard crashes through
Leaving the board to win
Deep in the dark Ardennes.

And so the gamer's drained
By carnage on the hexes
Where fantasy is pained
By nothing stark that vexes,
No bloated human meat,
Historical defeat.

The New World

Before they saw the shore
They smelled the sweetened trees
At fifty miles or more,
Cold England's pilgrim poor,
The lion's spoor, the lees.
The strange land held its course:
They drifted toward the source.
Then, by the scrolling roar's
Blank histories of the sea,
An old hint sent before
Out of a great cat's gore,
Wild swarms of scented bees
Filled honeycombs to please
All who would ask no more.

The Yeoman Farmers: North Louisiana, 1840-1914

for the Agrarians

We left the Carolinas in our prime
Exhausted by those bleak depleted fields
And like our fathers sought a virgin earth
Not on the eastern coastland with its waves
That brought us here from Europe's colder shores
But to the west far inland till we came
Beyond the Rio Flores to a place
Of buckled wolds uprisen from a sea
Whose salt and sand still glint in sandy hills
And saline springs that bubble from the domes.
We stopped somewhere beyond the Ouachita
In wilderness that struck bewildered eyes
As Adam's land unplowed six thousand years,
And there we swore to stay and break the soil
That we might eat its fruit as God's own words
And be at once the thing we taste and say,
Old cloven roots abloom in man and earth.

To all we saw we gave those common names
That brought the sheer appearances so near
In iron-capped hills braced against Arctic winds
Or bottomlands weighed down with graded clays,
And there in time the trees of Eden rose—

Red oak and blackjack oak, loblolly pine,
And spread along the green primeval streams
Or raft lakes rising and falling with the Red
The dogwood, hawthorn, cypress, water-elm,
Overcup oak, and willows near the bogs
Clotted with bloodroot, aster, goldenrod.
These things declared the seasons in their prime
And in their rugged coverture secured
That ground from which in our own tongue there came
Strains of an ancient anthem of the land,
A floral oratorio proclaimed
By plighted light so holy to behold:
The twayblade and the nodding indigo,
White mayhaws slashing wild through dandelions,
The early buttercups and lyre-leaved sage
Turning the springtime pastures pink and blue,
And resurrection ferns that feather the oaks
With leaves made green again in each new rain.

Such wonders trembled near us in a wind
Articulate with speeches of the trees,
And when we read the Bible and we gazed
From Holy Writ to this unbroken ground
We sometimes saw the olives of Carmel,
Philistia's headed barley, glinting grapes
Grown ripe across the bright Judean hills,
Or clustered pulpy dates of Jericho,
And as we gazed we tasted in a daze
A honeyed milk drawn sweet from salty springs.
But this at best was Eden unreclaimed,
Not paradise but forest where we shaped
By work that would have strained bent Adam's back
Each garden, orchard, pasture, pen, and field
Out of an earth no plow had ever turned.
And there the oxen dragged sharp coulter-blades
Through loam from which our seed-corn sprouted high,
Those tall green stalks long summers filled with ears
That dried in barns where like a harvest god
The welcome kingsnake slithered in the cribs.

The garden in its seasons gave and gave—
Spring's early peas and onions, summer beans,
Then mustard greens and collards through the fall
While orchards swelled the bins with ready fruits,
The apple, peach, persimmon, fig, and pear—
Riches that came alone from constant toil
In spite of storm and drought and pestilence,

Crops rotting in the shallow lakes of rain,
Then shriveled in the cracked and baking earth
Or feasted on by beetles, worms, and birds
And by disease for which we had no name.
Those years of mere subsistence fixed our wills
And we survived, thriving in privation,
Freeholders of the soul's created ground,
No longer pioneers who barely lived
Hardscrabbling day by day to eat and be
But yeomen so possessed by what we owned
The rhythms of the seasons made us sing
Plain verses turned in earth and heart and mind.
And from such work recalled in latest dusk,
The furrowed fields agleam with sweat and dew,
We washed, sat down to supper, and then praised
The Father whose great mystery remains
This uttered earth His Word alone sustains.

Baked ham from pigs made fat on homegrown grain,
Plates piled with turnips, field peas, lima beans,
Mashed potatoes with red-eye gravy pools,
Cornbread to sop pot licker from the greens,
That was the common fare we relished best,
And after, while the kitchen's built-up heat
Moved out into the early evening cool,
We settled on the porch and put in words
The customary wonders of the day,
Those stories children gathered in their hearts
To blaze in recollection like a faith.
And when at last we had no more to say
We watched the stars whose tale was like our own—
Old yeomen of the cold blue fields of space!—
And knew that deepest peace a freehold brings
Where all is seen and done as sacral act
As on those nights when we could faintly hear
Dry cisterns hiss with warm late summer rains,
While in the bed, flesh answering to flesh,
We filled the womb's rich ground with human seed.

And so we lived for years almost the same
As when we cleared the wilderness and found
High pasturelands still grazed by buffalo
And meadows where the startled bobwhites rose
In choral odes composed of their own name.
Then came that blighted time when cotton lords
Drove us into a war to save their slaves,
Men just like us, yet who had worked the land,

Not as themselves, but others' property.
And in defeat we, too, were all but slaves
Sold into debt and tenantry and lien
Long after Yankees burned our crops and stole
Not only from the planters on the Red
But us as well who might have called them kin,
Those farm boys from Ohio and Vermont.
Yet worst of all was something that broke free
From shattered chains which held it through the war,
A strange, detached, new terrifying mind
Both bestial and angelic in its pride,
A mind that we saw realized in acts
When loggers cut out all the yellow pine
Leaving stripped hills the rains would wash away,
Or when, in bright savannahs, where the pinks
Spread blushing in the flush of early spring,
Great metal wells made dreadful silhouettes
Like huge black praying mantises that bowed
Each time they turned their wheels and from the ground
Pumped up as holy oil the spoiled remains
Of creatures left for ages undisturbed.

In such a world but few of us still live
As neighboring relations on these farms
Whose graveyards bear the same repeated names
Through generations, stone by native stone,
And yet we stay in witness to a time
Before the long poled wires brought telephones
To tell us quick what might have kept a while,
A time when these as yet unclouded skies
Would darken when we saw the massive flocks—
Passenger pigeons!—casting on the ground
Vast shadows of themselves that haunt the mind
Because we still remember how they died:
The men who came by night with torch and rod
Slaughtering whole rookeries for the meat—
A thousand barrels daily to New York!—
The young left in their nests to cry and starve
Until the last bird perished in a zoo
That summer when the war to end all wars
Broke out in mad attacks that would not stop
Till mustard gas, machine guns, tanks, and planes
Blackened the trench-scarred farms of Catholic France.

The South

> I am afraid of those Great Suns.
> Emily Dickinson, in 1858, to a friend
> spending a summer in New Orleans

for Andrew Lytle (1902-1995)

Down here great Sherman suns burned up
The sweetest fields our Aprils bring,
Gay daisies blazed with buttercups,
The cavaliers of spring.

Then summer heat's oppressive strokes
Made drunken sons of memory
Raise Dixies under courthouse oaks
To the sober bust of Lee.

Soon Indian summers of the fall
Possessed them as the past was sold:
They swayed when northern plants grew tall
In goldenrod so gold.

Now trembling ironweeds rust and fold
At a touch of winter chill
While round the courthouse, green and old,
The pastoral oaks grow still.

Oak Alley

for L. P. S.

1

Having toured the house, old wood restored with care,
You walked the long green corridors of shade
Formed by those great oaks and drew out of the air
A history of the South your musings made.

Your mind went back three hundred years ago
To when an unknown Frenchman drained the land
Clearing virgin wood of ash and tupelo
Set thick in gumbo clays and river sand.

The modest cypress cottage long since gone,
Its trees, planted as saplings to enhance
A dwelling-place, grew massive on the lawn,
Seedlings of Eden, gigantic in their trance.

Perhaps you saw as well young trunks in their prime
Torched by autumn suns along the carriageway
Where sugar princes danced at harvest time,
Their bourbon glasses tinkling on the tray.

Or else a family dinner: deep blue plates
Of willowware filled from hot tureens,
Then placed by slaves in warmers near the grates,
Gravy ladled out over the pastoral scenes.

But most of all you listened for refrains
Sung by exhausted field hands, cries of the heart,
Burdens of an undersong whose strains
In time would tear their masters' world apart.

And though the planters had a case, a right
To their secession, it cannot be denied
That goods begat goods when slaves cut cane by night—
Acts of agrarian usury and pride!

Then, after the war, history and fiction,
Chronicling this world as though a single art,
Shared the metaphysical dereliction
Of houses they could enter, not depart.

Such disciplines, you sensed, but touched the mysteries:
What deeper craft could teach you more than these?

2

For years you probed to locate deep disease
In the Old South and New England, twin
Empires of modernity, each one at ease
With its own myth of innocence and sin.

Slave worlds of the cotton field and northern mill—
Both marked the bleak distinctions you refined:
The second fall of man from guilt to will,
The war of the secession of the mind.

Chiron's mythic school within the linden trees,
Platonic noons of stilled Ilissian planes,

Scriptoria, universities—in these
You found a third estate the intellect sustains.

Awareness of being, lost to the absurd
In closures of sophistic church and state—
Serving the realm of letters and the Word
You left those mute dominions to their fate.

Yet from your own domain there would emerge
A gnostic science no common tongues contain
But only coded symbols that diverge
From discourse into the wordless dark arcane.

Searching the twilight skies of Christendom,
Oppressed by melancholy and despair,
A wise man, yet a shepherd, you had come
To wonder if the Star was ever there.

Still, in all you wrote, you kept alive old norms—
Edited, annotated, codified—
Made essays that attained primary forms,
And mourned the prose renascence while it died.

Then, like Socrates, hearkening to the end,
You turned to poetry and lately sensed
In Tate and his successors some firm trend
Toward what your musing daimon had evinced:

A southern poetic, Thomistic, undeprived,
Apollo lost in Christ and glorified.

3

These things all held within, you came to stand
Beneath Augustan oaks—dense as the screen
Of history, remote yet close at hand—
And gazed upon the primal southern scene.

Here exiles lost to innocence betrayed
Two rooted peoples, black and native red,
And while the fields of paradise still paid
Heard none but the soothing words their serpent said.

And so, where the Mississippi's foaming mouth
Enters a sunlit gulf and voids its silt,
Rich earth brought forth the Matter of the South
Out of the seeds of chivalry and guilt.

That was the precious blessing: to be cursed
By Eve's plantations, green dreams of Adam's fall,
And thus made proof against the very worst,
A world that cannot taste its bitter gall.

Built in that place by artisans and slaves,
Oak Alley was abandoned, then restored,
Its servants and their masters safe in graves,
Untroubled by the raised or broken sword.

And there like one who versed and harmonized
Apollo's hymn and Aesop, in his cell—
Pure intellect and nature moralized—
You measured out a pastoral citadel

Far from those prose myths of Tara and Legree
Until at last poiesis set you free.

For John Finlay (1941-1991)

I met you on Good Friday at the wedding
Of a friend, and struck by your strong voice, broad
Forehead, wiry build, and penetrating mind
Determined to know you better.
                                        Later,
In Baton Rouge, we read each other's poems
Testing the rhythms, images, and rhymes,
Struggling to master this greatest of all crafts,
Craving the grace of one perfected page.
Truly a man of letters who could love
Blunt Johnson and the nuances of James
And ask how that which says "the mind is weak"
Can state its law and yet transcend the same,
You wrote clean abstract poems in plainest style
And sensuous descriptions charged with thought,
Probing toward the source and end of intellect
That marks our place in all the Maker wrought.
Both natives of the South trying to reclaim
Something of Greece and Christendom, we'd walk
To the Union from our desks in Allen Hall
Talking of Homer, Dante, Winters, Tate,
A "Stanford" or a "Simpson" *Southern Review*,
Finding ourselves as poets and as friends
There, at LSU, in those sweet-olive days,
Summer seeming endless in sunlit colonnades.

At Franklin

And where, O Allen Tate, are the dead?
Donald Davidson to Tate, 15 February 1927

for Charles C. Clark

1

The dead lie here beneath each measured stone
Anonymous yet known to Him alone
Who holds their souls while undecayed remains
Of dust and bone still touched by winter rains
Sink slowly to a buckled limestone bed
Whose sea had been a word the Maker said.
And opening the gate in autumn light
We come at dusk to know them as we might,
No Eleatic strangers made absurd
By loss of faith in action or the Word,
Nor elegizing hierophants who claim
To keep alive a waning sacred flame
But seekers who would bring to what they find
A loving objectivity of mind.
Such love would tell in time the dead had fought
Not only for the world the planters wrought
But for the sheer adventure, the élan
Of mortal battle called up by blood and clan,
States' rights, escape from boredom on the farm,
Concern that their own kin might come to harm
And at the last perhaps from some vague dread
That *things themselves*, as Davidson once said,
Were being rooted out from given ground,
Then floated in a pool the psyche found
Within itself, mere images displaced
From that full life with which they had been graced.
And thus the nearly fifteen hundred souls
Whose names would soon be stricken from the rolls
Had come to Winstead Hill where state by state
In closing ranks grown still as day grew late
Filled with the grim presentiment of loss
They saw that open ground they had to cross
Confronting Union guns and musketry.
And of these men the men of Tennessee
Alone could gaze again on what they craved,
A land four hundred battles had not saved
Yet held in memory's blood grown flush with love:

Uplands and plateaus once so clouded above
By migrant flocks of pigeons that the sun
Hid by the flapping blackness seemed undone,
Deep rivers and the mountain streams so clear
Running through woods where Indians would spear
The cornered bear or chase a white-tailed doe
In auric glades whose noon's archaic glow
Had lured those first explorers toward a ground
Of open gold the old long hunters found
When one loud shot flushed out a thousand quail
And brought the settlers down the narrow trail
With tools made by and for the human hand
Tempering wilderness to useful land,
This place of common riches—collard greens,
Glazed hams and buttered cornpone, young snap beans
And winesap apples, thick biscuits and the sweet
Spring water welling up, and bourbon neat.
Such memories, once theirs, we hold alone
Inside this fence, spiked iron guarding stone
Where leaves fall as they will and lichens spread
While high in the fluted cedars overhead
Winds carry the last male crickets' rising cries
Toward Franklin as the autumn twilight dies.

2

Hood stood on Winstead Hill as best he might
With crutch and stump, determined on a fight,
His field glasses trained, oblique to failing day
On Franklin where a Union army lay
Dug in on chosen ground it swore to keep
Waiting behind high breastworks and those deep
Empty ditches near which the cannon massed
Against the dream that held him to the last—
To Nashville! turning Sherman from the sea,
Then through the Gap to Grant, crushing him with Lee.
Such was the deadly rhetoric that Hood
Would see enfleshed in bodies dripping blood,
Hyperbole made lethal by a mind's
Wild Viking will that nothing ever binds
To truth but tragic acts beyond control,
Some Celtic fatalism of the soul.
And thus with no artillery, reserves,
Or plan but the dreaded gesture that serves
No further purpose—a charge doomed to halt
At earthworks over fields the blood-drops salt—

Hood ordered the attack as hazy light
Windless and warm gave way to early night,
And soon two corps of eighteen thousand men
Raised up with ragged battle-flags a din
Of hellish yells moving north again,
Gray and butternut over the bluegrass plain.
Ahead, in the coming dusk, rabbits and quail
Panicked as the yells became a wail
When Union guns tore Brown and Cleburne's lines
Mangling legs and torsos, snapping spines
With canister and ball in enfilade
While to the front behind each palisade
Riflemen poured forth concentrated fire
Riddling shattered ranks that staggered in a mire
Of their own guts and blood when the volleys told,
Whole men dissolved in gore no hands could hold.
The works were breached, then sealed, the battle lost
But not yet ended: night brought holocaust.
For pinned beneath huge headlogs by the bank
Of parapets men killed and died point-blank
In those blood-pits of sacrifice so steep
That in the end the dead lay seven deep.
By moonlight, rats and looters roamed at large,
Feasting on the carnage of the charge
While Schofield, as he planned, just slipped away
Leaving the consequences of the day
To one whom smoke and distance and the dark
So blinded that he could not watch the stark
Horror he caused or see how many died,
Including those four generals side by side
Laid out on Carnton's gallery while Hood
Moved on to Nashville, as he swore he would.
And there when ice froze light itself to ground
He saw an iron Zion ringed around
With batteries and breastworks to defend
Its powdermills and foundries without end,
A fortress of numbers, sheer materiel
From which, when pressed, the Rebels fled pell-mell
Their bare split feet streaking snow with blood;
By Forrest screened, they sang of John Bell Hood.

3

The army straggled back through Franklin where the dead
Lay tangled still in trenches while instead
Of marble slabs or tombstones with a name,

Each birth date, and the one death date the same
Which nearly eighteen hundred men now bore,
30 November 1864
Only a few small crosses in the snow
Marked where the frozen bodies thawed below.
Then, in the second spring, McGavock gave
A portion of his land for one great grave
Where state by state beneath each measured stone
The dead remain, anonymous and known.
Yet have we done them justice by the claim
That some "immoderate past" or conjured name—
"Stonewall, Stonewall," "Antietam, Malvern Hill"—
Damns us to inaction, paralyzes will,
Leaving us not wise Clio or the still
Visage of Mnemosyne but a fool
Jaguar leaping to his image in a pool
Or else a sidling Eliotic crab
Washed in a tidal life surely too drab
For any landed man—or by those cries
So partisan, yells rattling into sighs,
Old longings wandering solemnly at large,
"The Army of Tennessee knows how to charge"
(But to what end and under what command
And to defend what cause, to take what stand?),
Or wishing just to say as Cleburne then
"If we are to die, let us die like men"—
Or should we try to voice and usher in
Those truths which history's dead keep hidden still
From that twin face of fixed hermetic will
Whose gazes neither hold nor yet dismiss us:
Nostalgia and Narcissus as Narcissus?
For all the world is Nashville or would be
As seen by Hood before he had to flee
Like him whose deathless mother once revealed
What battle-smoke and matter had concealed,
"Dread shapes come into view—mighty powers"
Whose timeless minds decreed Troy's final hours,
"The gods, the relentless gods" behind the fire:
Neptune, Juno, Pallas, and The Sire.
Yet here, where Hood was blinded by the smoke
And solipsistic will, no goddess spoke,
Nor did the long campaign take us to Rome
But on to Appomattox, Durham, home,
Home to become a self-made bonded race
Compelled to build New Corinth deep in Thrace
And then to come to like it, just as these
Commuters through the twilight's last degrees,

Back now from Nashville, take to a tennis court
Beside the graves where catgut makes report
The ball pocking as the players charge the net
Trading shots in darkness through the set,
Taut muscles moving to a full steady breath,
Their dream the modern dream—to ace out death
Or take him strong with each deep lob and volley
To the final breakpoint—madness and folly
Spared the Mound-Builders whose village once was here,
These dead as well whose stillness draws us near.

Palm Sunday, 1865

for Shirley

Stirred ashes of the last encampment glowed
A moment in the dawn that Lenten day
After the night's bleak council had resolved
To try once more to break out to the west
And Lee took to his tent to wait and pray.
The spiked palmettos shivered on the verge
Of Holy Week when Lincoln like a god
Would move through Richmond hailed by faithful slaves
As their redeemer-king, no more than days
From comedy a plot turned passion play.
But as for us who tested federal lines
That Sabbath morning—pressing horse and gun
Until they melted back through those massed corps
Not even Stonewall, God's quick justicer,
Could then have turned and routed, had he lived—
We knew capitulation would confirm
Only what martial force and partial truths
Rooted in new taboos could realize.
And so, though all was lost, those four seared years
Became a demarcation scorched with fire
On breasts possessed by undivided love,
And our defeat just pickets driven in
Along a single front that since has spread
Across the earth in open total war
Gone far beyond the vaunted holocausts
Of Fredericksburg, Cold Harbor, Pickett's Charge.
And though we could not know it at the time
When Traveller passed between the still blue lines—
Surrendered Lee, immaculate in pain—
We sensed that Appomattox made no end

Of this sustained engagement to the death
Between the given world and wild desire.
And that is why Palm Sunday in a Lent
Extending past the fiery pride of those
Whose homes, now ash, had thrown their columned flames
High in the ancient houses of the night,
We rode beyond the lines that Gordon held,
And once more to affirm what we would be,
As truce flags fluttered white by our struck tents
And cherry blossoms fell like April snow,
Across the burning ground of our own lives
We turned and headed south with Fitzhugh Lee.

Thoreau's Farewell to Concord: A Mirror for Modern Magistrates

Richard Weaver, i.m.,
and for David Bovenizer, who once read Weaver by Walden Pond

Now that my shoes are mended, once again
I'll shake the dust of Concord from my feet
And follow whims that flutter from within
Leading my heart to drum its rebel beat.

I never joined the family, church, or state
And feel no guilt for duties left undone,
Though who but I was fit to consecrate
Myself as priest and regent of the One?

The pencil factory, Harvard, and the school
Are bodies of no consequence to me.
They served my higher purpose, each a tool
I used to forge a soul in secrecy.

How well I know the fate of Socrates!
Why should I stay to drink such poison down
Administered by those it did not please
To recognize in me a one-man town?

In truth, my night in jail was little more
Than time to eat and sleep and sense again
How right it is to publicly deplore
Each thing my private conscience deems a sin.

I'm glad, of course, my college had its books,

My pupils their tuition, and the Sage
Of Concord work for one on whom he looks
As friend and fellow prophet of the age.

And, yes, I'll wander far in mended shoes
Beyond the cobbler's hammer and his bill,
But that's all past: I'll pay no other dues
Except to follow fancy where it will.

And now some people wait impatiently
For me to lead them up a hill I know
On which there's no authority but me
To show them where God's huckleberries grow.

The Old Bank in Saline

> For what shall it profit a man,
> if he should gain the whole world,
> and lose his own soul?

The locked front door holds firm though broken panes
Above the worn brass knob go unrepaired.
Late afternoons the tellers' rusted trays
Take in the gold the sun deposits there
Descending through a haze of yellow dust
That settles far beyond all human care.
Beside a filing cabinet's empty drawers
A calendar for 1959
Cut from a southern almanac declares
A January holiday for Lee,
The weather and the moons, best planting times,
Aquarius and Christ's Epiphany.
And through the wavy blocks of jagged glass,
Peering with thick-lensed eyes made dim with age
I'm swept by love's great elegiac sway
Back forty years when I would toddle down
Past open doors and tellers to your lap,
Grandfather Sudduth, president and mayor
Of this small bank and sandy pine hill town.

And even now I seem to find you there
In plain white shirt, black coat, and straight black tie
Leaning over a ledger's columned page,
Your fountain pen dipped deep in purple ink
To reconcile and balance, rectify.

And when you read the numbers and the names
By signatures on mortgages and loans
You did not think of profits maximized
Through sharpness or severity but those
With whom you sat each Sunday as you prayed
Taking to heart the Baptist pastor's fire,
His bony finger tapping at the texts
About the widow's mite and Caesar's things,
Joseph enrolled, the tithe, a Wise Man's gold,
The temple's moneylenders, talents hid,
Or Judas' palm where silver burns the soul.

Thus humbled by God's justice and His love
And led by mercy's prudence you would try
To help indebted neighbors keep their homes,
Building up true community and trust
With honesty from that part mythic time
When handshakes were as good as papers signed.
The girls your loans would send to Normal School,
Come back to teach the farm boys thirty years,
Those boys' own fathers you would let hang on
When mortgage payments fell months in arrears,
Widows whose pension funds were placed so well
They'd all have gladly wed you if they could—
Such private happiness and public good
Defined a world you bettered on the way
Toward modest earnings hard and fairly gained.
And so, unchanged, your probity and word
Sustained you through not only those grave days
When FDR himself would have to write
To shut a bank untouched by panic-runs
But through Ike's richer '50s when you died
Leaving nine thousand dollars and a name
To those the name alone had satisfied.

And now as dying sunlight turns to gold
Those rooms that only memory can restore
To one who knows as you had known before
From what great depths the heart can overflow,
I walk back down to my blue Regal parked
Beside the modern bank that's since replaced
Those old gray walls condemned to slow decay
And see-through windows silvered in the dusk
Two young bank officers still working late,
Granddaughters of a man whose land you saved,
Now helping as they once were helped themselves.

And on a wall there hangs a photograph,
A gift I sent in 1994
To celebrate the founding of the bank,
Your image caught some forty years before
In honor of the first half century.
You stand erect in sober, formal pose,
Grandmother Mary Emma at your desk
Beside cut roses floating in their bowls,
Your firm hand on her shoulder gently pressed,
A patriarchal gesture, dated now,
Yet here the source of her contentedness.
Behind you two large pictures fill a shelf,
Grown children missed: Joe Lynn, a country boy
Scarred by fifty missions over the Rhine
Whose bombing left a time bomb in the heart
Exploding in his sleep at forty-five;
And by him in a golden oval frame
Anna Marie, my mother, who lives on
According to her girlhood's social code,
Expecting courtesy, good manners, taste,
Eyes saying all a lady has to say.

Long may such faces gaze from that new bank
As spirits witnessing to other days
And may the old bank building not be razed
For parking space or draw the tourists down
Who might have seen Saline in Newman's *Blaze*.
And may those yellowed ledgers in their dust
Remind us like the Bible that you kept
Beside the books to call you to account
How soon you'd have consigned to bankrupt hells
All loan sharks and those '80s S&Ls
By virtues made the coin of your just realm,
Their worth the legal tender of your ways.

Hurricane

All summer off West Africa the sun
Poured heat upon the surface of the sea
While coming from the jungle humid winds
Wove up my torrid torso as it spun.
By August I was headed for the South
Following routes the slave ships used to take
Until my spiral bands, great arms of rain,
Would lash across the waste of salt and foam

So I, the dreaded reveler of the waves,
Whose black locks raveled in the stratosphere,
Might dance my dance of death before the Keys
And in the upper Gulf when I broke clear.
And as my eye revolved, huge water-walls
Would trap tired egrets, frigate-birds, and gulls
Flown to the clouded center of my heart
Where swept in the drenched winds swirling around
They drowned aloft, then sank in Breton Sound.
At last I wobbled and stalled along the coast
Where the mouthing Mississippi's lips of silt
Curled as I drove the fecund waters from his bed
Slicing the barrier isles as I would blow
Through twisted willow, oak, and indigo.
Once over land, now holding you in throes,
I spread my fatal waves through salted grass,
Flattened the cane so sweet and green and high,
Tore wires that brought you cooling and the light,
Smashed the chapel spire, plowed up the buried dead,
And left your babies hanging in the trees.
Then feeling weak and mortal from the rage
Of such great dissipation, I drifted east
Breaking up somewhere just north of Boston.
And though again in that strange way you gave
Thanks to your Father-God for being saved,
Accepting devastation as a part
Of that inscrutable act you call the Fall,
Your weathermen are wrong to take away
From half of me those female names so real
For I am Audrey, Betsy, and Camille,
So cast aside that patriarchal myth
And worship me whose pattern is the pith
Of all that is, the brutal womb of things,
Closed systems of the woven dynamos,
And know me as the one who comes and goes,
A fury in the matter I have riven,
Myself the only giver and the given.

Hyacinth Song

for Leslie Alexius

From mother earth I came to you a gift,
An ornamental beauty rarely seen,
In lily pools and fish ponds set adrift
Where Buddhas smiled belichened and serene.

Once powdered by my pollen I soon grew
By flower and offshoot root till I became
A blossomed god flourishing as I slew
All things I could entangle in my name.

Then pulling me up and flinging me aside
In sewers or in streams you thought to be
Rid of a plant whose beauty you decried
The moment I defied you and broke free.

Spread wide by waterbirds and hurricanes
Who took my seed aloft on wind and wing—
Those lethal storms, great egrets, twisters, cranes—
I throve on death itself, my vital sting.

And blooming on from April until frost,
Changing my size and color as I will,
Choking your waterways forever lost,
I was the virulent mere that none could kill.

Your dynamite and arsenic and fire
Did nothing but disperse me more and more,
My yellow eyes made wider by desire,
My streaming leaves grown green from shore to shore

For beauty, sex, and death are Gaean powers
Aroused by the wheeling aegis of the sun,
These lavender and blue and purple flowers
Divided and dividing from the One.

The Duck Hunt

> Male and female created He them. . . .
> Genesis 1:27

for William Bedford Clark

Its ricefields bared beneath a hunter's moon,
For miles we crossed an almost treeless plain
South to the shifting edges of the Gulf.
Here doming beds of salt and crumbled marl
Had yielded to the diggers printed stone—
The primal forms of whale and mastodon,
Wide thigh-bones of a woman, shoulders of a man—
Such lay beneath a road of shell and clay

That took us into the marshes where we felt
Our senses heighten and found ourselves again
As hunters and providers, human males.

Black coffee for breakfast, boots pulled up snug
To the hips, in faintest dawn we started out
Driving beside scrub willow to the spot
From which, through silverling, elder, rattlebox,
And matted stands of man-tall yellow sedge,
Pushing out into the shallows we paddled
A light canoe, bearing by the stakes
That marked the cuts between us and our pond.
And there, knee-deep in reed-blinds, camouflaged,
We called to migrant flocks that passed above
This open wilderness of grass and mud.

By night and day, oblivious of time,
Offshore, distant rigs, ringed with warning lights,
Sent down huge bits to breach the ancient layers
And flush up oil a thousand ages made
Consumed in one short century of waste.
But here a saner pace of heartbeat and breath
Returned us to a place we once had held
In fealty to a shared apparent world
Of beast and plant, of mineral and star,
Things trusted to our knowledge, use, and care
Within the givenness of what we are.

Called back from such high musings by the cries
Of canvasbacks and mallards flapping down
To the water, we stood up, aimed, turning
As they wheeled away, firing just ahead
Of each stunned duck that arcing in dead drop
Floated in feathered wreckage on the pond.
Fair marksmen who reached our limit in the dawn,
We loaded the canoe, paddled back to shore,
Slung the chain of birds into the trunk,
And filled with a quiet archaic elation
Passed down from all our fathers, headed home.

Blue Herons

for Carolyn

The morning sun inclines us toward its light
Spreading above scrub willow and the sedge

Where swamp gives way at last to marshy ponds
Of pickerel, fire flag, and arrowhead.
And there in mangle-brush and roseau cane,
Black mangrove, matted bulrush, and the dense
Old water-groves of tupelo and gum
Or high within the doming cypress stands
We see the great blue herons in their nests,
Each platform with its clutch of pale green eggs.

Hatched out in June with softest natal down,
The birds become tall stalkers in their prime
Deliberate in movement through the pools
Darting at minnows, frogs, and dragonflies.
Their colonies remain throughout the year
Though when their northern kin who breed in cold
Then gaze toward polar wastes of ice and snow
Are drawn back south by some still hidden sign
Our residents call out while they return
Alighting on the islands and the coast.

We make no noise yet when we start to go
The herons cry and climb as toward a home
On columned drafts between the Gulf and sun,
Alive in fiery light above the foam.
Bright heirs of an almost winterless domain,
They hear our voices rising as they glide
Higher in time's elation and declare
That time is but a flyway to the side
Of one who calls all creatures by their names,
His timbre their intention on the course.

Beyond the Chandeleurs

islands reached and named by Iberville, 2 February 1699

Old channels of the river's sunken bed
Gone under shores black waters wash and tar
Ten thousand years have swung from side to side
For more than fifty miles through swamp and marsh.
And underneath the waves of Breton Sound
A buried delta settles on the shelf
Worn down by storms and tides nine centuries
Here, where the Mississippi found the Gulf
While Saint Bernard, for whom the place is named,
Inside remote Clairvaux, as tapers blazed,

Praised Mary as the mother of the child
Whose mortal flesh was hers and hers his grace.

And now, three hundred years from Iberville,
This frigid winter dawn the very day
Whose name he gave those shores toward which we sail,
We cross the sound to find the Chandeleurs
So luminous in moonlight, crescent dunes,
Bleak beaches without islands, miles from land,
Forever washed by waves that crash across
Their narrow breadth, channeling in the sand.
And as we pass by slowly, south-southwest,
We see in mingled gleams of moon and sun
Bubbling over the salt in windblown foam
The play of shape and chaos, our true home.

So, too, as that grim interim—the Break—
Rent Christendom in 1699
Iberville sailed on, blind through sleet and fog,
Threading the low marsh islands, mud-drift logs,
And those hooked spits of swirling sea and earth,
Moving through uncreation where his men
Would dig deep pits to make freshwater wells
And sleep on planks above the flooding strand.
Yet when at last he reached the Chandeleurs,
Whose myrtles yielded wax for Candlemas,
He tasted in the wind-borne glazing rain
Sweet water from the Mississippi's mouth.

And though we find no myrtles on these shores
We still can glimpse within each twinkling grain,
So near black dregs of marshes and the rigs,
Glimmering hints old Simeon discerned
In eyes that glowed with heaven's native light
Just as the stars, like whorling hurricanes,
Come from the vast galactic nursing-grounds,
Candles that burn in scattered grains of flame,
Now blaze the blatant purpose of the world
Beyond the Chandeleurs that still remain
Within this star-torched temple love preserves
Declaring till the end their given name.

THE HABITUAL PEACEFULNESS OF GRUCHY: POEMS AFTER PICTURES BY JEAN-FRANÇOIS MILLET

(2005)

Madame J.-F. Millet

Catherine Lemaire [1827-94]

ca. 1848-49

Each long precisest lash, each hooded lid
Protects in downcast eyes a mystery
Whose depths rise sympathetic to pressed lips,
This Breton Mona Lisa's dimpled smile.

You came to him at only seventeen,
Your dark bunned hair undone by pliant hands,
And bore nine sons and daughters twenty years,
Unwed, then wed in law, by church at last.

And though your only photo shows you glum,
Both staring at and past the opened lens,
This portrait, all those paintings, tell much more:
For you're the farm wife pasturing a cow,

Teaching a daughter knitting, shearing sheep,
Washing at dusk in waters of the sun,
A planter tending, gleaner bending down
Gathering field, hearth, garden into one.

Woman Pasturing Her Cow

ca. 1856-57

Too poor to let her cow graze rented ground
She leads the beast along a public way
To forage tufts beneath its line of trees
Whose stark trunks bar and mark off private land.

There, fecund herds eat grass in solar gold,
The one black bull mounting cow after cow,
A herdsman leaning forward on his staff,
Exhausted by this plenty he defends.

The woman stays beside her single charge—
Gaunt haunches and the marrow-harrowed bone,
The vivid ribs and skin like fleshly bellows—
And does not gaze upon those Helian fields

But stands erect with staff against her lap,
Knitting between her pregnant belly, breasts,
Contented with subsistence like her cow
Cropping in dark by arpents of the sun.

Knitting Lesson I

ca. 1854

Through windowpanes the filtered winter light
Passing over a basket's rumpled yarn
Covers a mother's radiant bent face
Whose cheek and chin rest on her daughter's head.

The young girl holds in small soft awkward hands
Long knitting needles glinting in the threads
Looped round a knuckle, woven, then pulled tight,
Part of a garment shadowed in her lap.

With palms grown rough in mastering her craft
The mother, from behind, now clasps and guides
Her daughter's pale pink fingers through their task,
Both bracing and embracing as the dusk

Gathers the light from bonnet, coat, and skirt
That muffle intensest women who themselves
Pull wool from sheep to card, then spin and knit
Into the well-made garments of their lives.

Shearing Sheep

1852-53

A green tree shears the dusky sun in half
Before a thatched stone barn and open hut
Under whose hill of drying, settled grain
A sheep is held and clipped on a barrel top.

The woman, young, well-muscled, bends and snips,
Her free hand braced in clutching uncut curls;
Meanwhile, an older man in peasant blue,

Grimacing, grasps the sheep's feet two by two.

The flock press their wet noses through the bare
Slats of gates where the next ewe on its back
Squirms in cold mud with lashed hooves lurching free,
All caught—these beasts and souls—in raw May air

And in an artist's dream of splitting suns
That die in trees, clumped wool, thatch-raftered grain
And fixed tellurian laborers who stay
Stray solar ghosts chthonian to the bone.

Washerwomen

ca. 1855

The sun still cleans its sky with parting light
Reflected in a pond though pond and sky
Turn turquoise now in evening's spreading stains.
Between them both a long green bank divides

The waters of the heavens and the loam,
Its strip of grass and clay floating amid
This earth and that unearthly realm of stars
Whose arras decks a grove of trees and homes.

By water's edge two washerwomen work
With things wrung free a while of dirt and sweat,
One bent beneath her burden, hand on hip,
The other gently loading on the clothes.

Soon night will wash faint sunlight from the stars,
The dredger pole his high-piled boat toward shore
To raise a sinking house on sand whose grains
No one can scrub from nothing's cloak of stone.

Potato Planters

1861-62

The plot is small, a patch of ocher-browns
Adorned by kingly purples where a man

Digs out a row of holes in which his wife
Drops seed potatoes from a white cloth sack.

Beyond them, Chailly Plain, that vast expanse
Of green and yellow grasses, fertile herds,
And in between the plot and plain, two trees
Whose yellows, greens, and browns unite the scene.

The trees bring gifts of coolness, quiet, and shade
To a basket's dreaming child where watchful eyes
Of a donkey seem to almost comprehend
This infant still asleep in Bethlehem.

The planters' clothes are streaked with clinging earth
That yields a crop some scorn as human food,
But not this family, poorer than the ground,
Their hunger numb to beauty's ocher-browns.

The Gleaners

ca. 1857

Two women bend, a third strains, back half-bowed,
Searching for stalks in well-picked-over fields,
Their meager gleanings clutched to spine, knee, thigh,
Leavings strewn in stubble on this shorn ground.

Paid peasants in the distance thresh and bale
The wheat and hay where a horsed overseer
Directs his laborers by voice or hand,
Boaz remote from these three silent Ruths

Or, more so, the Fates, stark daughters of Night,
Allotters whose dark word destines the child,
Who spin cut hay or wheat in auric weave,
Birth-spirits, from the Second Empire born.

In early drawings, they bow down toward us,
And children bind black sheaves in gay bouquets
While far carts, weighed with grain, are brought so near
We all must breathe the fatal golden dust.

Bust of a Female Nude

ca. 1847-50

Not any nude, but Catherine, we think,
Sometime between nineteen and twenty-three,
Model, or inspiration at the least,
In Paris or your exile's Barbizon.

We see you with your worn black crayon raised
To lift up from flat paper rounded breasts,
Sleek muscled arms, taut belly, and a face
Held fast by pure detachment and desire.

And so we sketch a scene in dusk's spent light,
Catherine's wrap descending from her hips,
Your dusty chalk-stub put aside at last,
The studio abandoned for the bed.

And thus she draws you down to what you'd drawn,
A woman flush beyond your crayon's art,
Now coaxing you to be a man alone
And know her in the mortal flesh apart.

In the Garden

ca. 1860

A garden dug in Barbizon—Millet's?—
Late spring or early summer it would seem,
Green sprouts from carrots, onions, beets, and beans
Maturing by the headed lettuce leaves.

Two children still in Eden find themselves
Either side of a twisted cedar tree.
The toddler waves a stick at hungry hens
Poised at the very edge of her domain.

The elder, twelve, leans back against the trunk,
Her hands doing the mending while her eyes
Stare far beyond squat beehives side by side
Whose stings and honey mark the garden's end.

Beside the girl a plain brown basket spills
Bunched linen like the horn of plenty's fruit.
She peers at clouds that soon will bring a rain
Of Adam's sweat and Eve's maternal tears.

Newborn Lamb

1866

The swung-back gate leans still against its hedge
Whose shrubs curl in a tangled darkened arch
Through which a girl bears off a tiny lamb
Before a flock led by the mother ewe.

The ewe's raised head strains up to touch her young
But the girl, gazing on her, swings away
Cradling between her breasts and aproned womb
The warm new life that fell in meadow grass.

The shepherdess is lost in mother dreams
Though she is but thirteen and does not see
By path-side rocks the spiny yellow furze
Whose thorns prick hungry sheep that eat its leaves.

A pastoral scene from Millet's Norman home
Where his dead sister Emélie could dwell,
Here is no lamb stillborn, no mounting ram,
But gates of life refined in soft pastels.

Little Goose Girl

1868

Perched on a bank whose meadow-grass gives way
To reeds and woody limbs of toughened shrub,
The peasant child, well fed, surveys her realm,
Her first job almost one with make-believe.

Ducks waddling on a path turn verdant heads
Ruled by her limp green branch whose shriveled leaves
Are fluttering just enough to shoo them down

To cool pond water sloshing on the sand.

The meadow crests in barn and farmhouse stone
Sedate between great swathes of sky and grass.
And there, contented geese grow fat on roots,
Then come to bathe and wallow in the wet.

This place, if east of Eden, cannot be
Removed by more than one or two degrees
Of swaying shades of overgrowth whose sheen
Startles the birds and girl from dream to dream.

Goose Girl Bathing

ca. 1863

Late morning and secluded in the cool
Of May's green banks and boughs, this hidden stream,
A girl perhaps fifteen sheds all her clothes
And rests beside the waters where she'll bathe.

Her geese and ganders paddle in the wet
Where she as yet but dips one ankle in,
Her gangling body rounding out in soft
Womanly contours–thighs, hips, belly, breasts.

She's been the family goose girl thirteen years
And knows her time as such is near its end.
Between the trees of life and innocence
She stares at her reflection's steady change.

Above her, in dense foliage, two white cows
See all that young men soon will vie to see:
Flesh warming toward its noon in rose and blue,
Those filtered sun-shafts rippling in the depths.

Madame J.-F. Millet (Pauline-Virginie Ono, 1821-44)

1841

He painted her for nothing but her love,
A Cherbourg tailor's daughter without means

For such a tender rendering as this:
Desirous, tense, yet teasingly serene,

Those earth-brown irises, that slightest smile,
Hair clipped, severe, tied in a ribboned cap,
The look of expectation, quiet surprise
Directed at this man her brother knew

Who stroked her with his oils and darkened eyes
Until she came alive on canvas threads
That held her there as in her wedding bed.
And though she soon would pass beyond recall

Like those two fruitless, brief Parisian years,
Millet remembered, kept till his own death
This image both relinquished and possessed:
And Catherine saw them kiss through widow's tears.

The Lovers

ca. 1848-50

The oval cameo with bank and tree
Frames nothing else but this most secret scene:
Two faces blurred as mind drifts into sense,
Flesh waking to its latent ecstasy.

His left hand from behind holds her left breast,
His right hand stilled for now beside her crotch,
His muscled back and buttocks, bulging thighs
Ready to root him soon in softest earth.

Venus and Adonis? Adam and Eve?
Old Master precedents or peasants glimpsed?
All these perhaps yet we guess something more
Hearing a Breton housemaid's climbing cries,

She who would heal him of his first wife's death—
Tubercular Pauline who had no child—
Spreading her legs to let her belly swell
When soul and phallus spilled their pent-up seed.

Woman Sewing Beside Her Sleeping Child

ca. 1858-62

An inner twilight deepens in the room:
The smoky oil lamp pegged high on its stand,
A child tucked-in beneath the blanketing beams,
The shadowed mother mending in her chair.

She pulls a woolen thread to close a seam
In the work shirt of a father still afield
Plowing his darkened rows until the stars
Gleam twinkling from the yielding fertile earth.

Behind the smoke that clusters into curls
A bed whose drapes recall a garden wall
Awaits her strong young husband and the night,
Her warm wet furrow eager for his seed.

The child will never waken from the bed,
The mother never finish like Millet
Who made of color-threads this scene he dreamed
Between the twilight times of dusk and dawn.

Faggot Gatherers on the Edge of Fontainebleau Forest

ca. 1850

They came when he had laid his brushes down,
Light passing from the palette and his face
As evening drew him near the forest's edge
To be at peace among his painted scenes.

But seated under finished winter trees
Whose wild fall fruit had fed both life and art
He soon saw limbs move stiff through Fontainebleau,
Huge bundled faggots bending backs and legs

Of stick-like human figures, crayon-gray,
Old women and the poorest of the poor
Gathering sheaves to stave off death with fire.
And when at last sheer pity took them in

Not as mere subjects for his craft but souls

Bearing the common burdens of this earth
He thought of one whose eyes, when half-repaired
By miracle, had seen men walk like trees.

Entrance to the Forest at Barbizon in Winter

1866-67

No springtime cows, heavy with milk or young,
Now pass the ancient gate to graze on grass
Beyond this wall of beeches dense and deep
Where birds peck up the snowflake-crusted seeds.

One stone gatepost remains, the other gone
Or crumbled into rubble in the drift
Where siftings upon siftings blow through trees,
Old matter's ghostly soul that roams the earth.

The beeches' topmost boughs branch up in V's
Outreaching to embrace down-gliding birds
Whose V-winged shapes alight on kindred limbs
Above the forest's darkened common ground.

The trees speak in a language all their own
Known only to interpreters, the birds,
Who leave their runic footprints in the snow
Before tall beeches standing there like runes.

Farmyard by Moonlight

1868

A full moon under tattered, speckled clouds
Shines down upon a courtyard where a dog
Stares back at glowing stone, yet hardly more
Aware of it than it has been of him.

The moonlight spills through gate-slats to the mud
Where a wheelbarrow with its load of sticks
Seems far from labors done or still to do.
A puddle's tufts take root in lunar seas.

Outside the yard a dead tree's scraggly limbs
Grasp ragged clouds and claw up to the moon
That stays above some central place unseen
Beyond the courtyard's blocking granite walls.

And here, though silence listens, no one states
Its blatant implications that surround
The barrow, dog, tuft-puddle, gate, and tree
Eternal in their mortal light and dark.

Landscape with Shepherdess and Sheep, Winter

ca. 1850-52

Her back against a talus topped with trees
Whose new-growth leaves and limbs have long been stripped
High as a sheep can reach, bare as her staff,
She seems as sheer and stiff as bank and trunk.

Her long plain dress and face, cape, hood, and shoes
Emerge from wastes surrounding Barbizon,
This over-cropped and well downtrodden turf,
Grim given no skilled rendering dispels.

A fallen branch lies blanched as cattle bones.
Two ewes snuggle for warmth where no grass grows.
Others pull frosted roots up where the sun
Grazes in winter dusk on frozen dew.

A draftsman mastering what he loved and knew,
First fully realized here in theme, technique,
He sensed at last his art's profoundest ground,
The pastoral raised to epic dignity.

Path Through the Wheat

ca. 1867

The hillside's tidal waves of yellow-green
Break downward into full-grown stalks of wheat
In which a peasant, shouldering his hoe
Passes along a snaking narrow path—

A teeming place through which his hard thighs press
And where his head just barely stays above
The swaying grain, drunken in abundance,
Farm buildings almost floating on the swells

Beyond which sea gulls gliding white in air
Fly down on out of sight to salty fields,
Taking the channel fish off Normandy,
A surfeit fit for Eden in its dawn.

Yet as the peasant moves through such high grass
Made edible in bread he will in time
Stumble upon a skull from Arcadie,
Abel's cranium anchoring the grain.

The Sower

1850

He strides with massive thighs and torso turned
Like Michelangelo's Adam now combined
At last with the Apollo Belvedere,
This Norman peasant scattering the corn

On broken hillside ground as twilight fails.
He binds his calves with straw against the cold,
Sowing winter wheat in mid November,
The earth disturbed again by human need.

Upon the furrowed crest a harrow dragged
By huge white oxen covers up the seed
While birds descend, black-winged, from threatening skies
To feed upon some gleaming unturned grains.

His clothes are red and blue, his eyes unseen
Beneath his low-brimmed hat, his look intent,
Inscrutable in fearful dignity,
Mysterious with life's prime mystery.

Two Men Turning over the Soil

1866

They work upon the untilled hillside soil
Rocky and uneven, all splotched with tufts
Of green and yellow grasses stark in March,
Shovels cutting and dumping lumps of earth

While midway in the distance plains seem set
For planting furrows streaked bright pink and blue,
Small piles of fired weeds making pure white smoke,
Some great estate long settled in its ways.

The father frowns and stares at bare turned ground
Beside his son who uproots turf observed
By eyes more full of wonder than despair
From those few springtime years he's labored there.

These are the priests whose solemn, common mass
Will raise up grape and grain from canvas-clays
Blocked out by Millet's crayons and pastels,
His stippled sweat saltwatering the rocks.

Buckwheat Harvest

1868-70

The ground is Norman—windswept coastal soil
As thin as seed-and-harvest time is short,
Too poor for oxen trampling out the grain
And yet a place where hardy buckwheat grows.

In stubble, bent-backed women bind and tie
The pink-white clustered flower-heads in shocks,
Then shoulder them or push square-basket sleds
Toward circled threshers raising up dead limbs.

Like some archaic pagan sacrifice,
Men thrash split stalks and chaff to free the seed.
One with a pitchfork tosses straw on fire
Whose winnowed smoke spreads high in cirrus skies.

The church in distant Gruchy's barely seen
Between these gatherings of germ and cloud,
Its steeple pitched, a shock of headed stone
To rocky backs that bow toward toil alone.

Harvesters Resting

1853

The pink and golden graindust spreads its mist
Glittering over the reapers' spare noon meal—
Water from red-brown pots of earthenware,
Mush that crude spoons scoop from a common bowl.

And while they sit or sprawl by wheat stacks swelled
Like many-breasted Cybele, one stands,
The scythers' overseer, whose arms link them
And a gleaner-girl come shy in Virgin-blue.

The tale is Ruth and Boaz now transposed
From Bethlehem to France's central plain
With Boaz no rich kinsman but the same
As these he drives for absent heirs abroad.

Though foreign, Ruth will find a husband here
And bear the common realm inside in her womb,
A Moabite at home in Israel,
Ancestress and descendent of its kings.

Gleaner Returning Home with Her Grain

ca. 1857-62

No blissful gleaner dreamed by Jules Breton
With bundled grain raised high on slender arms—
A beauty fleeing wheat fields for the town—
But one near such, in twilight left behind.

Her sheaf is balanced on her head by palms
And elbows crooked to bear her gatherings.
Beyond her, dusk's last harvesters still strain

To rake up, then haul off the fallen stalks.

Nearby, two plainer women lag behind,
Bundles shouldered or held by low-locked hands,
Climbing under a new moon's crescent rim,
A disc wedged bright in scattered ash of clouds.

The first girl's tucked-up skirt, bared petticoat,
Strong arms, broad haunches, modest ready breasts
Tell us she'll stay and be some farmer's wife
Gleaned from the leavings of her class and sex.

Return of the Flock

ca. 1863-64

Across the blue horizon that divides
Pale twilight skies from twilight-darkened earth
A shepherd leads beneath a crescent moon
His bending line of pliant moon-eyed sheep.

The laggards and the leaders, nipped by dogs,
Swirl from a formless mass of flesh and wool
Toward faces separated yet the same,
Soon lost to sun in starlight like the stars.

The shepherd in procession grasps his staff,
His right hand parting his cloak to show within
His long blue shirt, a bishop's under-robe,
Literal symbols speaking for themselves.

Both moon and flock are turning toward their homes.
This shepherd is his sheep's blind overseer.
His sheepdogs push and lead the column on
Till shepherd, prelate, moon, and flock are one.

Killing the Hog

ca. 1867-70

The painting is unfinished, rightly so,
For it depicts what never has an end:

A fat hog on her haunches pushed and drawn
Out of the barn to this small walled-in place,

Two men pulling a rope tied round the snout,
And a woman coaxing, showing the beast
A bucket's tilted lip of slop and corn,
November's emblem, bleak with our bleak need.

The hog has caught the scent of other hogs
On the butcher's stained apron and she squeals
So near the slaughter-board, the primal scene,
The long knife and the basin for the blood.

Huddled and wrapped against the wall and cold,
Two ghostly children—charcoal, not pastel—
Appalled yet famished, fix on death and ham,
This open abattoir, hunger's great I AM.

Bird Trapper

1867

The artist sets us here in this dark barn
Directed by perspective through a door
Opening on a yard now cloaked with snow
Where a propped shutter shades new-sprinkled seed.

Hard by the door a kneeling trapper peers
Along his stringy rope tied to a stick
Holding its shutter up above a bird
That takes from flakes this windfall autumn grain.

Beyond the trap and snow-topped garden wall
Warier birds watch from a leafless tree;
Others, foolish and lucky, walk the edge
Of boards that drop and smash one unaware

When a trickster yanks and the prop-stick flies,
The shutter crushing feather, beak, and skull
To add to a winnowing basket's limp heap
Of flesh well fed on manna and the Fall.

The Winnower

ca. 1847-48

for J. A. C.

Threshed wheat now rests in mounds where sackcloth frays
Threading in dark above a framework shed
Down channel winds that salt well-sweetened seed
A winnower tosses from his tight-weave scoop,

Grain beaten from light chaff that's swept a-breeze
Powdering yellow swells like stellar dust.
Beyond this unwalled hut far stars remain,
Sifted from drifts of chaos and the night,

Grist milled for heaven's bread, an astral staff
Risen from germs that spurn their dusky husks,
The wrenched essentials' dreaded separations
In fluted marrow's windblown bone and soul.

Implicit in this local Norman scene,
Such castings up of dross-and-gold sew winds
That loop and lash where flaring ashes fare:
The Winnower's Scoop, but woven of the air.

Peasant and Donkey Returning Home at Dusk

ca. 1866-68

Between raised ochre plains and low slate skies
Pressing against stray clustered tufts of trees
A tapered wedge is driven blue through light
Flaring from clouds that tatter in the air.

And on a scarred black path that blindly winds
Unoutlined at the utmost edge of dusk
A peasant, brown and dark on dark brown earth
Draws his tired donkey, burdened in the murk.

Cross-hatched, then rubbed and blended, well-stumped lines
Show sun-flecks streaming home from cloud and plain,
Escaping wraiths both radiant and grave,
Brightness incised, fleeing a bleak demesne.

These winter rows are sown with dusk and cold.
This man has bound and baled late wheat and hay,
Surd stalks fettered and pressed in night's blind vise,
Words stark as their unlettered dark and day.

Man with a Hoe

ca. 1863

He leans on the short handle, knotted oak,
Its flat blade pressed on brambled clay and stone.
A boulder shoulders thorns up from the soil
While oxen plow a far-off pastoral farm

Whose stubble-fires smoke white toward skies in haze.
He dominates the land as serf and lord,
The subject monarch of his stark domain,
His thistle-crown root-bound in freehold earth.

Not fallen from some paradise whose crops
Turned golden while he plucked a harp's ripe strings,
He's come down long hard centuries the same,
Man's bent-back state no revolutions change.

Millet made no more gestures after this
But concentrated on technique alone,
Placing his faith in color, shape, and line
To render such grim dignity divine.

Winter Evening

1867

A single oil lamp, hanging like a star,
Shines from its pole down on the hooded crib
Whose infant sleeps deeper than night and day.
His face unseen, the husband, with skilled hands

Weaves reeds into a basket like the one
Near him holding tools—chisels, mallets, awls?—
Employed through winter sabbaths from the work

That binds his sweat and seed to Adam's earth.

Beside his stool his wife sews in a chair,
Mending some plain white garment thread by thread.
Her full pink blouse and gray-green skirt reveal
A body fit to bear a farmer's sons.

What lies outside this Norman Nazareth
The fireside cat that stares at flames recalls:
Snow filling darkness with its cold white glow,
Each flake unique and common in its fall.

Watering Horses: Sunset

1866

Flared light in the dimming center radiates
Between low pink or higher turquoise clouds
And sundown browns that cloak the winter Seine
Soaking its banks' dead sedge near Barbizon.

A peasant riding bareback on a mare
Leads other tired draft horses down to drink
From waters crimped and furrowed like the fields
In which they left their lather's salty seed.

The rider tugs the heavy wingless beasts
Into their own reflections unaware
Of anything outside this thirsty dark,
Their history, like their lives, a twilight scene.

Such figures drift upriver with the night
Toward dawn-times when great Pegasus a-wing
Would fly pink-turquoise skies, then glide on light
To lap his bright face up from pastoral streams.

Farmyard in Winter

1868

From low gray skies slow streams of moistened snow
Whiten stiff limbs leaden above a hutch

Where fattened hens and cocks stay quiet and still.
Meanwhile, outside, on crusted sheaves and stones

Wild birds alight to search out frozen grain
Including one chill robin, perched, alert
Between the thatch-roofed chickens and the rooks
That sink down in a drizzle-glaze bone cold.

Below a smoldering chimney's topping-snow
A single hen, venturing from the rest,
Pecks lean gleanings under the flakes' bright pall,
Her crest and robin redbreast flush with want.

What farm folk do inside the distant house
Is unexpressed, though through the chimney-keep
Smoke slips from fires whose silent tongues caress
Baked chicken, apple brandy, sex, and sleep.

Twilight

1859-63

The sun's failing radiance draws the moon
Out of that dark a foreign light defines
In crescents which embrace its dusty stone
Reigning over the brown unplanted plain.

The cloaked wife on a donkey, unsold sheep
Returning from the market to their fold,
The husband on foot–a holy family
Going toward Egypt or toward Bethlehem?

No, here's no Joseph with some sheltered flock,
No Norman pastures greening channel cliffs
With heads of wheat tossed in the salted air,
No fig or grape to pluck from limb or vine

But bleak and unalleviated ways
Between the market cross and stark despair,
Blank cravings just to eat and sleep and be
In twilights of the cosmos and their lives.

Woodcutter Making a Faggot

ca. 1853-54

Cold light above leaves his grim face in shade
As does a hat whose pulled-down brim half hides
Eyes focused on the task: lopping off shoots
From branches on a tripod cutting-stump.

Before him lie more branches still to trim,
Beside him a crude-fashioned faggot-crib,
Behind him great bound stacks of bundled sticks,
Beyond him, dense and endless, Fontainebleau.

His work is also endless, bill-hook raised,
Then dropped to chop away dry sprouted twigs
Until the winter dusk's stark frost and dark
Grant timeless labor temporary rest.

The bare embankment swells toward huddled trunks
Awaiting bleaker winters yet untold
When even trees of knowledge and of life
May yet be felled to burn in utmost cold.

Cooper Tightening Staves on a Barrel

ca. 1848-52

His mallet raised again to strike a wedge
Forcing stretched vine-hoops down to brace the staves
And make oak barrels watertight for wine,
The cooper finds the rhythm of his craft.

The barrel rises higher than his eyes
That stare through his own cast shadow at the task
As though he nailed a silhouette on wood:
His artisan's blue tunic black with blood.

The worker and his work are all but one,
Descended from Burgundian books of hours
Through almanacs to picture magazines,
An emblem of September's ripened vines

For him who by the strokes of his poised brush
Raised up this mallet made of ink and oil
While wine-drunk craftsmen, come from Gothic stone,
Staggered across the Paris barricades.

Training Grape Vines

ca. 1860-64

The dresser weaves spring trellises with vines
Whose leaves and tendrils sprout out opposite
With each fifth tendril flaring into flowers
That bear black grapes for dry red autumn wines.

He bends away from ochre-shadowed grass
Toward ancient fruit-trees twisted like the shrubs
Either side of a lichened garden wall
Beyond which slopes his tilled and seeded field,

A ridge of stiff, still beeches without leaf,
And skies whose blue the clouds turn white and gray.
Above the wall pink petals seem to dance
Free of their limbs and trunks, a powdered paste

Of matter that no underlaid black sketch,
No Dionysus, Eostre, Christ the vine
Sustains as well as well-trained grapes persist
In making raisins, vinegar, and wine.

Woman Baking Bread

ca. 1852-56

She leans back, hunches forward, as she shoves
Over the baked-brick oven's steady flames
The long peel with its spade-head's puffed-up dough,
Her strained arms browned and muscled like a man's.

Green wheat made ripe and gold in solar winds,
Its threshed grain milled by stone grinding on stone,
Warm-water yeast cakes melting into foam—
These mix with milk and sugar kneaded in.

No longer hunter-gatherers who once
Plucked woodland fruit or brought down mastodons,
We tend our fathers' orchards, fields, and folds
Not for unleavened bread in exodus

Or doorways washed with blood or tempting loaves
Conjured from rock or in an upper room
But just for strength to push the yeasty seed
Into the rising wetfires of the womb.

Young Woman Churning Butter

ca. 1848-51

Her eyes turned down, absorbed by what she does,
Strong arms stirring the churn-stick in the churn
Over and over and over till cream
Makes butter from its water, fat, and air,

She labors as a Norman peasant would
Not for herself but others far away
In Paris restaurants and dining rooms
Where chilled squares melt on bread their *fleurs-de-lis.*

Yet here, in weary anonymity,
A woman works and works the buttered cream
In utter resignation, tired and bored,
Left in a world whose elements congeal

Those old emulsions mixed with grace and fate,
The curse of Adam fixed in her drawn face,
The black background, the shelf of waiting jugs
She rose at one o'clock to fill by dawn.

Morning Toilette

ca. 1860-62

Through diamond panes webbed tight in crosshatched lead
Pale strands of morning's pliant light are strained
Falling so soft on cheeks that none can see,
Obstructed by an upper arm and hand–

A harvest-girl just risen from her bed.
The rumpled single sheets, a pillow pressed,
Are wet with unkissed tears. The filtered beams
Reveal a pitcher, crumpled cloth, wood comb

Distilled upon the sill in gold and blue.
This is a private moment unconfined
By role or sex, unvexed and intimate,
The hidden inwardness that all possess.

And yet since there's no husband and no child
To call her wife and mother she must work
Into a knotted bun those gathered strands
That none caress, locks strained against the grain.

The Departure

ca. 1858-6

The solid granite farmhouse stands behind
A backyard garden where bright flowerbeds
Might well have thrived had not necessity
Demanded rows of shallots, cabbages

And carrots by an open-top Dutch door
Through which a father bends to work in dark.
Outside, walking a furrow-halving path,
A woman holds a basket and her child

Who reaches toward a hidden warm fresh loaf,
Intelligence and hunger meshed in flesh.
The mother's soft sage whispers curb the hand
Of one bundled in bonnet, dress, and cloak,

Conceived on sheets now drying on the slats
Of a picket fence that marks this fruitful yard
The girl must leave to bargain in the town
For rinds that once held seeds of paradise.

Peasant Children at a Goose Pond

ca. 1865-68

Her bent knee on a fence's lower pole,
Plump elbows on the upper in its notch,
A leafy reed her rod, the watchful child
Seems poised between the realms of work and play.

Her brother with his palms pressed flat on grass,
His back against an unforbidden tree,
Gazes on geese that take the worn brown path
To eat wild greens, then lap their splashings up.

Above deep banks of water, shade, and rock
The plowed spring ground awaits its maiden buds.
A worn-out mother leads two cows between
The seeded rows and homes of thatch-roof stone

Sinking amid the wrinkled fields and sea.
The Norman woman looks down on her young
Who wonder at these geese that preen and breed,
Then drift on the stilling ripples of the pond.

Motherly Precaution

1862

Translated onto glass from copper plates
As from Rembrandt or Brueghel or their heirs
In whose busy depictions such an act
Is incidental, some side-alley fact,

Now placed here in the center by Millet–
This all too human scene, both rude and true:
A mother wrinkling up her young son's gown
Before he wets himself on backdoor steps

Where his six-year-old sister, shrinking, stares
At the wobbly colossus, wholly exposed.
His soft hand grips his mother's muscled wrist,
Still nearer to the milked than milky breast

That manly hands will master, hard and warm,
Till old age brings him trembling to a crone
Who'll lead to the darkened doorway-stones once more
This human flesh incontinent with need.

Shepherdesses Watching a Flight of Wild Geese

1866

Sheep graze along a plain in twilight quiet,
Their earthward heads cropping dark clumps of grass,
And near them, by a hedge where yellow leaves
Grow golden in the evening's mellowed air,

Bent over yarn and needles knitting wool
From these same sheep for mittens—two young girls.
Then suddenly one rises, shades her eyes
And gestures to the other not to move,

One arm crooked and one stretched out like the V's
Of geese intent on their archaic way
Beyond the late fall cold toward Galilee.
The one who stands leaves raveled knitting spilled

But she who sits and leans back on the hedge
Holding the needlework she'll soon complete
Appears the more enraptured in her gaze,
Eros sublimed and climbing toward the sun.

Flight of Crows

ca. 1866

Their feathers lift them high through feathery trees
Tall, thin, and almost leafless far in fall
Before a small mauve pond from which the birds
Drink till startled, then scatter toward the clouds,

Their bent wings flapping black in blackened skies.
The sun arcs down below its curving earth
That crests in the wide rough plains near Barbizon.

A golden glow illumines as it fades.

Some landless peasant girl leading her cows
To feed between the cultivated fields
Stands with an arched back, steadied by a staff,
Watching crows leave the screening trees and glide

There in the middle distance where the air
Holds clay and flame and water till the dusk
Concedes these plains to darkness and its stars,
Those fire birds bright against the night's vast pond.

Shepherd Minding His Sheep

ca. 1863-66

This weathered wall that separates the plain
From forest when Chailly meets Barbizon
Is now itself divided where a path
Brings sheep between its crumbling, grassy stones.

They leave the baking orange sky and fields
Of high-stacked hay, the shepherd's picket-fold
For pastureland this side of fallen rocks,
Tall blades so green and cool in shade that spreads

From trees, which, undepicted, must be there
Behind our set perspective on the scene.
Some ewes crop roots while others nudge and bleat.
One lifts her head, impatient, wedged behind

Slow sisters nearing Canaan's verdant ground.
Atop the wall, the shepherd looks and broods
Like Moses on Mount Nebo, gazing down,
Amazed at deprivation's plenitude.

Watering Cows

1863

The moon's curved rim of pale reflected light
Shines blindly down on sheepdog, shepherd, sheep,

And on a cowherd with her stick to make
Slow cows drink up the rippling lunar gleams.

The flock heads toward a dense green clump of trees
Just past the far bank, Eden's final stand,
Protected, as we see it, by a stream
Flowing between its origin and end.

This side, the cows, whose milk and meat and skin
We feast upon and wear, move through the world,
Unmindful of their deaths, of drying hides
Or stench of entrails rent from roasted flesh.

Yet here as well the cowherd's rich pink vest
Sustains pure light and color as the west
Spreads everywhere its hueless gloom until
All colors fade in dusk's pervasive gray.

End of the Hamlet of Gruchy (II)

1866

The last house, made of granite, flowering slate,
Now shades a mother's chair and spinning wheel
Abandoned to the geese and afternoon's
Deep peace in which a restless child is held

Up close to a contorted cliffside elm
Whose roots clutch hard the stony Norman soil
Where stunted trunk and lashed limbs imitate
The primal clash of fire, earth, water, air.

The village lives in quiet. A single cry
Of goose or duck or gull is local news
Replete with common portents quickly grasped
As when the hind goose turns half toward the child

Who feels the elm's rough bark with softest hands
That when the years have toughened them will reach
In dream toward wind-whipped limbs which at the last
Embrace him in his manhood's spinning end.

Millet's Birthplace in Gruchy

ca. 1863

The chiseled, wedged, and mortared pale red walls
Rise up from granite hardened by those dawns
That stain each shutter, window, porch, and door
Opening on the well-tracked village street.

The stony ruts are furrows where the birds—
Domestic geese and ducks, wild rooks and gulls—
Peck seeds and pull up worms until a wife
Sweeps out dust and ashes over their heads.

Between two doors, one opened and one closed,
A child of seven seems to brace his house,
Hands pressed against recessed and jutting rock
Long settled on the still unsettled earth.

The child has eyes for color, form, design,
And fingertips he'll roughen like a brush
To paint, when deep gray wrinkled brow and brains
And heart and mind combine, these things redeemed.

House with a Well at Gruchy

ca. 1863

The scene is what it was when he was born
Across the street: the deep-dug village well
Protected by its squat turret of rock
Topped by a stone cone cap and rounded knob.

Beside the well, where worn-down stairs meet ground,
A Norman woman in her peasant dress—
White bonnet, blouse, red bodice, full blue skirt—
Feeds geese with bread crumbled from loaves she holds.

The gathered birds soon gulp a puddle up,
Then strut by the granary toward distant pools
Outside the village where they bathe and play
In rains that welled from heaven's fountainhead

Kept pure for those who draw from stellar dells
Or else from clay beneath the deepest graves
Waters that once had rolled through burning foam
Till fire made salt bring crystals from the waves.

Cliffs at Gruchy

1870-71

Downward from Gruchy, past its wind-wrenched elm,
The path drops under pastures to a cliff
Where outcrop boulder-stones glint blue and iron,
Breaking above great sweeps of sea and sky.

Below the rocks, rowing in close to shore
The fishermen, no bigger than the gulls
That turn above them crying at their catch,
Glide over green and lavender to sand.

Outside the scene, a higher, flatter rock
Provided the perspective for these stones
That point toward the horizon's shining line,
Insight's limitless limit bound by sight.

The boulders are an outpost in between
Earth's umbers, turquoise seas, and azure skies,
Distinguished by the mind that from its cliff
Brought fire inside this elevated cave.

Coming Storm

1867-68

Piled up to great black heights like an anvil
Struck by Thor till Viking lightning thundered
On Chailly's plain, cumulonimbus clouds
Roll over seabirds buoyant in the wake.

A farmer far below pulls the unyoked team
Of stout draft horses through the thin green strip
Of common land still his, the turned-up plow

Left out in rows the deluge sweeps away.

A road curves and crests where the torrent pours
Flooding an unseen slope down which it runs
Like chaos in creation, dust raised up
As ash by the bolting fire's electric jag.

This is the road that toward the coming storm
Of trenches drenched, storm-troopers, blitzkrieg springs
Will lead on from a blasted natural plain
And *Sturm und Drang* to a radiant mushroom rain.

Priory at Vauville, Normandy

1872-74

The coarse and common quartz-and-feldspar stone
Named for its hard grain *granite* dominates
The scene: William the Conqueror's priory
Rising up rock by rock from solid earth.

Abandoned when the guillotine blades fell
On royal and revolutionary necks
The chapel has no altar candlelit,
No chalice's or paten's elements

Of holy blood and flesh but serves instead
To store a farmer's grain and Christmas wine.
Outside, a peasant leads toward pastured cliffs
White cows he fattens for their milk and meat.

The gate creaks in the worn long-sunken wall
As man and beast move to their given ends.
Nearby, the channel's sea gulls search for prey
Above the chapel's crowning salmon arch.

Le Puy du Dôme

ca. 1866-68

These billowing hills crest green in grassy froth
As they have done two thousand years or more

Between some goat-girl and *le Puy du Dôme.*
Older than both the Alps and Pyrenees,

The cone's dark peak is crowned with smoldering clouds
Where radiant glaciations, molten flows
Blazed long ago from *le Massif Central.*
Here goats bed on a precipice or crop

The bedrock's outcrop-stone while a girl knits
With legs outstretched, feet splayed, turned well away
From crater lakes and crystalline plateaus.
Her face is featureless, hands indistinct,

Her dwelling brief among these granite swells
Out of the heart of France where basalt veins
Streamed from their peaks when Vercingetorix
Met Caesar on a hill in Burgundy.

Sheepfold by Moonlight

ca. 1856

Low at the dusk's far edge a blunted moon
Descended from its fullness dimly glows.
The night abides again on Chailly Plain.
A wandering shepherd labors in faint beams

Till picket-fold and hut rise up once more
From parts kept in a cart that no one sees.
A raised staff comes back down to guide and goad
Each sheep dissolved in darkness and a flock

Shadowed by light but not the source of light.
The bleating of a lost or straggling lamb
Will go unheard in deep exhaustion's sleep,
For here is no Good Shepherd but a man

Staking his claim to rest, then pass away,
His hutch and fence a flimsy citadel
In these Arcadian wastes like Paris, Troy,
Or any other city of the plain.

Young Shepherdess / Captivity of the Jews in Babylon

ca. 1870-73 / 1848

for Deborah Cibelli, art historian

i

She sits alone upon a hillock-throne,
Wholly composed of her own history—
The colors of her sculpted woolen skirt
Marbled in knee-splotch greens and blotchy grays,

Her distaff like a queen's rod on her lap
Or lyre wound tight, plucked by the thorny comb,
Her cloud-brimmed hat crowned bright in aureole—
A peasant girl attended by the myths.

And there where rows stream brown away behind
To burst on the horizon white and blue,
Two sheep pause, one haunched up and gazing down
Toward pastureland, the other a blunt head

Rising in dream between the fields and hill,
Almost aware of who this woman is,
The Virgin, Eve, and Ceres of the plain,
Her antique face impassive as a mask.

ii.

And underneath that mask x-rays reveal
To scholars of its art this history:
Bearded Assyrian guards whose proffered harps
Make Judah's highborn maidens turn away

In anguish, hiding naked tears that fill
The Tigris and Euphrates with their streams.
No psalms will echo back from garden walls
Where kings hang foreign blooms for foreign wives

Nor would Millet submit to the Salon
Another many-figured Bible scene,
Only Chailly or his own Normandy
To which the Prussian war exiled him home.

And there, short on supplies, and near the end,
He painted out those maidens for a girl
Whose scepter is the distaff in her palm;
Behind her, Eve, beneath her, Babylon.

Hunting Birds by Torchlight

1874

They make their way by starlight to the trees,
Then light and thrust up torches into limbs
Where settled pigeons stunned with flaring flames
Are bludgeoned by their hundreds to the ground.

Two children fall down scared below a bird
Descending into darkness set ablaze.
One grown-up summons others to the kill.
His helper waves the paralyzing fire.

The earth is full of broken wings and cries,
The flapping back and forth and back again,
Then silence of a fledgling Armageddon,
Creation stained with cruelty, hunger, greed.

Remembered from his childhood near the end
In white and charcoal chalk on rosy gray,
He knew such things had always underlain
The habitual peacefulness of Gruchy.

Self-Portrait

ca. 1840-41

Such portraits in your works are early, rare,
Just two in fact—that Cherbourg fantasy
Tailored to Ono in-laws, white shirt starched,
A black cravat, cheeks shaved like sheep well shorn

And this arch countering image, full rich beard,
High velvet collar, right eye bright, urbane
And frank, the other warier in dark,

Bohemian and peasant, sundered, one—

Yet neither does you justice, your true face
Disclosed in self-effacingness alone,
A model artist modeling on God
Your kingdom ringed by Ptolemaic stars.

And in these poems I've disappeared in you—
Or is it that you've lost yourself in me?—
Our shapes and phrases so alike composed,
Your Channel in the Gulf, my South in Normandy.

The Angelus

1854-59

The Angelus of evening, distant bells,
Three for Ave Marias, versicles,
And nine for every collect low-entoned
By priests inside the far-off village church

Built up from Norman stone. The sky stays gold
Although the sun is gone and shadows pass
Over potato fields where standing still
In attitudes of prayer a man and wife

Think of the Incarnation of their Lord,
The flesh redeemed, a graced creation saved,
Bells pealing from the New Jerusalem
Through history back to Eden's speaking leaves.

Yet here between these dreams of paradise
Potatoes must be planted, tended, dug,
Then sacked on barrows pushed to winter bins
To feast on till the final angels come.

THE FIDDLER OF DRISKILL HILL: POEMS OF LOUISIANA NORTH AND SOUTH

(2013)

Bonfires on the Levee

for Burt Cestia

Late autumn days we labor in the swamps
Or by the riverbank's entangled brush
Gathering cane and willow wood to dry,
Then cut and stack and soak in kerosene,
Towers showing the way to Papa Noël
Riding over the beaches and the bluffs,
Lining the River Road near Baton Rouge
Where north Louisiana yields at last,
Though stubbornly, to customs of the south
White cotton bolls becoming sweet green cane
And the Mississippi, ready for the Gulf,
Foaming in salt beyond the salted marsh.

Then when Christmas Eve recedes into a night
So distant from the shepherds and the Star,
We torch the settled base-logs one by one
Watching fires rise more like the beaconed peaks
That spread from Troy to Thessaly and Thrace
Than candles of the body and the blood.
Unchristened constellations made to blaze
Beyond the last millennium's passing end—
The stars' coeval gleamings in the dark
Appear as faintest signals from a source
Whose love would touch each bonfire's sparkling bark
Even in this remotest holy post.

And by such light we glimpse what sense commends
In this strange state subsiding like our lives
From foothills of the Ozarks rippling out
In gardens of the strong-stemmed Shreveport rose
Down through the dense Kisatchie once preserved
By Carrie Dormon's will into the central farms
Of soybeans and corn then further on below
South to the bottomlands whose fallow mold
The wild strawberries redden every spring
And plump mushrooms make white in autumn dawns
Where settlers three short centuries ago
Parted man-high grass and saw the buffalo.

Such are the chief ingredients of our roux—
The mantled sands and gravels, oil and gas
Welling from ancient deltas, rising domes
Pushed up from the mother-bed of primal salt
All thickening this rich gumbo eons stirred—
The fossiled olives, laurels, hollies, figs,

Gullies of maidenhair untouched by spring's
Chill sun, late winter's early mallows
Trembling in a telic realm where bears
Coming to fish under a Hunter's Moon
Paw deeply in the streams for goggle-eyes
Or maul dried hives for honey in the noon.

And now as the last charred logs collapse in ash
Blown twinkling in the cindered distances
Over the farther arpents' sunken clays
We give ourselves to what we had possessed
Too rudely in the day, this drained estate
Through which the river straining at its banks
Crests like the fallen waters Noah rode
When Chaos broke again through its black crevasse
Out of the leveed heavens whose bonfires
Like our own declare the drifted silt
Poured off a shelving continent's worn edge
To lie undredged over DeSoto's bones.

Winter into Spring

Thibodaux, Louisiana

We drive north to New Orleans this far south
Where land and sea both lose themselves in marsh
And spring breaks through mild winter's brittle cold
When pansies blaze over the noon-light's ice.
We know, of course, the rare unsparing day
When sovereign Arctic blasts sweep south-southeast
Freezing the boughs of budding fig and pear
As in the fall and summer kindred winds
Bring down from mobile thrones of blade and air
Our ladybug and monarch butterfly.

But these are open winters where the sun
Tempers the sleet to rain and makes a dew
Of snowflakes on the maiden maple leaf.
And even in a January dawn,
Awakened by the salt breath of the Gulf,
Dutch clover, yellow mustard, and a thin
Unbending periwinkle on a stalk
Deep-rooted in its terra-cotta pot
Spread hues and scents across pale frosted lawns
Till once more spring's green regency has come.

In Waking Dream

Nicholls State University, Thibodaux, and Grand Isle, Louisiana

for Alice

Most days I pass your open office door
To find you grading papers, rubber band
Bound sets of awkward adolescent gropings
Toward classic architectures of the soul
Where sentence, clause, and phrase and single words
Build paragraphs that should support the whole.
And with your desk lamp bent toward each white page,
Your pen now poised, now marking faults in red,
You seem the good physician of our tongue
Gazing with your intense yet gentle face
On all those grave contagions of the human
Heart and mind—wrong cases, fragments, run-ons,
Letters and numbers somehow gone astray—
And you would make it better with your mild
And sterner cures, a justified D-minus
Balanced by mercy's note: "Karen, you have
Ability and often write quite well.
Please see me in my office. I can help."

Yet when at times you tire of both diseases
And their physic, you drive down to Grand Isle
Leaving a while the disciplines of speech
To walk the beach at evening as graceful
As a heron but with movements all your own.
And there you stay and look upon the Gulf—
Stars rising in their fires through lakes of space
Out of the ocean's swelling salt and dark,
Storm-petrels taking sea-trout from the waves,
The wild oats sowing seeds in windy dunes—
And sense in that one place all mystery,
Creation's ancient language no one knows,
That elemental syntax of the world
Still roaring in the seashell and the sea.

And in a year long past my given days
I picture you retired at eighty-five,
Still teaching part-time, walking with a cane
Then indispensable, those Grand Isle nights
In wonder on the beach just memories.
And if I may permit myself to dream
Perhaps you'll make your slow bone-aching way
To my old office down that narrow hall,
A room by some young colleague occupied,

And think of one who wrote about the surf,
Those breakers and the kingdom of the things.
And when at last the past will have its way,
In spite of shortened breath and stiffened knees,
Knowing you have to see Grand Isle once more,
You'll charm that nice young man who had usurped
Unwittingly the office of a poet
And make him drive you down to watch the Gulf
One clearest winter evening (though only
From the window of the car), and you will walk
In spirit on the beach and think of earth
As that grand isle of all the life we know
Worn down by time and space's steady waves.

And if your driver sees warm welling tears
Filling the deepened wrinkles of your cheeks
Perhaps you'll tell him as he looks aside,
"It's nothing, just a few remembered lines,
Some verses someone sent me long ago.
He'd see me grading papers, I suppose,
From what he wrote and left me on my desk.
He was a southern gentleman, standing
Up for ladies still in 1999.
I never guessed he thought of me at all
But poets see right through you when you don't
Even know they're looking. Then you waken
To the world's unending mystery again.
He touched me at a depth no one had touched
That way before. Perhaps I did the same
For him as muse, although he never said.
The poem is lost. I can't recall his face
Except in dream, or now, in waking dream.
I walked these Grand Isle beaches as a girl
And found that words, to which I've pledged my life,
Lay latent in the soundings of the waves.
He knew that much about me. Take me home."

The Breakers

Grand Isle, Louisiana

Late afternoons we walk upon the sand
Where breakers make the world that we desire,
This meeting-place of air and sea and land
Washed from the bright prime element of fire.

Pelicans heading westward with the day,

Shells rolling in surf, the shifting dunes in flower
Never knowing when we come or go away,
These stay within their changes hour by hour.

Near twilight we wade out beneath pale skies
That darken till the stars at eventide
Let flow upon the foam about our thighs
Faint rays from those far homes where they abide.

So noble in their hallowed altitudes
The stars withstand the breakers of the waste,
Lords of the lunar dunes their light includes,
Now braced against the void they once embraced.

And though no cold, remote, untainted mind
Can free us from these nights through which we roam,
The salted blood is stellar, like in kind
To wisdom's salt come shoreward on the foam.

Old Maker, who still binds in tidal rhyme
The rhythms of poiesis and this place,
Your metrics measure heaven where in time
Things burst in holy closures of your grace.

North Louisiana Country Church in Flames

Bienville Parish, the mid 1950s

Late Christmas Eve and now long hours begin
For a boy whose mother's welcome hearthside kiss
Closes old tales of no room at the inn
And leads to dreams of lighted trees and this:

A sleep disturbed by strangely glittering gifts
Waiting under the bubble-candled fir,
Then by a wind that through a cracked pane lifts
Curtains the faint smoke-traces lace and stir.

The child in time awakens, sniffs, and peers
Blearily through the window toward a flame
Climbing far steepled timbers till his fears
And eyes fix on a church's gleaming frame.

The rest his roused grandfather, whom he'd tell,
Related hours after when the splash
Of dawn-light drenched the still flickering hell
Where tongues unnumbered babbled in the ash.

Stunned deacons first crushed-in the smoldering doors
Meeting a Red Sea blazing in the nave
Uncrossable to reach those Jordan shores
Beyond the scalded baptistry's raised wave.

Then bearing lists of weddings, births, and deaths,
One dashed by the pastor's study and the choir,
Glimpsing the pulpit Bible's dragon breaths,
Its Book of Revelation laved in fire.

The smoke-choked deacons stumbled out for air
As winds took up the holocaust that spread
Under spiked railings' incandescent glare
To lay its pall of flame upon the dead.

And as those gathered watched each cindered grave
Glowing below a stone's seared name and date,
The church's crackling rafters cracked and gave
In to the great cremation uncreate.

That Yuletide night no cows or oxen knelt,
No cocks crowed evil spirits well away,
And no one knew what then a child had felt
Walking those charred foundations Christmas Day.

Yet there beside a melted cross and bell
Clutching his gift, a book of tales, the boy
First saw that world in which each man must dwell,
Aeneas bearing Vesta out of Troy.

The Singing Wires

Saline, Bienville Parish, north Louisiana, December, 1960

The Christmas giving over, he strolled in the great mundane,
Sad aftermath to wonder, the same old world again,
A boy not yet twelve but with a man's imagination,
Waiting for the muse's fatal instigation.

And going down the welcome-walk where pink wood sorrel grew
Long summers when he wandered, prince of all he knew,
He smelled no blazoned fragrances from blooms withered and gone
But gazed on high-pitched phone-wires, stark and taut in dawn.

The walk led to a gravel drive with pebbles gleaming bright—
Translucent yellow, rust, and pink, gray, black, and cloudy white—

And up above them, some ways off, those telephone wires strung
One line above another, pole to pole, straight hung.

The scene looked like a lined white page or like a music sheet
Designed for sounds of words or notes high above the street.
The boy scooped up a good handful of many-tinted stones
To hit the wires and set off twanging monotones.

He threw sidearm and overhead—rocks jagged, flat, and round—
Some zinging wires that whined with vibrant cadenced sound
Though most stones arced and fell away through silence to the sand
Washed from pinewood slopes to build up watermelon land.

The boy soon tired of what it took to keep the wires singing
And so the lines grew still again although they kept on ringing
Inside the mind of one almost ready to comprehend
The muse had chosen him that day as hers for her own end.

And so in time his lines like wires would thrill with carol, song,
Eclogue, georgic, elegy, and anthem set along
This wold's millennium-rhythms, iambic hills one hears
Measured out in eons like the music of the spheres.

The Deep End

Cedar Grove Pool, Shreveport,
Louisiana, 1955

for my father, David V. Middleton, Jr. (1922-1996)

So tentatively stepping to the end
Of the limber board until my clenching toes
Felt for the edge while counterpoising hands
And a twisting torso sought the balance point,
I stared down at the water where you stayed
Treading slowly, waiting for me to leap
Or dive into the deep end and your arms
One Sunday afternoon when public pools,
Like all the blue-lawed town, were closed all day
Except to you, their summer manager.

I knew my way around the shallow end
Where first I bobbed in inner tubes and then
Went under after pennies on the bright green floor
That sloped down as I floated toward a rope
Beyond which lay the great unwaded dark,
Emerald and unending in the eyes

Of a scared boy standing on the diving board
Hesitant as you yelled for him to jump.

And so, trembling and teetering on the edge,
Wavering between pure trust and total fear
I weakly sprang collapsing in a splash,
Then looked up paddling with my gasps and cries
Toward you who had removed yourself a ways
To make me swim through dead brown water bugs
And sand flies stinging as I rose and sank
Toward where you held your hand out from the bank.

And now for three long years you've swum alone
Breathlessly through death's unfathomed pool
While at your gravestone's marble board I stand
Trembling and looking down to find you there
Treading the darkest depths we'll ever know,
Waters through which my soul must also go
With faith and fear that bore me up before
To clasp a hand extended from the shore.

Hand-Me-Downs

She wheels her chair beside a locked oak chest
That holds both christening and wedding gowns,
Her mother's things she's always cherished best
And worn herself, love's heirloom hand-me-downs.

Her husband far afield pushes a plow
His father made to break this fertile land
That he as father works with his son now,
The well-worn handles passed from hand to hand.

The son's put on his father's overalls,
Now come to manhood and a grownup's size;
A daughter wraps her mother-woven shawls
Across full breasts no shawl or blouse disguise.

This family knows that little's really new,
That most of life's comprised of hand-me-downs
Someone before us thought or made or grew,
Then gave or left us like a mother's gowns

Or Bible with its ever-spreading tree
Whose limbs bear names like those oak limbs outside
Young grandsons calling mount with that same glee
Their grandma felt who wheels to watch them ride.

Leaving Drexel Street: A Wife's Goodbye

August, 1990, 942 Drexel Street, Southern Heights,
Shreveport, Louisiana

for my mother, Anna Sudduth Middleton (1922-2022)

The sun is going down on our last day
As on the first in this the only house
That we, as man and wife, have ever owned:
Stacked boxes packed and numbered once again,
The wedding service worn with use and love—
Cracked china, tarnished silver—wrapped in sheets
Of *Shreveport Times* whose syndicated reams
Say nothing of this home I kept and made and dreamed.

Outside, the front yard's red-brick flowerbed
Still blooms with portulaca planted there
When these splotched hands were rosy as the heads
That bow and close in latest summer dusk
While I, as my sick husband, sitting, waits
For movers to remove us from our world,
Must walk one final time these rooms I share
With ghosts that speak and breathe in memory's breathless air:

The parlor where we met in formal dress
The pastor, salesman, candidate, new friend;
The dining room where fasting met repast,
Those bowls and greens our kiln and garden gave;
The kitchen whose bright rites of knife and fire
Prepared the table's meat, fish, leaf, and root;
This bathroom where we washed, then drained away
The soil and oil and dust—refuse of all our days;

The bedroom where we lay to gaze and love,
At deepest peace with seasons of the stars,
Where, when our son was born, we snuggled up
To read him lore of Mother Goose and Grimm,
Of Greece and England, Rome and Bethlehem—
Fathering wonders hidden in the words
That call all children home from the absurd,
Great stable tales that lift the bidden heart and mind.

But now the movers come, the dark van waits
To haul off all these recollected things
In one blank clanging chamber to our boy
With whom we now will live in love's last rooms
Near far Acadian marshes well below
This river bluff's crimped hills, these Southern Heights

We'll leave when one more watering is done,
A parting bride's moss roses still touched by setting suns.

Summer Ending

Green blades grow pale and still
Below this windowsill
Whose clearest panes
A sheer light stains,
Then passes where it will.

The grass's crickets cry,
Compelled to mate and die,
And thus to share,
Though unaware,
In my more chilling sigh.

For here I rock and stare,
Grown old in this old chair,
Alert to what
Crickets are not,
Hope woven with despair.

The first leaves reach my door,
Pecan and sycamore,
As summer ends
And fall portends
What winter knows before.

In Allen Hall

Louisiana State University, Baton Rouge, Louisiana

1. Of Textual Editing

for R.W. Crump

text < Lt. *textus, texere*—woven, to weave >

I pass among the stacks in those cool rooms
Where manuscripts stay dry in box and dark,
Papers laid out on shelves like family tombs,
Dated by ink, hand, font, or watermark.

My task is daunting, haunted by defeat,
To guess the last best words an author meant—
Collating each saved draft, each printed sheet,
Blue-penciled proofs—the matter of intent.

And though today loud Humpty Dumptys claim
That words mean only what we *say* they mean,
Yet I in quiet will weigh them just the same,
By Pilate, Cain, and Eden's snake unseen:

For editors of texts have always known
How tentative, unstable words can be—
High tongues of Babel dumbstruck on the stone,
Tragic ash in the Alexandrine sea.

But if we cannot fix by imprimatur
Platonic absolutes, some perfect verse,
Penelope by Homer woven pure,
We still believe in better texts and worse

Unlike those who declare all words absurd,
Corrupted wits unfit to serve a king,
The Word Made Flesh, suffering to be heard,
His life a holograph whose psalm we sing.

2. Near Viareggio

in memory of Annette McCormick

16 August 1822

il buon tempo verrà

The waves that left him bloated on the shore—
The wet pale skin, the red salt-streaming hair—
Washed yellow toward the shallow grave that bore
Beneath its three spaced stakes what brought them there:

Trelawny, Byron, Hunt, the helpers hired
To dig up flesh white lime stained indigo—
Fish-eaten face and arms now furnace-fired,
oured wine and oil soaking logs stacked below.

s his ashes floated high in light
t winds toward the whitest Apennines
his body died into its night,

Soul overwhelmed by Adonais' lines,

The unlocked Bible, Jesus freed from priests,
Prometheus and his Asia come as one
Spirit to sing at Demogorgon's feasts
Till Harriet's and Mary's pains are done,

He found perhaps that marriage he had dreamed
Among them all—Platonic realms above,
Necessity within the things that seemed,
Substantial shadows hallowed by his love.

Upon the Publication of a First Book of Poems

The Burning Fields, LSU Press, 1991

To see them here brings humbleness, not pride,
Poems so well printed, jacketed, and then
Braced by comments made by generous men
Whose works my own could never stand beside.

Here also is that absence, black despair,
That stared from blank white spaces at my face
Until the courted muse released her grace
And words flowed into verses like a prayer.

Such moments of eternity-in-time
Confirm the Maker in each maker's rhyme.

Warren in Thibodaux

The Southern Literary Festival and Fletcher Lecture Series,
April 1985, Nicholls State University, Thibodaux, Louisiana

You flew down to New Orleans, then drove south
Into a trembling prairie, sea and land
Unstilled by any maker's word or hand
So near the Mississippi's silent mouth.

And there you shared your poems one final time
Unaided though when stage-light beams would blind
Your one unblinded eye you spoke your mind—
"Hopeless! Hopeless!"—yet then read on in rhyme.

Later, at that plantation where you stayed

Night thickened with your whiskey-tales that strayed
From rooms Jim Bowie owned to where a knife-
Sharp wit cut sheer through dank moth-hours still rife
With bearded oaks that once more made you feel
"After Louisiana nothing seemed real."

Rapture at Twilight

not far from Driskill Hill,
north Louisiana

Far down a winding hillside road
Under the chapel-ground
Where she'd inclined and heard explode
Revival words profound

About the end-times' final night
In which the chosen few
Would be uplifted to the light
While those left got their due,

A woman steers toward Christ alive
As from the town below
Pumped frat-boys in their pickups drive
Toward some snug bungalow.

They've stocked back seats with smokes and beer
And hit sex shops as well
For blow-up dolls they'll hold so dear
When phallic egos swell.

The dolls, tied to the trucks' flat beds,
Float high in twilight skies
Toward which one unsuspecting heads
Till wild revival eyes

See unclothed bodies rising free—
The Rapture come at last!—
And so she slows ecstatically
Up-gazing at The Vast . . .

And finding there a sermon's proof
Above her thrilling sighs
She stops, disrobes, and on the roof
Raises her arms and cries,

And when the wafting rapt-dolls pass

She leaps, then falls pell-mell
Back on her cracking tailbone ass
Waving the saved farewell.

Janitor

< Lt. *ianitor*, doorkeeper >

Nicholls State University, Thibodaux, Louisiana

for the custodians

I work these rooms before and after class,
Picking up dusty *Cliff Notes*, pencils, gum
From this tough stage where boredom spiked with sass
Grew quiet at tragic wisdom's podium.

Most students, like professors, pass before
My busy broom, well faded shirt, frayed jeans,
My presence what they pay for to ignore,
A lowly ghost of their high ways and means.

They never think how much depends on me,
Blocked water fountains cleared, the scoured johns,
Light bulbs changed out, the heating or A/C
Kept up in this base age of iron and bronze.

And none would dream that I was one of them
Until my father's death made me a man
Who dropped out to become the man I am,
My texts exchanged for bucket, mop, and pan.

Yet in that office-closet where they store
Strong chemicals with implements I use
A long shelf holds books left on desk and floor,
Collaterals abandoned to their muse.

And there, through lunch, door closed, I open doors
Unlocked yet shut to all who hesitate
To run with Heathcliff, Cathy on the moors
Or fall with Milton's Satan to his fate.

Such was my education: words and dust
Together in the depths of bone and brain,
Those sweeping strings of straw and verse that must
Be one in some harmonic final strain.

The Courtyard Plum

Nicholls State University, Thibodaux, Louisiana

It stands alone inside stone courtyard walls
Of this small southern college, close confined
By generator, bench, and all that falls
From cloud or sun or rises from the mind.

The tree moves through its seasons with a grace
That comes of being grafted, pruned, and bred
In China, then Japan, and now a place
Exotic on its semi-tropic bed:

White umbel clusters opening in snow,
Petals of February's winter-spring
Dropping before bronze leaves break green and slow
And yellow fruit turns blue in ripening

From May until July beside the halls
Where young bards trying haiku pluck a plum,
The season-word for which each haiku calls,
Its images deep hints that quietly come.

And there amid the bending mellow boughs
Still reaching down from Eden creatures feed–
Bumble- and honeybees, jay birds in rows–
Together in the weather of their need

With lizards, crickets, squirrels, and dragonflies
All drawn to feast on craving's bleak predation
And on the tree of life that bears and sighs,
By silence weighed, dying in creation.

The plum tree spreads its branches, roots, and leaves
Just like that tongue in which its petals sing
High psalms of heaven's courts no one perceives
But shapers when their balmy rhymings ring

In praise of manner, port, demeanor, air
By which the plum declares itself a liege
Caught up in this fraught world once whole and fair,
Made better by its bred noblesse oblige.

Before and After Reading

in memory of Leo Luke Marcello, 1945-2005

New Orleans, February 2003

We sat there as an early evening fell
That winter on the old St. Charles Hotel,
Sipping dark coffee, polishing a line,
Community in grounds and sounds ground fine
For rarest listeners, those local rolls
Of Christian scholars, critics, poets, souls.
It wasn't always thus. We knew the tale
Of readings where smart smirks and sighs assail
Verse fleshed with images that bear the Word,
Staves staving off the utterly absurd,
Shunned by some smug editors unannoyed
By changes tolling into a tongueless void.

But not tonight. And so we took our place
Behind the podium-pulpit, sacred space
For poet-rectors, humble yet ordained
To lift up all they hoped their work sustained.
And when you read your elegy for John,
Our brother maker lost to AIDS, then one
About your priest-friend, near here beaten dead
By those young men he prayed for as he bled,
Your smile and twinkling teardrop eyes would shine
As ever in this comedy divine
Where souls untold will hear your poem-bells, pealing,
Say Christ made even death itself a healing.

The Fairfield Gnomes

Fairfield: an elementary school in Shreveport, Louisiana

They grace the Gothic archway to the school
As they have done for more than sixty years,
Those gnomes of education's constant R's,
All numbers, letters, words, and their close kin
In axiom and syntax—diagrams
Of grammars where the mind can know the world
And know itself through radiant translations
Of sentence and equation's golden codes.

The Gnome of Writing prints his alphabet
Raised up by marble pen from marble page,

The building blocks' block capitals that spell
Synonymous tautologies of God,
The Logos' *fiat lux* and *finis est*,
His squinted eyes, cramped fingers, drawn-back face
Grotesques of body's discipline by mind.
And opposite, Arithmetic's balked Elf
Fixing his dumb attention on a row
Of numbers half-abstracted from the slab,
Treasures of weight and measure and degree,
Latent gradations, quiet hierarchies,
A Ptolemaic cosmos after all,
The music of the atom and its spheres.
Then, last, above the ciphers, ABCs,
The Gnome of Reading, given to his book,
A creature's stirred alertness to intent,
Each person, mood, case, number, voice, and tense
A trace of One indwelling yet alone,
His page of thought and nature caught in stone.

Such elements exposed to rain and sun
Still grace the Gothic archway to the school
As they have done for more than sixty years
Guarded by dwarfs transfigured into giants
Whose minds forever strain by earthen light
Dug from the mother veins of brain and ore
To parse and tally, point, and reckon sums
Till number, letter, word, and world are one.

Daddy

after Sylvia Plath, author of "Daddy"

Shreveport and Thibodaux

for my father, David V. Middleton, Jr. (1922-1996)

Some afternoons I waken from a dream
To dream on to the rocker's to-and-fro
And the tick-tock pendulum of a clock
That holds me for a moment out of time
Till long lost scenes come welling from the depths
By happy access in creation's play.
And one such afternoon when winter chill
Brought stillness to each autumn leaf and blade
Stiffened by winds that dry their dew to frost
I saw you making clay pots in your shop.

It took you all your life to reach that place,

The eldest of five brothers and at times
A stand-in father even as a child
Who if you swung your bat and got a hit
Would have to let another run for you
So you could hurry back to baby boys
Card-playing parents left in your sole charge.
On Fridays you would skate down Egan Street
Then over rippling hill bluffs toward the Red
And back again, library books in hand.

At home, in a rocking chair, you'd sit and read
Those books in stacks each weekend, left to right
The piles of read and unread up and down
Till Sundays when you skated back to town,
Your father baffled by his egghead son.
Then after graduation you would work
Some months in Faulkner's world, your weekends spent
Shooting pool in New Orleans till the draft
Found you at last and you became a cook
On Asian ships till A-bombs brought you home.

And there, although the West still drew your blood
(Cooled by a mother's clutching reluctance)
By grace at Highland Baptist Church you met
Saline's Miss Anne, small-town nobility,
Who loved you for yourself, helping you evade
Maternal suffocation just enough
To be the artist you were meant to be
After those long tough teaching days at school
Or summers as a lifeguard at the pool
That kept a wife and child from poverty.

And as your youth gave way to middle age,
A principal at Judson you opposed
The peewee football dads and sanctioned games
In which they all could play, both girls and boys,
And with that stubborn hand-pressed ribbon machine
Cut even eighth-place ribbons so no child
Who tried at all would lack some accolade.
Coach, umpire, fan for soccer, softball, track,
You found that childhood you had been denied
With children whose respect grew into love.

Each year, guided by you, a sixth-grade class
Made murals for the cafeteria wall,
Our New-World story told in grout and tile,
Columbus, Indians, pilgrims, soldiers massed
In clashing blue and gray, a settled West,
And then this century from Kitty Hawk
To Cape Canaveral, pictures no doubt

Too innocent yet made for innocence,
Each panel immovable, fastened tight
By hidden bolts still known to you alone.

Years later, drained by central office stress,
Administrative politics, decrees,
At fifty-six you gave up and retired,
Taught college art at Centenary two sweet years
And ran your boyhood's bases when you won
10K's and marathons till Parkinson's
Slowed you to a shuffle, walker, chair
Whose wheels your weakened fingers clutched and pushed,
Great-hearted racer who pressed on and on
Toward death's black tape broken with your last breath.

And now a decade later I still see
So clear in heightened musings, deepest dreams,
Two images of you: one near the end,
Painting in your wheelchair, stiffened hands
Then capable only of dabs and streaks
That filled a tautened canvas primed in white
With colors pure in form and formlessness,
"Trying something new," you wryly said,
Almost like a child learning ABCs,
Your primer's words of yellow, blue, and red;

The other, thirty years ago this fall,
You singing in your workshop, shaping clay
In male and female obelisk and pot,
Then glazing them in colors of the earth,
Late autumn shades of gold, brown, orange, gray
Fired in a backyard kiln you fenced against
Neighbors afraid to feel creation's heat,
Cones melting under kiln gods undisturbed
By matter's agony or by a love
That forged them too, your passion made serene.

Mother Among the Graves

Magnolia Baptist Church,
Saline, Louisiana, April 2000

for Anna Sudduth Middleton (1922-2022)
who was born in Many in Sabine Parish and died at age 100

So early in the morning we had come
To stand once more before the Sudduth graves,

For four years now, a Middleton's as well,
By spiderwort and spider undisturbed,
His leveled mound as grassy as the rest,
Stone stained by broken shadows, summer rain.

Your parents' stones lie tilted, sunken, worn,
Their birth and death dates, verses, even names
Obscured by climbing grass and fire-ant mounds,
Your only-sibling brother's much the same,
And you, almost eighty, the last one left
Ungathered to the ashes of your kin.

And right beside my father's stone there lies
Another stone, put down to save a place
In the crowded ground, bearing your own name
And birth date but as yet no Bible verse
Or that last date whose chiseling-in I dread
When you too come to rest among the dead.

But now, though so much given to the past
That waits beyond what time there's yet to be,
You smile and turn in fortitude toward me
To live on as a mother till the end,
Grandmother to your one grandchild whose name
And spirit are your own: Anna Marie.

And as we close the rusted graveyard gates
On plots where our own plots will one day be,
We gaze on pines made radiant at dawn
And on that tree the years have nurtured here,
An old magnolia whose broad leaves at noon
Cover the graves with deep unbroken shade.

Deep Country Epitaph

Here lies untouched by sun or snow
The flesh of one content to go
Out of a place of age and pain
To which she'll not return again.
She rests beside her husband now
Who kept, like her, his wedding vow
Nor thought of any other course–
Neglect, adultery, divorce.
Standards upheld without complaint–
Denial, duty, self-restraint–
She needlepointed that first fall,
The Ten Commandments on the wall.

Six decades took her through each state
That plighted troths enumerate,
The bumper crops, the barren land,
The strong and then the trembling hand,
Rare days she wondered at her choice,
Those fertile nights, the mastering voice,
Nine sons and daughters whom she saw
Become themselves by natural law;
Debilitation, fading, death,
Her husband's last faint kiss and breath,
Long years there living on alone,
Spring cleanings of his house and stone,
Tending blue stars and marigolds
By Mary's rose the dawn unfolds.
Such sacraments of sky and flower
Sustained her in her final hour,
The doctor's, then the pastor's hand
Upon her brow, the funeral planned,
The simple coffin made of pine,
The great King James's *thee* and *thine*,
The nineteenth psalm and twenty-third,
Our Father and St. John's The Word,
Interment near her husband's dust,
And one still doing what he must,
Her eldest son, who, now grown old,
Plants blue star mixed with marigold
In earth that covers the remains
Of one whose love his life contains,
A soul with virtue deep imbued,
Commandment and Beatitude,
Spared late in this most graceless age
That worships its own pride and rage
Modernity's depraved embrace,
Fled far beyond this time, this place.

Two for Life

in Acadie

i. Late February

2/22/86

Sleeping alone in a farther room
This morning's mother-to-be
Leaves for now the tragedy
Of ruptured blood and the voided womb.

The husband, nursing coffee, still sits up,
Shocked by the quick miscarriage,
Bitter first fruits of marriage,
Black dregs settled in an empty cup.

He shakes as a grave equation sears
A heart too long in mind's control—
Each lost child: a human soul—
And weeps in quiet his manly tears.

ii. Chemo Refused

dying mother to unborn child

I only did what Christ himself would do:
I gave up life to give your life to you.

In Winter Prime

Near Lent the winter deepens toward its noon
When sun-flakes twinkle keen in snow and grass
And stars beyond the stardust of the moon
Pass on within a dark that cannot pass.

Yet even then may come a milder time
When ice sweats cold gold beads that swell and run,
Their melting felt in earth as early prime,
Some subtle fluctuation of the sun.

And in that radiant glade where warm light glows
A yellow dandelion and butterfly
Wake to a false brief spring that comes and goes
Between long afternoons of frosted sky.

Such blooms and wings soon stiffen in the dusk
Of matter's endless winters that still hold
Each fall and spring, each summer's greenest husk,
All caught in plots that plot a tale untold.

Black Lake Tales

Bienville Parish, north Louisiana, 1959

for my uncle Joseph Lynn Sudduth (1919-1964), Lt. Colonel, US Army Air Corps

Sometimes, though not in wakefulness or sleep
But that strange state just after piercing dreams
When memory traumatically reveals
Objective truths, we find forgotten scenes
Are brought up from the depths like fabled prey
On some taut line, each mythic fish just held
By time's bright hook a moment and then lost
Returning once again, through deeper reeds,
Into those beds no light has ever found.

*

They moved through humid blackness toward the shore
Before the dawn disclosed their ghostly forms
Clutching limber poles, damp cans of worms,
A tackle box and rods, and jangling chains.
The forty-year-old uncle and the boy,
His only nephew, ten, a city child
Deep in the summer country of the soul
Soon made their way across a rotted pier
Whose firm planks they remembered yet would test
Until they reached the roped post and the boat.

Unsteadily they stepped from seat to seat,
Rocking the solid bottom with their weight
Until they settled down amid the faint
Black lappings of the little shoreward waves.
They chucked the mud with paddles, pushing off,
And in a quiet no motor would disturb
They pulled and pulled then glided in the trees
Whose names and forms were clarified by light:
Old water oaks and locusts, tupelos,
Bent willows, and the sun-drawn cypress stands.

Then drifting near an over-woven grove
The uncle and the nephew baited hooks,
Lowering bobs and sinkers from the poles,
r from bent rods flicked the shiny spinners
r the glittering surface of the lake.
here until the noontide in full bloom
med them with its blazing fragrant rays
the vibrant line or plunged bob ran
from the wordless depths first words reclaimed
bluegill, and buffalo.

Sometimes the boy would glance aside to find
His uncle fixed intently where a trail
Of water lights sparkled across the dark
In silent rhymes of brightness and the night:
Creation's radiant twinkling in the sheen.
And in such moods the uncle often spoke
Not to the child alone but to the man
The child's ripe innocence barely held within
Of what had long possessed his heart and mind,
Things gleaned from books and from the book of life.

He said he did not live within the state
But in an unabstracted known domain:
Crests of the buckled uplands, fractured folds
Lifted from the dried primeval seas,
Wrinklings of eons shriveled into hills,
Old salt beds exposed as sour lakes, salines–
Expressions of a depth where nothing grows–
And sandstone ridges, facing inward, steep,
Their sloping backs declining toward the Gulf,
Outcroppings of the logic of the rock.

Such forms he'd seen and dreamed on Driskill Hill,
Lulled by the undulations of the pines,
Gazing toward far Arcadia and those
Enfolded wolds–Kisatchie, Nacogdoches–
And the great Sabine Uplift under the Red
Where ice floes once brought boulders from the north
To lodge upon the risen inland coast
And where the Raft grew thick to such a reach
That over its rich width from bank to bank
Green willows flowered southward like a stream.

Grappling in bafflement at what he'd heard,
The startled nephew hardly made reply,
Recalling other times his uncle seemed
A voice the spirit uttered from its core,
Speaking of the unspeakable as when
At LSU with Brooks in '41
He studied that same irony he'd feel
Bombing the place from which his fathers came
Till down flak-alley's length he seemed to hear
Cries rising from the Rhine to curse his name.

Later in vital nightmares as he screamed
Fully awake and terrified in sleep,
He flew again beneath a bomber's moon
While all around the skies, like shooting stars,

In molten cockpits fighter pilots fell
Flaming through cindered heavens to the ground.
And yet within those broken smoky clouds
On one most terrible run the dark grew clear
And night's unmeasured beds became Black Lake
Twinkling in winter twilight's brightest stars.

These tales the boy had heard and now again
Saw pain the rugged uncle's sullen face,
A face that once had gazed upon a scene
Come up from unimagined depths of hell:
The death-camps' mangled hills of fetid flesh
Pushed by bulldozers over the lime-pit's edge.
Then, too, like all the world, the uncle lived
Minutes away from total holocaust,
A terror told again when sonic booms
Rolled from targeted Barksdale over the wolds.

And there amid such dreaded recollections,
While baitless lines lay tangled in the weeds,
The uncle found new access to a past
Now called back in full poignancy by grace,
And so he told the boy till latest day
Gave way at last to twilight and the dark
Of what had scarred an unsuspecting heart
When like his nephew he was barely ten,
And as he spoke, his nephew rowed alone,
Listening as his building muscles ached.

The uncle was a boy in '29
Though little of The Crash had touched those hills
Whose poor stayed poor on grim subsistence farms
That yielded corn and greens and black-eyed peas
To brutal toil and hunger's constant pain.
And here within a triple history
Of nature, Holy Writ, and humankind
He knew he had been made from Adam's clay
Dug from the salt-domed valley of the Red,
A place the Rebels held until the end.

The things themselves, familiars of their names,
He saw as science and Genesis and sense:
Creek water pure and cold from leeched gray clays,
The cottonwood, crab apple, sassafras,
The purple morning glory, goldenrod,
The black-eyed Susans, cat-tails, chinquapins,
Loblolly bogs where rare white arums thrive,
Celestial lilies, star grass, spiderwort—
Such uttered substance once had been a speech,
A rhetoric made tremulous with love.

It was the only world the uncle knew,
And there he roamed alone through Eden's trees
Or with his dog, a young mixed-breed named Will.
At times they ran with dancing, lost in joy,
The dog and master chasing each in turn
Across the ripening watermelon fields
Covered with prickly nettle, stickers, ticks
And fire ants' built-up hills that just fell in
When Will pranced through their nations till he sank
Chest-deep in the crumbled tunnels, stunned and stung.

One late spring day adventure led them on
Farther into the woods than ever before
Beside old dogtrots claimed by rot and vines
And past the deadened fields of girdled trees—
Now glades with bramble berries overgrown—
Then farther still, beyond those hidden rows
Where Indians once grew maize from Adam's loam,
Until they reached a place whose given name
Had lived in tales kin told as though a myth,
Two hills in massive collapse: The Big Ditch.

The uncle and his dog drew near the ledge
Gingerly peering straight down sixty feet
Into a dense entanglement of names
Now teeming up from chaos into light:
Black alder, sugar maple, oak, and ash,
Magnolias lifting blossoms toward the sun,
And dandelions so golden on a rim
Filled with the noise of crickets that would brush
The silence of the yellow butterflies,
Their mundane strains the music of the spheres.

And standing in a trance upon the brink
The uncle saw his dog a moment late
First leaning toward a hare that hopped below,
Then trying to backtrack from a sliding edge
Of bitterweed and honeysuckle vines
Where he yelped and fell into the undergrowth
From which repeated whimpers pierced by howls
Scared one who stayed till nightfall looking down
Where soon the autumn's galaxy of asters
Would rise in pitiless beauty toward the stars.

Thus caught between pure terror and pure love,
The uncle hesitated and then fled
Running by panicked instinct through the woods,
Lashed by the bramble-briars and nameless dread.

And when at last bounding onto the porch
Breathlessly babbling he hardly knew what
In a house as quiet as midnight on the lake
He roused his father who would take him back
Into the deepened evening, with flashlights,
Lengths of rope, and a downsized .22.

They made their way by impulse, faith, and fate
Back to the ditch in thickest midmost woods,
But then restrained elation was displaced
By instant fear when not one howl was heard
Or whimper as they whistled, called, and cried.
Instead, within the ditch, a bobcat moved
Eluding the long beams, and, over the brink
From which the dog had fallen there arose
A great horned owl in almost silent flight,
Its hard pinched talons dripping bits of meat.

The father turned his son away in tears
Just as that son as uncle now would turn
From tales recalling things forever lost
Toward paddling to the shore and driving home
While stars and fireflies mingled in the trees.
And when at last the uncle and the boy
Had scraped and gutted the fish, sitting outside
They gazed awhile, in silence and the night,
On old unsounded depths of earth and sky,
Black lakes whose beds no light has ever found.

Flies and Grounders

Jonesboro, Louisiana, 1963

in memory of my cousin, Gordon Stille Sudduth (1952-2019),
Southern Baptist pastor and Christian counsellor, who died on his birthday

We played on that grass lot beside your house
All afternoon through long green Easter springs,
The shortleaf pines marking off unmarked lines
With plated bark and wind-swung oblong cones.
And there, where silent heads of clover tolled
In gusts that brushed the latest April blades
So tender now, so hard in summer light,
We came with simple gear—bat, ball, and glove
Well spat on, worn, laced, oiled, and broken in—
And took up our positions on the field.

The game was flies and grounders—one to hit
The other to snatch, scoop up, or body-block
Till three caught in the air or seven stopped
Dead cold on earth switched out the one-man teams.
Up first, I chocked, spun, bunted, popped up balls
That you knee-skidded, leapt, or dove to clutch
Before they rolled on past you and away
Over the lane toward moldy, sunken woods.

And as you vanished into that dank dark
Stumbling to chase a seventh grounder down
I saw your father's bomber on its run
From England to the Rhine and back again
Past swinging batteries, banked fighter planes,
And acrid flak that even then in sleep
In that front room so close to where we played
Could blind him like black fire in flashback dreams
In one of which a year hence he would die,
Gliding aflame toward night on smoking wings
To join at last lost buddies in the waves
Crashing below chalk cliffs that called them home.
But as for now such nightmares let him be,
Next to his bedside window in a chair
Watching you, like a plane, return to base,
Mission fulfilled, an errant grounder found,
The stained ball raised triumphant your glove.

And now, four decades later, on a cane,
Though only fifty, lungs and bone and brain
Infested by those toxic molds that spread
Throughout a church whose souls you've served so well,
You, like your father, pass through flak and flame–
A homeless congregation, some who've left
One who, though ill, did not abandon them,
Delayed insurance settlements, huge bills,
Unsteady mind and body, and your own
Wild flashback dreams to innocence and health–
Your bearing graced by faith and fortitude,
Still fielding flies and grounders in a glove
Yet one not made of leather, oiled and laced,
But magnanimity and guts and love.

–2002

In the Bleak Midwinter

Christmas and St. Stephen's Day

Angels and archangels may have gathered there
Christina Rossetti

to my daughter, Anna, at eleven, to read
years hence when the times
of faithful doubting come

Staying up late to play
Once more on Christmas Eve
The role of Santa Claus
For one who would believe
(Though doubt now gives her pause)
In reindeer and the sleigh,

The toyshop gifts, the bells,
St. Nick in white and red,
The elves, the ho-ho-ho's
All dreamed while snug in bed,
Tucked in for years by those
Strong hands where safety dwells:

I know the glittering veil
Of fairy tale and myth
As literal and living
Must be stripped to its pith:
Spirit of Christmas giving,
Love's light that ought not fail.

But then when midnight nears,
My job as Santa done,
I gaze up at the crèche,
The Mother and the Son,
Where myth and history mesh
Or so it now appears.

Yet what if this tableau
Of God's redeeming love–
The Wise Men and the beasts,
The great Star poised above
The shepherds' hillside feasts
With angels in the snow–

Were nothing but a dream,
The deep heart's deepest cry,
Fulfilling fantasy

That though we all must die
We never cease to be
As soul and mind would deem.

So might this story told
Of such a human gift–
Bright fictive mystery!–
Still leave us set adrift
In St. Nick's history,
This bleak midwinter cold.

"If I should die before I wake": Of a Daughter Who Died at the Age of Ten

for David Mills

So many nights I sat beside your bed
Tucking you in and brushing back your hair
When "Now I lay me down" and books we read
Could bring the sleep of fairy tale and prayer.

And though you seemed untroubled I would say
Before your droopy eyelids closed for good
That if some fear had built up from the day
To tell me and I'd quell it if I could.

And once when winter's early darkness fell
On Dolly's twisted leg and rolled-back eye
Awry from tightest hugs old frights compel
You asked me "Daddy, am I going to die?"

Then pressing both your hands in one warm palm
As I had done the morning of your birth
I told the truth in terms that left you calm
With dreams of many years on mother earth.

Yet now in this dread antiseptic place
By monitors that measure my despair
Too soon I stroke these teardrops from your face
And brush a head strong medicines make bare.

Meanwhile in flesh I know so chastely well
My drawn blood and your own flow vein by vein
In wars between each pale and crimson cell,
Our long defeat's slow holocaust of pain.

And from such pain in frightened eyes that scan
The face of one whose strength was ever there

To soothe you when some fevered dream began
I see a fear grown far too deep to share:

A fear that stays awake in aching sleep
Brought on by drugs too weak for this disease
Which will persist through any watch I keep
And love's great rage no grace can yet appease.

And when the night, departing with your breath
A floor below the floor where you were born
Leaves me those things that I must leave to death
I'll hold them till the soul's last threads are torn.

The Latchkey Child

north Louisiana, the late 1990s

i.

He felt within his pocket for a key
That slowly through the school day's set routine
Of study, lunch, and play had settled down
Below soft clicking marbles won at keeps,
A worn buffalo nickel and a knife
Whose ivory handle bore his father's name
Spun to a blur in games of mumblety-peg.
Meanwhile the yellow school bus which had stopped
Now flashed with bright red warning lights and signs
Before a darkened house where no one was.
The driver pulled the stick back and the doors
Swung open on a place long gone to seed
Since that green spring some forty years ago
When mothers by their gates would wait and gaze
Eagerly down the street each afternoon
To welcome home missed children with a kiss,
Sweet brownies, milk, questions about their day,
And supper cooking slowly on the stove.
Yet for a lonely boy this place was home
Or all of home that he had ever known
Since that cold day four Christmases ago
When taking his shaken face in shaking hands
His mother said things never said before
Of which he could remember only one:
His father would not be there anymore.
The boy slid over the seat and grabbed the strap
Of a heavy see-through schoolbag that had passed
Hand-searches and door signs the teachers' bells
All drew him through: "NO GUNS OR DRUGS ALLOWED."

Then stepping down into the shadow-web
Of January's crackling sapless limbs
He passed the gate whose iron pineapple cups
Had rusted through the years of rain and snow.
The house was from the '40s, cheaply sold
By two who raised four happy children there
But then, becoming frail, at last agreed
To all their children's wishes and moved in
With one of them hard chosen from the rest.
A lovely, warm, and lived-in atmosphere
Still lingered in those rooms through which the boy
Soon made his way into a lightless hall
Where on a ledge an answering machine
Gave out a number greater than his age.
He pushed the message-button, then a click
Began a long sad catalogue of sounds
As messages played back from twelve to one,
Voices of men his father never knew,
His mother's last, apologetic, vague.
The one become a zero, he erased
The disembodied presences and turned
Into the empty kitchen to remove
Another frozen dinner from the stack,
And while it warmed inside the microwave—
The processed chicken shaped like chicken legs,
Thin instant mashed potatoes, greasy peas—
He went alone into the family room
And surfed the hundred channels on the set.
Promiscuous soaps and violent cartoons
Flickered by eyes looking for something else,
A moralistic tale in black and white
Of life within a Carolina town—
Warm, humorous, humane, love's faithful way—
The mothering aunt, the sheriff, and the son.
And when the loud commercials' color came
To interrupt the pleasing pastoral scenes
And tiredness of the day and half a life
Brought glazing eyes toward that deep healing sleep
Where all is lost in symbol and desire,
The boy would gaze upon a photograph
Contained in an ornate Victorian frame,
A woman turning toward him with a smile
Out of the world of memory and dream.

ii.

Within his mind that place would never change
From what it was before the great divorce,
Those summers happy parents left him there

With one both bride and widow of the land,
Too old to have a care for anything
Except for life remembered in a pipe
Like one her great-grandmother loved to smoke
Long winter nights before the Yankees came.
Then rocking on the porch until the stars
Appeared in constellations of their names,
Like some wise angel versed in perfect rhymes
She told him in the language of the heart
Of things and ways of things a later age
Could only dimly sense in primal signs
Now taken to be less than what they seem.
A virgin woodland's clustered buttercups
Scenting the fountainheads of icy springs,
The baking fields of maize in dry July,
Blue herons bearing north through Chestnut moons,
Midwinter pansies blooming wild in snow—
These were the things dumb wonder made her praise,
The evident perceptions love would know.
Yet from that realm where word and thing are one
The boy would wake in tears to some blurred world
Where broken words break hearts and egos breed
Evasions, ambiguities, and lies.
He saw the time displayed upon the face
Of a faceless modern watch whose hands would pass
Unnumbered marks above the open gears,
But in his mind another kind of time
Recalled yet ever-present took him back
To June's starred Arcadie, that country house
Where by a double window as he lay
Under a comforter made before the War
He'd waken to his dream: an antique clock
Whose numbers, etched in silver on its disc,
Were circumscribed by those revolving moons
Bright-eyed in animation—quartered, halved,
And full—and one no more than closing eyes
Black as the mattered night in which it sank.
Beyond, a slower disc bore through the years
Its fine, exact depictions of the signs—
The Argo's Keel, the Centaur, and the Cross—
And after these the fixed stars in ascent
Below the empyrean's blazing arc.
Such stars the boy had witnessed from the porch
Those deep clear nights a dying voice recalled
The two of them to something that sustained
His all but broken soul through bitter years—
A father gone, a mother barely there—
Years passed alone in some suspended state
From which he would awaken in good time
To live with other kin in that green place

Where recollective prose and measured verse
A small yet steady readership would buy
Provided him enough for those few needs
Beyond what chickens, pigs, and tended rows
Of string beans, sweet potatoes, peas, and corn
Would yield to sweated knowledge of the laws
That govern all from Seraphim to seed.
And so he gave himself to toil's routine,
A lay monk of the Benedictine kind,
Subsiding in the silence of the rites
Whose counterparts, night's brightest heightened fires,
Were elegiac lights that still declared
Prime things that shared in timelessness and time
As did a rusted antebellum clock
Which, when a frail grandmother passed away,
Would come with her estate to him alone.
And by such time as Gothic numbers ticked
In lucent moons, the zodiac, and stars
Contained by the fiery zone's embracing flames
He measured out his life until its end.
And by instructions left beneath the key
That wound the antique clockworks he was placed
At last beside the matriarch he loved
Under a massive oak the pioneers
Had spared from those first woods to shade their graves.
And there, in twinkling leaves, the summer stars
Intense as on the evening when he died
Still warm the night whose doming spheres contain
In lordly ordination, names proclaimed
As brimming emblems shaped by One above
To grace a clock whose winding key is love.

Home

> It is a kind of total grandeur at the end.
> Wallace Stevens, "To an Old Philosopher in Rome"

> I am going to the inevitable.
> Philip Larkin, near death

Late middle age, late autumn when a sense
Of ending heightens all we see and are–
The crimson maple leaves now down and dense,
Cane-stubble flames that flicker in the char.

Inside, a clock tocks out the times that rhyme
With measures poets set against a dark
Which brings each season deep into a mime

Of silence where all things grow bleak and stark.

The house for now displays its old décor,
Familiars of the candle and the stars,
Pale rays at twilight fading on the door,
Hearth's ember-ash, the zodiac's marked cars,

The memory with its notches, halls, and nooks,
Scratched records on the antique gramophone,
The keepsakes and the heirlooms and the books,
Those walls of verse from Homer's to our own.

And there we watch again the last gold glow
That far in autumn falls on everything
In turnings of our lives and lines that go
Toward one great end that all beginnings sing:

This mystery of the house in which we dwell,
These cradling graves of starlight and the loam,
These seeds of earth that flower in heaven's dell,
Love's valley where we pass toward love's first home.

The Farmer's Almanac

"for planters, farmers, workers, gentle folk"

Its cover graced by fine antique designs
Year after year printed from those same plates
Whose long dead craftsmen grasped the things they fixed
In etchings pressed so deep on each inked page—
Black edges splashed by dissipating waves,
Four cornered winds blowing the ghostly foam
Of matter's atoms splattered in salt and air,
And spreading in the center, yielding fields,
Wet furrows urged by patriarchal rays
While farmers plow beneath a smiling sun—
Such pictures bear fair witness to a time
When heart and mind could know the world as one.

And though three hundred years have brought us far
From Harris and those first plain almanacs
Of astral tabulations made for souls
Who crossed the sea and earth by plotted stars,
They still contain what we have never ceased
To yearn for in the long divided nights
Of reason and the fancy's fatal sways—
The news of what's too precious to be news,
Perennial predictions, natural laws,
The times to fish and plant and watch for rain,

Tables of weights and measures, zodiacs
Whose houses match the likened plighted signs
Of heaven and the body, zone by zone.

These brazen correlations well aligned
The later almanacs would decorate
With properties of curatives and lures,
Remedies mixed where faith and science combine—
Foxglove for palpitations, burdock's surge,
Skin glowing with aloe vera, bladderwrack
In thinning and those bilberry brightened eyes,
Mullein for easy breaths, garlic to open
Arteries, cayenne for circulation—
And near these rendered simples long dispensed
By pastoral physicians, happy ads
For weather-sticks bending in ice and sun,
An eight ball's love prognostics, sexy shots
Of would-be virgin brides from Singapore,
And all those notions, lotions, potions, sprays
For bumper crops of greenbacks, beans, and hairs,
Flat muscled bellies rippling, stirring bowels,
And prostates raising cocks up from the dead—
Snake oil of the medicine show Asclepians!

Yet why if now we've come so far beyond
Old pictures of the heavens and the flesh
And tall-tale claims the almanacs still run
Do we keep faith and heed them when we have
The Weather Channel, *Playboy*, CNN,
E-mail, the Internet, and FAX machines,
The Hubble telescope, the AMA,
Wall Street and Wal-Mart drugs, and A&Ps?
Perhaps, as the cover says, for "the great
And little secrets of the world, visions,
Divinations, nostalgia, curious lore"
Not only in the nostrums and the charts
Of solstice, syzygy, and equinox,
But in the long dead etchers' finest lines—
Ripe apple orchards russet in the dusk,
A Bible verse cut deep on family stones
By names that stay through centuries the same,
Sealed jars of golden peaches on a shelf
Put up against a window filled with snow,
And most of all in noonday harvest fields
When hay wains pause amid the windy rows
Of hissing ricks that lift the drivers' songs
Till music breaks in silence toward the light
And parted fact and fiction blend as one
In metrical conversions of the heart,
Transcendent transpositions never done
While farmers plow beneath a smiling sun.

The Sniper

Last Report from a Louisianian in Lee's Tigers

northern Virginia, winter, 1864-65, and after

When snowflakes gray with twilight and the smoke
Of Yankee guns now south of Petersburg
Fall quickly in a windless winter night
Blurring my huddled body crouched so still
Behind this virgin oak's half-blasted trunk,
I think on that warm spring of '61
When Ruffin pulled a lanyard and the shells
Screamed over Charleston harbor toward the fort–
A wild high rhetoric of iron and fire
That set a course to further Lincoln's end
And draw us off a thousand freehold farms.

And with our cows too tense to give their milk
When cannonades disturbed their primal sleep
I joined a corps that Stonewall Jackson drove
Across the Shenandoah at a gallop,
Read Presbyterian tracts, then knelt in prayer
Before shocked Yanks were turned and in detail
Routed again by hard side-hammer blows.
But when in that dark reconnoitering
Jackson was shot by his own jittery men
And one chance death then turned the flank of war
I left my hard-earned colonelcy to try
To be that cause by which the Cause would trace
Its pure effect in one all-telling shell
Like God's creation triggered by his will.

And so for eighteen months I blended in
With summer grass or muddy winter snow,
By silence and my stillness camouflaged
As much as by my worn uncolored clothes,
Discerning through a telescopic sight
Insignia, weapons, marksmen, officers–
Patches of acorns, diamonds, moons, and shields,
A captain's bars, a major's oak-leaf gold,
A general's triple blue-field silver stars,
My counterpart sharpshooters better armed
With Whitworths accurate beyond belief,
And those defining traits I knew so well
From newspaper sketches, stories, and reports
Of "Private" Grant's cigars and Custer's curls–
Heraldic signs I'd shatter with a crack
So that our own St. Andrew's Stars and Bars
Might flutter from the White House and the Dome.

And in those grim extended intervals
Between each precious bullet hoarded well
I thought of all my role and mission meant—
Precision, patience, causes and effects
Of almost infinite complexity,
Archimedes' lever, Zeno's paradox
Converging in intention's mystic act—
And wondered whether I would be the one
To squeeze the trigger till its clicking hurled
Fate's lead upon its set trajectory
High arcing from the muzzle to the blood
In some great death to balance Stonewall's own.
And so in that last winter of the war
I picked off careless officers and sent
A whizzing Minié ball past the slouched hat
Phil Sheridan had flourished as he burned
The furrowed Shenandoah farm by farm
Torching the tall dry stalks of summer corn
Whose scarecrows' tattered butternut and gray
Blazed heavenward, then shriveled in the flames.

Toughened thus by battle I lived to dread
What grandsons witnessed in extreme old age—
Destroyers built at Newport News to dwarf
The Merrimack, Richmond a Tredegar
Whose iron has been transformed and magnified,
The sprawl of car-choked highways, shopping malls,
Smog drifting through the Wilderness toward those
Stark nuclear reactors whose dark power
Compels the natives and late immigrants
Who made the Mid-Atlantic of our South.
Such technocrats, the planters of their day
With cash-crop data mansions spread across
The Blue Ridge to the fall line and the coast,
Can never now redeem a chattel-mind
That finds the North and South a single thing.

Yet when my memories surface in the souls
Who bear my name and nature we still gaze
On red men who brought corn in "starving time,"
The first word, *Croatoan*, on a post,
Small farms of ripened peaches, wheat, and oats,
And one young king who came to be a king
With that last word "Remember!" in his heart
As it had been upon his father's tongue
When his stark martyrdom for church and throne
Drew outrage from the New World Cavaliers
Whose heirs would see another Charles declare
Their company's seal be painted on his shield
Not as some mere possession of the realm

But that same Old Dominion which lives on
In steepled villages and freehold fields,
The better dream of Lee and Jefferson.

Song of the Overseer

Louisiana, the 1920s

Gk. *episkopos*, overseer; *skopos*, watcher

the whole assembly of the congregation of Israel
shall kill their lambs at twilight
Exodus 12:6

I sat there on an easy swayback-mare,
My shotgun, pistol, bullwhip by my side,
Watcher of those brown hands well trained to tear
White bolls from stems that blackened while they died.

No bondsmen then but tenants holding on,
In debt to those who paid them day by day
By sack and weight, some broke in soul and bone,
Time's fugitives who could not run away.

The big house in the distance and the row
Of cabins where each freedman stayed a slave
To keep the planters' sons from plow and hoe
All weathered what their seasons took and gave.

Yet sometimes, plagued by heat in mid July,
We seemed to be in Pharaoh's stricken land
With loam for bricks but no straw gathered by,
The Mississippi's Lower-Kingdom sand.

And there we toiled between the shack and hall
Till bits drilled deep through earth's sufficient soil
Toward poison-fumes, dead creatures that appall,
The fathers' arpents leased for gas and oil.

Our children will grow gray in that new age
Where factory and plantation are at one
Under no flag that rallies love or rage,
Old Glory and the Stars and Bars undone.

And I, no more the overseer of fields
Where huge mechanic insects grasp and pull
Seeds from seedpods—weevils of their own yields!—,

Am pastured now, late autumn's slaughter-bull,

While blight spreads wide across the Promised Land
Driving us back to Egypt, mile on mile,
Not plowing forty acres well in hand
But killing lambs at twilight by the Nile.

The Reenactor

upon the centennial reenactment of the Battle of Lafourche Crossing,
fought near the cane fields on Bayou Lafourche outside Thibodaux, Louisiana,
June 20-21, 1863

The day could not have been more like the one
A hundred years ago at this same hour—
Precisely placed, each soldier, horse, and gun—
Even the second day's great thundershower!

And from such fine exactitudes of mind
Came history's images in flesh and blood,
Prophetic elegies by time combined,
The past and present welling in full flood.

Black cannon-smoke pinned down by steady rain
Where Rebels flinched and fell in the riddling lead,
Yankee repeaters firing again, again,
Until time's empty chambers claimed the dead:

These forms deployed within a substance changed—
Authentic blanks instead of hollow shells—
Made ranks to follow namesake ranks that ranged
Over a ground where nothing ever dwells.

And though I know our reenactment's not
Enmeshed in time's iron fabric just the same
As history blind to what time hasn't got—
Things rooted in a transcendental name—

I nonetheless can sense when mustard-flowers
And sugarcane through vital cycles grow
From chronic sleep below those battle-hours
Where what might be awakens and we know

Edenic blends of timelessness and time
Swept back and forth in one still riverbed
Like war and war's depiction in a mime
Till none can tell the living from the dead.

The Given World

I had not seen your face in thirty years
Until a dream released me once again
To be a child upon that columned porch
Watching you as you walked with limp and cane,
So luminous in day's new-risen mist
That hung between the garden and our house.
I always found you there in late July
Whose suns would brown my skin and leave you soaked
As all day your black muscles moved in work
Through rooms you kept yet never could possess.
And where you went I followed deep in play
Watching the red bandana you'd adjust
On hair whose curls made ringlets like my own,
And when you ran the lemon-scented cloth
Softly over the tables and the chairs
Until the fine-grained oak and walnut shone
You sometimes hummed or murmured low and long
Songs of an ancient people of the law
Who once made Pharaoh's bricks from mud and straw.
Midmorning on the porch you had a rest,
Drinking a tall iced glass of lemon tea
For which by the shady hydrant I would pick
Fresh mint as green and tender as our love
And you, with such a fuss, would give me hugs.
Then in a quiet that deepened to a calm
Where reason finds its peace by grace alone
You watched the sun pour heat upon a slope
Whose ripened melons darkened in the light
And heard in distant whisperings of the pines
Archaic strains, creation's common tongue.
In time you rose and took me to the field
And while I held the pail you gathered in
By mundane sacral acts fresh elements—
The purple hulls, snap beans, potatoes, corn—
Then left me with your son to play outside
While you went in to make the midday meal.
His name was Louis Gene, "Blue Jeans" to us,
And jeans were all the two of us had on,
Barefooted and half-naked as we tried,
Where rain had left some pools beneath the swings,
To raise up Camelot from southern soil.
We sank our hands together in the mire,
Our black-and-whiteness swirling into brown
And from such well-mixed substance we would shape
Sludge towers crudely scooped from shallow moats,
And then a central citadel we topped
With oak-twig poles and leaf-flags from pecans

And black grasshopper-guards who kept their watch.
Brothers-in-arms from old Round Table days,
We made up tales of Arthur's plighted knights
Who rode forth side by side, the Celt and Moor,
Against the evil kings of south and north.
And when we tired, the hydrant washed away
Caked mud that casually splattered on the mint
While we stood spellbound by the heady smells
Come from the kitchen window with your song.
The floured chicken frying to a crisp,
Milk gravy browned with drippings in the pan,
Potatoes boiled and pealed, then mashed and mixed
With whole fresh milk and butter to a cream,
Sweet rows of golden kernels on the cobs,
The snap beans steamed with pork chunks, purple hulls—
Such flavors and aromas drew us on
In common hunger peaked by common fare.
Yet once you'd placed the platters and the bowls
Upon our dinner table you withdrew
With Louis to a smaller, farther room
And said a separate grace to our one God.
The table cleared, the dishes washed and dried,
You helped my kin to bed and quiet naps
Those long unairconditioned afternoons
In whose great baking light the world grew still.
And on the screened back porch you had your chair,
A rocker where you nodded off and dozed
Until the others woke and called your name.
Sometimes I sat beside you on the floor
Playing with Minié balls and arrowheads
Dug on our autumn walks from those high banks
Down which the sweet blackberries we would pick
Fruited outside of history in their time.
When older I would fight the Civil War
Lining up Rebs and Yanks beneath your feet,
A hundred painted soldiers blue and gray
Yet of the southern slaves no figurine
Except a picaninny stable-boy
Smiling and holding out an iron ring
Toward horsemen in the mansion's columned shade.
To such flawed reenactments of a dream
In which the Rebels always yelled and won
You uttered nothing, having heard the tales
From great-grandparents who had known them all—
Fire-eaters, carpetbaggers, scalawags,
Knights of the White Camellia, demagogues,
Sadistic overseers, racist Yanks,
And shysters in the Freedmen's Bureau frauds.
And yet I still recall one afternoon
When turning my attention from the War

You told me of a far-off summer day
When playing by the Cane at Grand Ecore
You found in crumbling bluffs of primal clay
Old traces of a Caddoan canoe.
Later the archaeologists who came
From Baton Rouge explained how it was made,
And after, in your being's inmost core,
You dreamed of those who lived here for an age
Before the world of masters and their slaves,
Humans whose skin was neither black nor white,
A native race, at peace with plain and glade.
You saw them burn an oak around the base,
Then push the dark trunk sparkling in the dust
To be scooped out with shells and launched at dawn
Through moonbeam-ripples gleaming in the stream.
Your dream would end when nighttime brought them back,
Those fishermen who worked with hand and spear,
Weighed down by bass and perch for which they sang,
Their paddles swirling starlight on the foam
As though they flowed along the Milky Way
Through chaos and creation toward their home.
But your own world was no such stable place,
Nor those canoes the vessels where in chains
Below the decks your fathers lay enslaved
By evils Appomattox did not end,
Nor did those Sixties when my kin would die
And you and I, so close, would seldom meet
Although at times I wrote and sent you verse
That flowered from a grounded pastoral dream.
For then the two estates that forced the War
Saw all your children victims of the wind—
Sons lost to sprawling cities, gangs or drugs,
And daughters to desertion or divorce,
The slaves, like all of us, to race and sex
In Egypt's bleak new kingdom of the dead.
And in those days, in hospital, alone,
Legs lost to diabetes, almost blind,
Your husband and your children long since gone,
You cast your mind back forty years or more
To one with whom you'd shared a given world
So far from English elms and tropic palms
Yet rooted in the manor and the clan,
The chieftain and the village, not the town.
And so, in that last season of your life,
Remembering my verses and your dream,
You made a will that gave your land to me—
The cabin, corn patch, garden, sandy road—
That lay beside my dead kin's great estate.
And when astonished lawyers made it known
That you had left the earth itself to one

Who rented out rich fields he'd never turned,
Even that house you kept so long ago,
I felt within the depths of heart and mind
A love no ideology can know.
And standing at the center of our world
Along a grassy path once sand alone,
Grains drifting from my hands in changing winds,
I knew the only thing that I could do.
You had a single child who'd come back south,
Escaped from some dread ghetto of the north,
A youngest son who labored in the mill
Stacking the long sawn boards of yellow pine
That round the lake would stand again in time
When oil-and-gas men built their summer homes.
This son had been included in the will
Inheriting the little you had left
In heirlooms, cash, and goods, but not the land
Unless by that late scribbled codicil
You added when you heard he might return,
Shakily made by a trembling palsied hand
And witnessed by no one save God alone,
Your son would leave the mill and work the soil,
Not only his, but mine, which we would share
As stewards of a place three races claimed.
And when he saw me cross the lumberyard
One dusk as he was quitting for the day
He heard a nickname grown so faint with time—
"Blue Jeans! Blue Jeans!"—that he was slow to turn,
But then his cautious walk became a run,
And we embraced: knights-errant of your love.
That night we slept as brothers on the floor
In your abandoned cabin, side by side,
And in a month, the tenants' lease expired,
Moved in that house where you had cooked and cleaned
Restoring your old place for guests and kin,
Joint masters of a land we both would serve.
And when the first-year fields lay gleaned and still,
Frosted under a distant autumn sun,
We made our way together to the plots
So far apart, my family's and your own.
And though we had to walk the greater way
To find your woodland resting-place we stayed
In prayer and meditation by your stone
Until a heightened brightness of the sun
Blackened the undersides of deep green leaves
On oaks that slaves once planted as a sign
Of that well-tempered realm of dark and light
Where we live best in exile till we come
From Eden to the New Jerusalem:
That dappled ground beneath each yeoman's trees.

Epiphany in Lent

The last parade has finished in the dusk
And all the floats come back through Thibodaux
From downtown to the college parking lot.
The king and queen and princesses have gone
To dance at fancy balls till midnight brings
This dark night of the liver to its end.
Like witches, ghosts, and trolls at Halloween
Banished on All Saints Day, these costumed gods—
Bacchus, Venus, Mars—now vanish into ash.
The power lines and trees are hung with beads
A few of which will be there in July,
Dry, cracked, and bleached through Caesar's summer reign.
The air still smells of beer and barbecue—
Elements bodies bless at Mardi Gras—
And diehard revelers head to bayou bars
While I, with curtains drawn, remain apart
As I have done for more than forty years
Both from the Protestant north and Catholic south,
Louisiana's European divide:
My '50s Shreveport with its endless Lent
Of guilt and blue laws regnant in between
The red-light streets and "game" ships on the Red
And Thibodaux's high feasts of flesh and blood
Lashed to a passionate abstinence,
Those twin sad aftermaths of Christendom.
And there I stay, secluded with the muse,
Heeding the poet's calling to withdraw
So that he can more fully come to be
The alien celebrator of his home
Shown in the heartfelt psalms his mind refines,
The native foreigner who carries on
As crafter of the wordsmith's mysteries
Forging with fire and sweat his image-beads
Like throws that hang on lines like lines of poems
Or pollen riming spring's Bienville hills,
Fat Tuesday, thin Ash Wednesday, hymned as one.

Parishioners

1. The Wretched Sexton

Divorced and difficult, a grumpy man,
On Saturdays when no one ever came
Except the ladies of the altar guild
Gracing the chancel's ledge with autumn grain,

You worked alone weeding the flower beds,
Cursing the lilies causing all this fuss.
Your wife was Lily, her new husband Gus.

2. The Lay Rector

Dressed in clerical black, his collar white
And high, shirt buttoned up, no tie,
Ascetic, severe, malicious, pale and fey,
A giver of record—advice, the widow's mite—
Though his inheritance had made him quite
Well off, he had a calling, he would say,
To tell new priests, who may have had misgivings,
That they were only curates of his living.

3. Sacrificial Giving: Old Miser Makes a Pledge

Watching my dollars, quarters, dimes
To pledge my share to help repair
Our church, I've switched, though near despair
Jack Daniels out for Early Times.

4. A Lady of Tradition

Having held with Eliot through change and strife
That "the spirit kills, the letter giveth life"
She wrote in the new prayer book that upset her:
"I'm against all change, even for the better."

5. R.I.P.

Old Harridan lies here most peacefully.
She's in a better place. And so are we.

6. The Yuppie Archdeacon

Determined that youth would never pass me by,
I lived clean till one day, just hitting my stride,
I broke through to the runner's apoplectic high,
Clutched my washboard gut, doubled up, and died.
Go tell my wife, who mourns me in black crepe,
That not all husbands die in such great shape.

7. The New Priest

Looking across the pews on that first day
He thinks of sending out his resumé.
But no. He's tired of moving. And, in time,
Each face will make a sermon or a rhyme.

White Wings

Of Kate Mulvaney, Irish-Acadian Traiteur

As the deer longs for the water-brooks,
So longs my soul for you, O God.
Psalm 42:1

15 December 1915
Louisiana State Museum

Curator:

I know the kind of deer that trapper brought
For me to see, shot near Lake Maurepas—
Odocoileus virginianus—
A spindly-leggèd, short-tailed, hoof-toed beast
Widespread across the state, this one a male,
Its rack of antlers ready to be shed
Now so near to winter, an albino
With rare pink eyes and with two teeth knocked out,
A bullet-furrowed tongue and riddled side,
And something I had never seen before,
Six buds along the spine where feathery hairs
Seemed set to grow and lift toward Seraphim
Or Parnassus an angel-Pegasus,
For this must be a living legend dead,
White Wings, the mythic vicar of the swamp.

December 14, 1915

Kate Mulvaney:

December's winds leave even cypress iced
In flooded wetlands by Lake Maurepas
Where I have lived in this unpainted shack
Ten years with my mulatto friend, LaBasse,
Concocting cures for asthma, burns, and pains

Of flesh and soul and mind and thankless love.
My potions came from simples of the swamp:
Palmetto, goldenrod, and mistletoe,
White-petaled poison hemlock, gentian,
Red milkweed, elderberry, pennywort,
Hackberry, pumpkin ash, and buttonbush.
And there as well were animals I loved:
White ibises, screech owls, and ruddy ducks,
Red bats and twilight bats, the cotton mouse,
All slinky salamanders, newts, and toads,
The slider turtle, snapping turtle, skinks,
The racer snake and mud snake, moccasins,
The bird-voiced and the gray and box-tree frogs—
Familiars of the witch some thought I was.

But they were wrong. I was a city girl
Whose father once taught Dubliners their Greek
And who, come home from that dark Quarter bar
He tended after some obscure disgrace
Forced him to quit our Ireland's snakeless green
For this green world of snakes and water-fields,
Would read Theocritus till I could hear
Far shepherd pipes that gathered-in the sheep
Bleating below the slopes of Helicon.

And then I met him, Irish to the core,
That fair-skinned Daniel Weyman who would drink
So much my father pushed him from his glass
Only for him to sprawl out by my door,
Begging me hard to let him be the one,
A charmer in whose face I'd look and see
Myself reflected—blue-eyed, russet-haired—
His voice a wind that left its seeds in me
Where Celtic roots would flower into love.

Or so I thought. But Dan soon turned morose,
Not drinking now, not doing anything
But reading, smoking, railing at the past,
Damning Atlanta where he'd been disbarred,
Spending his last few thousands, slighting his wife
Whom (though he'd not divorced her) he called X,
Expecting me to labor, as I did—
From passion, then from pity, then routine.
At first I worked at home as best I could—
Making plain goods of flour and eggs to sell,
Teaching the little rich girls notes and scales,
Then peddling vetiver's sweet Asian root
Or salves and powders drawn from plants I found,
Gathered on wetland walks all summer long
Between Lakes Ponchartrain and Maurepas.

Five times evicted over fifteen years,
We parted when he left me for the gold
And diamonds his dead uncle had in mines
In Africa, Australia; then he wed
A nineteen-year-old girl and ran a bank
While I, his "gift" wife, never even "kept,"
Had smallpox as his teenage bride had twins.
And so I found myself at Maurepas,
Talking no more to any but LaBasse,
My fellow-soul, companion, confidant
And to those creatures whose dumb Eden tongue
I understood as none since Adam had:
Swamp rabbits that ate carrots from my lap,
White-striped gray mockingbirds perched in my hand,
Quail preening as I stroked them on my knees,
Squirrels nesting in my ragged stocking-socks.
And though I with my pustule-pitted skin,
Soft snowy hair, claw hands—a drag-foot hag!—
Would seem beyond redemption's loving grace
There came a dying doe that had a fawn
Beside my cabin door—albino, male,
Pink-eyed and deaf, and either side his spine
Six nubbin humps for wings to bring me home
To that Seraphic circle round the throne
Of One who spoke those words that made the world.
I called him White Wings for his wings I dreamed
Would waft me into heaven's meadowlands,
But though he gave me hope that I could fly
Beyond the common burdens of this earth
One day he suffered for and with me here.

It was near mid-December on a road
Between the swamp and lake where I had gone
To gather fruit from holly, mistletoe
For red-and-white late winter Christmas feasts,
When a long black chauffeured car first slowed, then stopped,
And from the backseat lunged an angry Dan.
His younger wife, twin daughters saw me plain
And one girl, scared, cried "Swamp Witch! Swamp Witch! There!"
And Dan, to justify his guilt and fear,
Chased me into the razor grass and yelled
That I had haunted him his whole new life.
But rather than atone for leaving me
He smashed in, with his pistol, my front teeth
Then shot me in the mouth through cheek and tongue,
Pushing me deep into the soggy ground
Beyond the matted blades, though loath to kill
A "witch" whose power, from death, might reach him still.
They drove away and left me there to die,

But soon I felt a breath so soft and cool
Above me and I saw White Wings alight
With two teeth gone, a bullet-plowed blood-mouth,
And bruise-wounds on the same side as my own.

January 6, 1916
Epiphany

Curator:

That much we know—or heard from Kate's LaBasse
Whom my young helper interviewed at length.
She said that Kate was buried in the swamp
Among those things she spoke both with and of.
LaBasse called him "the white one" and she swore
That late on Christmas Eve their White Wings came
To bear Kate's soul, as his flesh took her flesh,
Through air to hear the hymns of Seraphim,
Those six-winged angels like this six-nubbed back,
This carcass of one dead yet who still lives
Beyond the farthest stars, this mythic fact
That my hard earthbound science cannot explain.

After Katrina: Noah's Raven

Noah . . . sent forth a raven; and it went to and fro
until the waters were dried up from the earth
Genesis 8:6

[in the new age] Noah was the first tiller of the soil
Genesis 9:20

He loosed the window-latch
And then he loosened me,
My grim cavort
The first report,
Now made belatedly.

From gopherwood and thatch
I plied by eye and wing
The ruffled weather,
Wave and feather,
Black froth the sea-winds fling.

Yet there was nothing there
But fountains of the deep

And heaven's wells
Washing great swells
Of salt the drowning weep.

Then hunting everywhere
Below a rounding moon
I felt my screech
Grow Eden-speech
We shared in that long noon

Whose fallen silent leaves
With Adam's clacking bones
Are swept through seas
My singing frees
From brine's dumb undertones.

And though a dove retrieves
From olives on the heights
Her leaf and lands
In Noah's hands
To coo away wild frights

And though she be the high
Meek queen of that new realm
Of peace and love,
The Holy Dove
No flood will overwhelm,

By foaming star tides I
Still fly unsounded ground
That only sweat
Makes fertile yet,
This raven-dark profound.

Hurricane Baby

They lie there in the golden afterglow
Of hurricane and twilight and the slow
Powerless hours through which they'll stay so still
Till air moves cool past each wet windowsill.
Outside spent gales adrift in sweet release
Blow mild by flattened cane until they cease.
Blue herons high in cypress preen and sleep,
Their hours those primal hours all beings keep.
And with the clocks, A/C, and TV dead,
No light for books, they have the dark instead
In which he turns to touch, then kiss her there
Lost in a gentle storm of flesh and hair.

The Fiddler of Driskill Hill

Bienville Parish, north Louisiana;
Driskill Hill: the highest point of elevation in Louisiana

for Ann Gresham, who, as a girl, played on Driskill Hill

and now

for my wife and soulmate, Fran, who climbed this "mountain" with me in September of 2022

Midnight in mid-July I come
Climbing through short-leaf pine
Up Driskill Hill to practice this
Old craft of staff and line.

The weathered greensand top's a stage
On which alone I thrum
These country numbers dark barred owls
Detect in oak and gum.

Below the crest none hear those notes
My bow brings from the strings
For I'm the fiddler of that dance
Where stars go round in rings.

So I slick up my horsehaired stick
With rosin from these trees,
Performing pastoral ballad-psalms
For pines and cypress knees.

I sing of winter winds that rime
The hill's hard ironstone cap
And of a young spring dawn that draws
The prime trunks' rising sap.

I sound deep summer's long green tone
That stays inside my head,
Then sweep harsh strings for fall's dry leaves
Blazed orange, yellow, red.

Sometimes I climb the highest pine
On this our highest hill
As daybreak breezes play through limbs
Where light and silence spill.

I spy the natural gas fields there
Ignited by the sun,

Sweet water filling Sugar Creek
Below Mount Lebanon.

Mount Olive, Jordan Mountain, too,
Are not that far away,
The Bible mapping wilderness
When settlers came to stay.

And though they lie by parish lines
Far north and south unseen,
I praise a name and holy place,
Arcadia, Saline.

And thus atop green Driskill Hill
Each year in high July
I sing what is and ought to be
And will until I die:

For that's what bow and strings are for,
To raise things up in song
Between The Fall and Paradise
And urge the world along.

THE DWELLING PLACE

(2003-2013, 2022)

north Louisiana

20–

saying the grace of names

The Dwelling Place

Being

An Epic-Pastoral and Country-Estate Poem,

Also, a Dream Vision and a Catalogue Homeric,

Containing Other Catalogues as Well,

Wherein Is to Be Found a History,

Imaginatively Conceived,

Of North Louisiana

As Seen Through the Prophetic Eyes

Of a Yeoman Farmer

Of No Small Memory, Education, Knowledge

Who Ponders

Astraea and The Golden Age and the Loss Thereof to Mankind,

And, Most Particularly,

To North Louisiana, Revealed in Its

Geology,

Indians,

Settlers,

Planters and Their Slaves,

The War Between the States,

The Tragic Aftermath of That War and the Coming of Modernity,

The Superiority of the Family Farm

As the New World's Answer

To the English Manor and Estate, Honorably Established,

And Ending with a Revelation

Of the Return of Astraea and The Golden Age,

Or, as Christians Say, Eden before The Fall,

This Return Also Being Mimed,

As to Syntax, Grammar

By the Poem as a Single Sentence

Without Period,

Returning Upon Itself,

The Line That Makes the Circle

Without End,

Therefore Forever

Being

The Dwelling Place

for the farmers of north Louisiana

who plowed by horse and star and Pegasus

and

remembering Donald Davidson (1893-1968), author of "Woodlands, 1956-60"

Catalogue of Epigraphs

Now is come the last age of the song of Cumae; the great line of the centuries begins anew. Now the Virgin returns, the reign of Saturn returns; now a new generation descends from heaven on high.

Virgil Eclogue *IV,* 4-7 (Loeb, H.R. Fairclough, trans., 1916; revised, 1935, pages 28-29)

He greatly helps his land who takes a mattock
To break the sluggish clods, and drags bush-harrows–
Ceres looks down from heaven and rewards him–
He too who, having first upheaved the surface
In ridges, breaks them down with angled ploughshare,
And disciplines the acres he commands.

Virgil, *Georgic I,* 94-99 (Penguin, L.P. Wilkinson, trans. 1982, page 60)

And then this race was hidden in the ground,
But still they live as spirits of the earth,
Holy and good, guardians who keep off harm[.]

He is truly blest
And rich who knows these things and does his work,
Guiltless before the gods, and scrupulous,
Observing omens and avoiding wrong.

Hesiod, *Works and Days,* 123-25 and 825-28 (Dorothea A. Wender, trans., 1973, pages 62 and 86)

. . . Astraea, the tutelary deity of the golden men, dwelt last among farmers before leaving earth for good.

William Alexander McClung, *The Country House in English Renaissance Poetry* (1977), page 8

You will die in an unclean land.

Amos 7:17

They refused the pleasant land and would not believe his promise.

Psalm 106:4

I have not changed any of my views on Agrarianism since the appearance of *I'll Take My Stand* [1930]. . . . I never thought of Agrarianism as a restoration of anything in the Old South; I saw it as something to be created as a result of a profound change . . . in the moral and religious outlook of western man.

Allen Tate, 1952

I think it's fair to say that *I'll Take My Stand* is a gross understatement of the conditions we face today.

Lyle Lanier, 1980

Tate and Lanier as quoted in Wendell Berry, "Still Standing," *Oxford American 25* (January/February 1999), page 68

(To Mary Chevillette Simms Oliphant)

Late, by a hundred years I come
To walk these paths of sand among your live oaks,
Oh, unseen host, whose shade my heart invokes.
A stranger, yet not strange, I gather wood
 To light again the flame
 And bid it bear your name.

*

To that unearthly logic must we yield
This rooted tree, this house, this storied field?

Donald Davidson, *Woodlands, 1956-1960, Poems 1922:1961* (1996), pages 19, 21

Each day of thine, sweete moneth of May,
Love makes a solemn holy-day[.]

Hymne IV. To the Month of May

*

Exil'd Astraea is come againe,
Lo here she doth all things maintaine
In *number, weight*, and *measure*:
She rules us with delightfull paine,
And we obey with pleasure.

Hymn XXIII. Of her Justice

Sir John Davies, *Hymnes of Astraea*, 1599

Now, *Penshurst*, they that will proportion thee
With other edifices, when they see
Those proud, ambitious heaps, and nothing else,
May say, their lords have built, but thy lord dwells.

Ben Jonson, *To Penshurst*, 1616

Now the last age of Cumae's prophecy has come;
The great succession of centuries is born afresh.
Now too returns the Virgin; Saturn's rule returns;
A new begetting now descends from heaven's height.

(Penguin, Guy Lee trans., page 180; 1980, revised, 1984)

The Dwelling Place

i.

Late autumn twilight leaves these fields and hills,
Rays paling where the gathered summer corn
Ripened on stalks that crack when dry winds rise
Toward Justice long suspended and ensphered,
Her faint stars gleaming down on candle flames
Whose trembling gently marks the stilling air
Finding in time its way along the porch
Where I in age rock back and forth alone,
Pondering these old commons of the gods,
Breathing in deep the verses of the rows
Well-turned by hoe and coulter, foot on foot
In rhythms that a memory-keeper knows,
Harvests of word and heart cut to the root—
Sole dwellers in the past of house and land,
Familiar spirits of this cadenced place—
And I, an elder son who has no heirs,
My father, mother gone, in settled graves,
My wife and child, my brothers, sisters too,
My fiddle and its fiddlestick high hung
On hooks like willow limbs of Babylon
Yet taken down to raise a story up,
A music blent with chronicle and psalm
For one who left her constant farmers last,
Her fairness, just and lovely, ghostly grown,
Her purple tassels raveling on the breeze,
Star-Maiden of the scales of gold and corn
On whom I call to appraise an age debased
And give true weight and measure to my song:

ii.

And so I dream where memory cannot go
Of shallow tides that washed the fossil-bones,
The mastodon and elephant and whale,
Extinct for eons in these inland beds,
The sand and silt and clay rolling in wolds
Uplifted from the prehistoric sea
With gypsum, limestone, sulfur, and the marls,
Tectonic plates down-warping, tilted, worn,
Streams shaping hollow, mountain, bluff, and bend,
Kisatchie, Nacogdoches buckled up,
Steep ridges ironstone holds on sloping peaks,
Their backbone crests molded by wind and rain,

The great ice sheet retreating toward the lakes,
Meltwater in the Late Wisconsin Age
That made the Mississippi, flowing cold,
The flyway of the heron and the crane
And other birds that died without a name,
Its thawed banks bringing northern flowers south,
The snowdrop and the crocus and the rose,
Seed, root, and bloom taking the king's highway,
Keeping the holy days as each day was—
Things undivided, cleaving, other, one,
Their speechless *be* uttered in time's prime tongue—
Old father of the waters going slow
On progress through his realm of flake and hail
With sun-bowed blossoms glacial in their pace
From Louisiana's flooding delta plain
Toward marshes and a sparkling star-grained shore
Where breakers leave the driftwood and the shell,
Dark waters of the flounder, crab, and gar,
The stingray, shark, and jellyfish, each thing
A harsh gulf holds, gives up, then takes away,
Its dunes of sea oats heading salty-sweet:

iii.

And there, from Asia, walking on a bridge
Of rock and ice to a land no man had seen,
Indians, who for twenty centuries
Ate mayhaws, grapes, pawpaws, chestnuts, pecans,
And honey sticky on the limbs and tongue,
Made golden in the hollow trunks of gum
All sweetening the meadows where they fell
Between wild streams and fields that tamed the corn,
The prickly squash vines fruiting near the roots
Of beans twining up stalks toward tassel-light,
Together called Three Sisters by the tribes,
A kindred whole, the soul's first metaphors,
Enwoven in their world ten thousand years,
Come from the Sun who fathered all there was,
Even the Father of Waters in his bed,
The deer and bear they honored as they killed,
Their foreheads daubed with dead and living blood,
Their tattooed images the signs of clans—
The Wildcat and the Panther, Wind and Bird—
Full brothers of the eagle and the wolf,
Vast grasslands where the long-horned bison grazed,
The saber-tooth and mammoth, born and gone,
The maiden woods that shaded pool and creek,
Persimmon, blackberry, walnut—bass and bream,

Great mounds of dirt, grit, skeleton and shell,
The funerary urns on which they cut
A double-headed vulture, shoveler duck,
Middens of trash and ashes, graves and waste,
The raids for scalping, plunder, slaughter, rape,
Their neighbors kept and left, the slaves and slain,
The beehive house of wattled grass and mud,
Packed earthen steps of flat-topped pyramids
Where priests and healers, one in name and bond,
Tended in that dark room the tribal flame
And pine-hearts, dipped, took home the sun's own tongue
For warmth and meat stone-boiled in deerskin pots,
Adopted as their blood-kin by the gods,
Roaming the great domains of near and far,
The Hunter-Gatherers of glade and range
Who found a ground that never had been lost,
All dancing to a brink that linked them all,
Bright likenesses in constellated night,
Fire-temples of the village and the sky:
And though they did not mark as we have done
The houses of the zodiac or days
Made sacred by the stable, cross, and tomb,
They sensed the measured essence of the land,
The weather of the heavens and the air,
Of animal and plant—bird, beast, and seed—
Lakes burning with the waters of the stars,
High cycling rites they thought would never end:
The winter Bear, Cold Meal, and Chestnut Moons—
Snow twinkling on ground corn, the baked coiled clay,
The sloshing pans they raised from sandy creeks,
Their salt grains leached to whiten in the sun,
The springtime's Walnut, Deer, Strawberry Moons—
Chill hoeing for the "little corn" and beans,
The honey and the onion gathered wild,
The robin's mating-call, the migrant skies,
The catfish and the crappie and the perch—
The Small and Great Corn Moons when summer comes
And leaves and in between the warmer nights
Of Watermelon, Fish, Mulberry Moons—
The peach and pumpkin, squash and sassafras,
The turtle and the grosbeak and raccoon,
The time for basket-weaving, building homes—
The cooling moons at last that autumn brings—
The Turkey Moon and then the Buffalo,
Dry days of torching brush to widen fields,
Elderberry mellowing, chinquapin,
Tracking the bucks for antlers, flesh, and hide
When hungry, roused, they butt, fighting for does,
The clacking racks they thrashed with, even locked,

The purple huckleberry's winter fruit,
Then Bear, Cold Meal, and Chestnut Moons again,
The air that turned to ice their tears and breath
Like stars falling in glitter from their spheres,
The whole of things each household kept and shared,
The common meals of birth and life and death:

iv.

And then three hundred years ago there came
Out of the coastal South's depleted fields
Long salted by the Atlantic's windblown foam
Wagons of yeoman farmers–Irish, Scots,
Welsh, English–freehold kindred–to a land
They cleared of virgin cypress, longleaf pine,
Their cabins made of notched logs, timbers squared,
Of local oak and native hickory,
Their acres staked by grave- and boundary-stones,
Corn golden grown without the old corn gods,
Cradles and chairs both rocking by the hearth,
The only book they needed their King James
In this far place they sought to flee a king,
The family tree whose branches bloom and fruit
Between the Testaments, their matter blessed
And ringing true, those stories timeless, new,
The marriages and births, baptisms, deaths,
Ur-stems of every sur- and given name,
Preserved as well by untaught chroniclers
Who kept the weathered ledgers, journals, notes,
Tied letters, clipped obituaries, curls,
Printed or cursive words of heart and mind,
Crude portraits framed by genealogies,
The tall tales handed down by mouth and ear,
The Highland tunes transposed to these low hills,
Legends for wide-eyed hearers by the fire,
Their cedar chests' quilts, ribbons–keepsake worlds,
A black slate's chalky numbers, ABCs,
The facts of gossip mixed with gossip's lore,
Plain histories of the meadow and the lane:
And when in time they tore their cabins down
They put up manors worthy of the land,
Farmhouses made for living, not for show,
The boulder-stones dug up, bricks shaped from clay
Shoveled from steep red walls of river bluff,
No foreign architect with fine designs,
Just neighbors and themselves, with knowing guess,
The feel of right and rightness in the thing,
Of heft and touch and balance, grain and cut,

No etched designs or compass, leveling plumb,
Old-school their only rule, the rule of thumb,
Like pinching this and that in recipes,
No granite from Carrara or New York,
No balcony or widow's walk or dome,
Parlor, gazebo, secret garden, maze
But kitchen, bedroom, living room, and hearth
Near which they dined, a long-benched table planed,
Porch swings that raised their parlance toward the stars,
A southern drawl so slow it almost paused
Before a stillness gracious and sedate
Even when pests and weather made them fail:
And there for years they showed, undispossessed,
Set hospitalities of sweat and blood,
Earned gifts that virtue's manners yet demand,
Pouring out water cold and pure from wells,
Buckets pulled up, spilling from hidden springs,
Abundance on the table's high-piled plates
For travelers unnumbered and unnamed
No porter looked down on or turned away,
No walled *hortus inclusus*, gated, barred,
But unlocked doors that opened to a knock,
The ample board that fed them if they stayed—
Tomatoes picked, potatoes dug that day,
Cream-mantled milk drawn mornings, ready cows
That only death could sunder from a dream,
The sudden nothingness beneath their sleep,
Late autumn slaughtering, the pail and blade,
Cobs hollowed for a pipe stem's smoking-bowl,
Churned butter cold, then melting gold on gold
In window-light come tawny from the corn,
The bass that sometimes struck a baitless hook,
Baked pies scenting the kitchen's windowsills,
Cool orchard-winds blown in to curl and go
Returning apple sweetness to the trees,
A table fit for governor or mayor,
Field hands, kinfolk, wayfarers where a prayer
Would grace the fixings, leavings of each meal,
Salt pork and greens, pot licker, dipping bread,
The ladled gravy, mashed potatoes, peas—
Lady and purple hull—the honeyed ham,
And children taught their "Yes, Sir," "Please," and "Ma'am,"
Then, next day, farewells said, the turning back
To living roots they thought would never die—
And will not die until they die in me—
My father casting seeds before the dawn,
Plowing the earth the way his father plowed,
My mother tending garden, orchard, hens
Whose new brown eggs lay wet and warm in straw,

Her fingers deft, adept to pull and loop,
Sewing with flax and cotton, carded, dyed
With petals, berries—cultivated, wild,
No ornamental myrtle-beds or planes
But marigolds and dogwoods bred and read
For beauty's use, the book of leaf and bloom,
Home remedies of mint and sassafras,
By store-bought goods then setting little store
Except for what they could not make or raise—
Pens, paper, needles, coffee, sugar, ink
And panes to let the sun alone come in,
The light divine of Indians, Genesis—
Both sons and daughters helping when they knew—
Through hand-me-downs of craft and thrift and love
Binding mind and bone—the manners of the land,
All bearing in themselves the fruits they bore
From meadow, row, and pasture to a place
Where rank and worth were one when fathers carved
And served grandparents, mothers, children last,
Blessing the simple feast with simple words
They spoke once more in verses shaped and phrased
By Tyndale, Cranmer, Coverdale and all
Whose graced estate was England's common tongue,
A Holy Writ for ages and the age,
Words learned by word of mouth and well-turned page
In house and church and school and court of law,
Heard best in pinewood chapels made of pine
By yeomen who still spoke as Shakespeare spake,
The Thames and Avon flowing in the Red,
Who, like the Caddo, built by river-creeks
In scattered hamlets, farmsteads set apart,
Provisioned by their labor, stock and ground,
Until past mere subsistence far enough
To grow a market-village for their crops
With cobbler, blacksmith, wheelwright—skills and wares
That matched their own—by barter, bill, and coin
Exchanging handicraft and shaking hands,
Their word made good by all they were and made:
And as they rode their wagons home again,
Wheels clacking in dry ruts or stuck in mud,
They sensed what only sense can wholly know,
Saying the grace of names each season brings—
Day-flowers blue and moist in April shade,
Pink morning glories climbing toward the sun
On green June limbs of locust, elm, and gum,
September's feather bells spread white in pines,
December's mistletoe in bare pecans,
Red holly fruit the cedar waxwings love—
All speaking for themselves, the Maker's way,

Things Englished that the Indians once named
In languages now lost as Adam's tongue
When being gleamed and God's first song was sung:

v.

But all too soon along old hunting trails
That widened into lanes, then wider roads
(Indians left to wander pathless woods
Of small pox, whiskey, syphilis, and tears)
Appeared what seemed another kind of man
Until he rose within ourselves as well,
Who bought up narrow arpents still untilled
In floodplains that the natural levees fed,
Alluvions overflowing, soil so rich
Their pride's Corinthian splendor laid a base,
Their capitals' acanthus-leaves and scrolls
Like offerings raised, the columns of the gods
Guarding great lawns whose graveled alleyways
Grew oaks to cool the ladies when they strolled,
Gentlemen sipping bourbon on the porch
While slaves dragged burlap bags of cotton bolls
The north and Europe bought with bags of gold,
Estates that rose above the estate of man,
A world in which no yeoman could have lived,
Far from a hearthside mantel's flintlock, clock,
Framed samplers made of home-dyed cloth and threads
With numbers, letters, woven from the earth,
The barn dance and the fiddler, bow aglow,
The hock-cart gold in golden harvest moons:
Instead, the planters built a kingdom kept,
But only for a time, by chattel slaves,
From modest, meet proportion, due degree:
The long halls, ceilings, galleries bedecked
With glittering chandeliers and painted stars,
Zodiacs, busts and statues, portraiture—
Maecenas, Martial, Caesar, Cicero,
Bright Pegasus and Lyra and Orion,
The Heavenly Shepherd—and those maidens loathe
To sing the songs of Zion in Babylon,
David with his harp, dodging Saul's quick spear,
Moses' stone tablets shattered at the calf,
Shy Amos tending sheep and sycamores,
Preaching against the kingdom of the north,
Christ bowed to write his lost words on the ground,
The wife of Pilate turning toward the truth,
Or else commissions from that place and time,
The family patriarchs in formal dress,

Black waistcoat, black cravat, white ruffled shirt,
Hoop-skirted ladies poised atop the stairs,
Their sons at ease in military dress
Of West Point, VMI, The Citadel
With sash and saber, hand on hilt for war,
And near the walls on which these portraits hung
The daughters skilled in needlepoint and keys,
A gamboling lamb of Eden on its leash
And hymns whose verses judged them as they played,
"Awake, Jerusalem, Awake," "O Word,
That Goest Forth on High," "Our Bondage Here
It Shall End By and By," "Repent, the Voice
Celestial Cries," "That Awful Day Will
Surely Come," "The Lord Who Truly Knows the Heart,"
"This Is the Field, the World Below," "Watchman,
Tell Us of the Night," and as night took the day
And parlor-light one final hymn was sung,
"There Is a Happy Land Not Far Away,"
The ladies unsuspecting, in a daze,
All dreaming of a planter's eldest son,
Dancing at spring cotillions to the strings
Of violin quartets while in the fields
The aching strains of slave songs lingered still—
"Roll, Jordan, Roll," "Follow the Drinking Gourd,"
"Wrestle on, Jacob," "Hunting for the Lord,"
"I Want to Go Home," "The Sabbath Hath No End,"
"The Old Ship of Zion," "Satan's Camps A-Fire,"
And "All My Father's Children"—without cease,
Faint undertones of calling and response:
And there, sedate in pride's entitlements,
Liqueurs and not pot licker to their taste,
Wines, French, expensive, in a fine-cut glass,
Not jars of moonshine snuck from hidden stills,
Long mornings and the longer afternoons
Comfortable in their study's easy chair,
The feathered cushion, scroll-arms, padded back,
The fathers soothed by brandy, pipe, and port
With drowsy browsing eyes through bookcase panes
Saw gilded, marbled, leather-bound fine tomes,
In Latin, Greek—Horace and Hesiod,
Theocritus and Virgil—pastoral dreams
Of first estates they never understood
In eclogue, georgic, elegy, and ode,
The uncut pages splotched with rust and mold:

vi.

But then a nightmare woke them from their sleep

When blue troops bled through butternut and gray
To torch those mansions where from flute and flue
Of pillar, chimney, black flags billowed white
In winds that strewed their soot across our fields,
Stark columns pointing darkly toward the stars,
Whirled ashes of the crackling zodiacs,
The walls' and ceilings' blazing paint and frames,
The patriarchs aflame, the statues, busts
All shattered by the ax and rifle butt,
Charred volumes curling wordless in the air
(Simms' library at Woodlands drifting east
As dust toward Alexandria and the sea)
While quartermasters took off all our stock
Marauders had not slaughtered, whiskey-fired,
Who razed farmhouses too and raised the dead
To steal a wedding ring or pearls unstrung,
Our kin long shrouded then in sleep and light—
Parishes we'd name Lincoln, even Grant!—
Though for a time struck clocks would strike us dumb,
The present, past, and future closing doors
That only opened when we turned away,
This aftermath effected by the Cause,
Our Stoic code Aurelius and a cross,
Our memories seared with history and myth
Beyond the good and evil of the war—
Antietam's Bloody Lane, the Devil's Den,
Armistead, hat-on-sword, leading the colors up
That slope where thousands fell upon a name
And Cemetery Ridge received its slain,
Petersburg's winter trenches, long and deep,
Then overwhelming numbers, Sayler's Creek
And Appomattox where a conquered Lee
Rode Traveller through salutes of blue and gray,
The whole war but one battle in a strife
Unending still, the country's great divide,
Tense armistice with snipers, picket lines—
And yet so many gone before their time,
Those farm boys doomed—Rhode Island, Maine, Vermont!—
Sowing with stones the lawns of Arlington
Where, pensive, at a post he cannot leave,
Last guardian of the Old Republic's tomb,
The ghost of Lee surveys the Union dead,
His shadow gray where blue wool stained young bones
Forever buried deep in southern soil,
Fable and fact in endless combat coiled:
And all across the South's blood-seeded fields,
The ploughshares, beaten back from melted swords,
Turning up settled relics of the war,
Exhuming with their bright abrasive blades

The scattered Minié balls and gilded hilts
Or buttons stamped US or CSA,
Brass letters worn away by rust and rain,
There, too, the planters' chapels, crumbled, burned
By men a pure high righteousness had made
Angels of their own rage that freed the slaves,
The altar's stolen chalice, pyx, and plate,
The shot-out azure panes of Mary's face
All twinkling in their shards, the Virgin's tears
(The splendor of their Anglican restraint!),
Tears for all her children—black, white, blue and gray—
Fort Sumter, Appomattox, prelude days:

vii.

Yet what of this plain farmhouse never named
Like Old South mansions called Felicity,
Mount Bountiful, Heart's Rest, the Muses' Grove,
Arcadia, New Eden, Avon Glade,
Belle Mont, Fair Haven, Stronghold, Reverie,
Clear Vistas, Tanglewood, and Waverley—
But only *home*, only a dwelling-place,
Familiar spirits—bellows, tongs, and wood—
The Lares and Penates of our hearth,
The kindled memories so far beyond
A world in which the dead are left for dead
While rigs pump up from under sea-floor sands
And bedrock the remains of layered graves,
Agribusiness in bondage to machines—
Their rattling chattel chains—topsoil worked thin,
Strong chemicals the Mississippi drains
From northern farms, a toxic underflow
Spreading The Dead Zone further in the Gulf,
Great kills of crab and flounder, shrimp and bass,
Bottom-rotting or scooped by swooping gulls,
The bumper crops of protean new strains,
The blight and pests that weather every change,
Unplanted tracts left fallow for a price,
Slaves of the banks and futures and the exchange,
No garden near for this day's corn and beans,
No family graveyards but the graves of farms
Once seamlessly beseeming, apt and fit,
Collations of the gods of sod and star,
Likemindedness and lovingkindness one,
Both comely and becoming, well in hand,
The culture of a cultivated earth,
The coulter's tropes no curses can reverse,
Tillers grown still to take in the long view

And keep the ancient sabbaths of the land,
Playing the fiddle brought down from the wall,
No longer hung on crooking willow-hooks
The pioneers wedged deep in fireside stone,
Songs with Scotch-Irish, English, southern roots—
"Carry the News to Mary," "Sally Ann,"
"Frosty Morning," "Over the Waterfall,"
"Lost Indian," "Sourwood Mountain," "Shady Grove,"
"Wild Mountain Thyme," and "Sugar in the Gourd"—
The words and music keeping souls attuned
Through evening when the shadows gather in
Plowmen walking tired plow-horses back,
No bells rung hard for slaves or tenant-serfs
But goat bells tinkling deep in pasture grass,
Each human life a human sacrifice,
Its modest state the right estate of man,
The trusted customs, valid habitudes,
A village made of names recalled and lost,
Proportioned to those roles this roll proclaims:
The farms of Martial, Horace, Penshurst kept
By Sidneys whom Ben Jonson praised the best,
Appleton House of Fairfax and de Vere
Where Marvell taught the daughter of those walls
Its history he'd commemorate in rhyme,
Croft's Saxham and Worth's Durrants, G.N.'s Wrest
Where Carew saw a "usefull comelinesse"
Grinding "the Yeallow Goddesse into food,"
Coole Park where Lady Gregory walked with Yeats,
Home places celebrated in their time,
Even flawed Woodlands dreams of Gilmore Simms
That Donald Davidson would dream anew:

viii.

And now as my own dreaming nears an end
And rocking slows to stillness on the porch
I lay my fiddle down in quiet hope
That one day we might fully know again
God's hospitalities, sojourning zones,
Old houses like my fireplace, starry hearths,
The candles and the anthems and the choirs,
The song of was and is and yet to be—
Elegant delegations of a love
From Mind to minds undisinherited,
The givenness of magnanimity
Whose breathless essence breathes a universe
Expanding and contracting to its end,
The prime rhyme turned and turning, fixed adrift

Between the stuff of nothing and the One,
Pegasus drawing the Plowman toward the Lyre,
His twinkling wings appointed star by star,
Cain's wheat and Abel's lamb near Eden's trees,
Both spared the altar-fire of stalk and blood,
New grain on the cedared peaks of Lebanon,
Jerusalem's crumbled walls of rubble-stone
Rising again in Nehemiah's eyes,
The pelican of David and the owl
Flying beyond the wilderness and ruins,
Noon deserts where the dunes will flower out,
Those early rains and late that never fail,
The bones of Joseph carried home at last,
Christ's private writing published from the dust—
While Ceres in the breasted haystacks sleeps
Until she wakes to Saturn's second reign
When Justice comes to raise a world debased,
Descending with a wind now mild and kind,
And farmers see what they were last to see,
Her scales balanced again with coin and corn,
Our cause not red, white, black or blue and gray
But only graded shades of meadow-green
As daybreak burns off darkness from the land
And all we long have longed for draws us home,
The ripened light, the harvest of the stars,
First fruits that only dawn-time tilling yields,
Astraea's rays over the golden rows,
The fall's last twilight leaving fields and hills:

Author's Note

on

The Dwelling Place

The Dwelling Place is a poem in the ancient "pastoral" tradition as well as in the tradition of the "country house" or "country estate" poem traceable to Horace and Martial. It makes use of history as well as myth and, as a pastoral poem, presents, at times, a happy picture of country life; at other times, however, it addresses and depicts suffering, war, death, problems of modernity, other evils, and other themes. It differs from other country estate poems in English in having as its setting not an English or Irish manor or the mansion of a plantation in the antebellum South but a family farm and farmhouse, in this case in north Louisiana.

The pastoral mode of the poem and its central themes are also deeply rooted in the southern agrarian tradition. The poem tries to evoke a world that may well lie just beneath, beyond, above, beside, within, or barely out of sight and reach in relation to what we are perhaps too quick to call "the real world." As Coleridge said of Wordsworth, the poet–in his true self–has the power to pull the scales of custom from our eyes so that we may once more see the world in its persisting wholeness and in all its primal wonder.

The Dwelling Place is dedicated to traditional north Louisiana farmers and remembers Fugitive poet and Southern Agrarian writer Donald Davidson (1893-1968). Two immediate sources of the poem are Davidson's own country-estate poem, "Woodlands, 1956-60," Woodlands being the South Carolina plantation home of southern man of letters William Gilmore Simms (1806-1870), and M.E. Bradford's essay "Donald Davidson and the Great-House Tradition: A Reading of 'Woodlands, 1956-60.'"

Of particular interest in Bradford's essay is his quotation from Lewis P. Simpson's *The Dispossessed Garden: Pastoral and History in Southern Literature* (1975): "as nearly as the South had a center in the Republic of Letters following the age when Monticello was such a place, Simms's plantation (called Woodlands) was it." The dependence of that plantation system in antebellum days on chattel slavery is addressed in my own poem.

The Dwelling Place is divided into eight sections, numbered 1-8. These sections may be characterized as follows: (1) Introduction–the speaker, his family, the setting, and the invocation of the Muse (Astraea); (2) Description of prehistoric north Louisiana and surrounding areas north and south thereof; (3) The Indians; (4); The Settlers; (5) The Planters; (6) The Civil War; (7) Modernity; and (8) Conclusion–including a return to the Introduction's setting and Astraea, then ending with hope for a renewal–or a new vision of–the human condition insofar as that is possible in a fallen world (noted in the poem's "final" line).

The Muse of the poem, Astraea (Star-Maiden), is the virgin goddess of Justice with her scales. When The Golden Age ended (some say also the Silver), Astraea was the last divine being to depart from the earth, and the last human beings she departed from were the farmers. She then became a constellation. Her return to earth would signal a return to The Golden Age–something like Eden in Christian terms.

The speaker is a farmer in present day north Louisiana. He is well educated, a fiddler-poet, and is in accordance with the pastoral tradition that grants to its rural speakers a knowledge of things usually beyond what a farmer or shepherd would need to know in order to perform his daily tasks.

Readers might recall the conversation between the shepherd Pierce and the shepherd-poet Cuddie in Spenser's "October" eclogue in *The Shepheardes Calender*, an eclogue on the nature and role of poetry and the poet. Cuddie and Pierce discuss Maecenas and Augustus Caesar, seem well-versed in the classics and Greco-Roman myth, apparently have at least indirect knowledge or intimations of Plato's philosophy, and discuss the major poet's attempt to rise from the pastoral lyric to the epic poem–as did Virgil, Spenser, and Milton.

The speaker in *The Dwelling Place* also has at times the voice of an Old Testament prophet, such as Amos, a simple shepherd and a tender of sycamore trees who was inspired both to know and speak of things beyond his normal ken. The speaker's voice is indebted as well to voices in Blake's prophetic books and the rhetoric of southern Fugitive-Agrarian poet Allen Tate.

The Dwelling Place is structured as one long catalogue, and within the poem-as-catalogue are local catalogues: Indian moons, titles of antebellum hymns and slave songs, the names of manors praised by other poets who wrote in the country estate tradition, Civil War battles, names of southern plantations, and several more.

Most of the items in these catalogues are real and of their period so far as the author can tell. Two exceptions are some of the names of the southern mansions and some of the artwork of the planters. As with T.S. Eliot's names of Tarot cards in *The Waste Land*, the reader will find in these catalogues real names and subjects together with invented but likely seeming ones, introduced for symbolic purposes.

The ultimate philosophical-theological nature of the catalogue as a literary device going back at least to the list of ships in Homer is implicitly argued throughout: its invocation and evocation of pure being, things perceived as *what* they are and *that* they are (with a divine Maker also presumed). It should be noted that "the dwelling place" of the title, a north Louisiana farmhouse, unlike other dwelling places in the country estate tradition in English, has no name but *home*. Whether the poem as a catalogue with catalogues is effective or simply tedious will be up to the reader to determine.

The poem, though long, is, grammatically, a *single sentence*. There is no period (.) in the poem. The colon functions in the flow of the poem as a weir does in a stream, slowing the poem at crucial moments but not fully impending its onward going as a period (like a dam) would do. The last line of the poem rounds back onto the first; thus, the poem is both a circle and a line, the ancient symbols of eternity (the circle) and time (the line) or idea and history. In fact, one might wonder whether the poem is a "sentence" at all since it has no period, cycles back into itself, and, thus, but for the mortal reader's necessary abandonment, has no end.

Throughout the poem are echoes, translations, and transpositions of details from earlier poems in the country estate or pastoral tradition and from other sources. One example is at the end of section 6 where a north Louisiana plowman turns up sunken Civil War relics. This detail comes from Virgil's *Georgic I* where an ancient Roman farmer does the same. Historical echoes include the phrase "overwhelming numbers" in section 6, words taken from General Robert E. Lee's well-known General Order No. 9 (Farewell to the Army of Northern Virginia), an order issued at Appomattox but with implications that go far beyond its original use and context.

Certain symbolic images may be followed through the poem. Three examples are wind, stars (including constellations and the zodiac), and fire. The old trope of "versus" as the poet's turning of verses and the farmer's (or poet-farmer's) turning of rows is also woven into the poem from beginning to end.

Music and paradox, too, are important in the poem. When sound begins to challenge sense as central to a word, phrase, or line or when paradox is used frequently to indicate that we have reached a point beyond which language and the mind may not be able to go, then we know that the brink between a golden age or perfect garden and our age has probably, at least for now, been reached. Nevertheless, a reader may perhaps be able to peer over such a brink into what English poet T. Sturge Moore (1870-1944) once called "the unknown known."

The idea of the Poet as Linker whose metaphors are devices of a deep (re)-connecting between all things is also present in *The Dwelling Place*. This concept comes from the verse of fellow Louisiana poet Wilmer Hastings Mills (1969-2011), whose family has farmed the same land in Louisiana since the 1790s.

In addition, *The Dwelling Place* can be read as a defense of poetry in the spirit of Sir Philip Sidney (who is mentioned in the poem) including a defense of the deep interrelationship of poetry and the natural order, especially farming (culture and agriculture). It is a poem about poetry and poetics in addition to other subjects.

Finally, speaking more personally, *The Dwelling Place* brings together themes, phrases, tropes, and strategies that have appeared in many of my earlier poems as well as in the poems of poets who have influenced me and to whom I owe a literary debt of one kind or another. *The Dwelling Place* seems like a culmination that has been coming for a long time. I prepared for writing this poem by reading earlier pastoral verse, country estate verse, and scholarly commentaries on such verse for nearly a decade. Especially important were the works discussed and cited in M.E. Bradford's essay.

The Dwelling Place itself was drafted and revised from mid February through mid October of this year (2013).

*

The Atoms of Democritus
And Newton's Particles of light
Are sands upon the Red sea shore,
Where Israel's tents do shine so bright.

William Blake (1757-1827)

OUTSIDE THE GATES OF EDEN

(2023)

Night Watchman at the Zoo

Audubon Zoo, New Orleans, Louisiana

The day's last visitors have left the zoo
Taking the golden autumn afternoon
Along with gift shop toys their children hug–
Stuffed lions smiling wide, soft cuddly bears,
Limber rubber snakes showing rubber fangs,
A windup ape beating its plastic chest–
All headed home to nightlights, bed, and prayers.

And here, as gates lock shut when sunset flames,
My flashlight, cell phone, pistol close at hand,
I walk the narrow pathways as they fade
Between these artificial habitats–
Savannahs, caves, pools, jungles, waterfalls–
A wilderness constrained by moat and bar,
A red wolf kept from swamp hares by the wire,
A cheetah's caged eyes fixed on still gazelles.

By each exhibit, tilted on a post,
An illustrated plate states what we know
Of origin and range, defining traits,
The boney abstract Latin, English flesh,
Cemophora coccinea, scarlet snake,
Zoologist and poet nearly one.

I watch for quiet intruders who provide
Stolen calves and cubs to the roadside zoos
Where they will languish, maddened in their cells,
Or offer them as curios to those
So rich and bored they need menageries,
Pure spectacle, a conversation piece.

But I'm on guard to thwart them as the heir
Of Adam who tamed animals with names,
Addressing them in ur-speech, early words,
The owl's prime Eden screech for colloquy.

Such animals still speak, their language maimed
As hisses, hoots, growls, bays we try to learn
As some of them can learn our blunt commands
Though most live in a state beyond recall,
Detecting with their feelers, bristles, tongues
A lessened world by appetite confined.

They're fed enough to keep them satisfied,
Their habitats shrunken to this small space,

Too captive-bred ever to hunt again.

I hear them eating far into the dark,
So seemingly at peace with humankind
That knows them as they cannot know themselves.

And yet I often think of Trajan's games,
Massed gladiators spearing crocodiles,
Or Nero's where starved tigers slaughtered bulls
As bulls did tigers, hundreds at a time
And how in our own day we still permit
Chinese safari parks where those who come
Pay to toss goats alive to waiting lions
Who kill and eat, feeding a savage glee.

Such images disturb me as I move
Between flamingos swirling water-stars,
Walking with grace through pools while overhead
Old houses with their Lion, Serpent, Bears
Mark gardens walled from floods the heavens hold,
Flaring against a ground no word declares.

Soon dawn will hide the stars-beasts in its light
And visitors will gather at the booths
Eager to walk the daytime's crowded paths
Till I, like Adam, waking from his sleep,
Return to watch the night out once again
While dreaming children clutch their gift shop toys,
Loved animals they hug and kiss by name
So far from Michael's sword and that first sin
Which drove us out of Eden to a place
Where closing gates lock shut as sunset flames.

Before and After Sleep

Late afternoon. Then twilight. Then the night
When nightmare-sleep and sleeplessness contend.
No Lethe-drop to drink. A heart not right
With what the mind alone would comprehend:

The first and final question, where we go
And where we come from, why we sojourn here,
The Big Bang and Big Rip the bounds we know
Around these flat-earth plains of *mere* and *sheer*.

Yet from some prime elusive shadow-seed—
Its physics welling in the seen-unseen—

Unfold proportions noble in their breed,
The Golden Numbers and the Golden Mean:

The spiraling florets of flower heads,
The curve of shell and beak, of horn and claw,
The whirling squares a logarithm spreads
Through everything by Fibonacci's law,

Or Pegasus, whom Ptolemy could trace
In radiant matrices—the fountain's sheen—
Descending star by star through time and space
Till hooves struck rock and freed the Hippocrene.

Alabama Correspondences: Winter into Spring

1

Flowers Hospital, Dothan

2/17/91

Somewhere in Flowers,
Some antiseptic room,
Too weak to keep on breathing
You finally died of AIDS
This first Lenten Sunday
My old poet-friend
Of almost twenty years.
Miles west, near Enterprise,
Across the family farm
Through quiet trees outside
The house you thought and wrote in
A sinking wind still cries.

2

Huntsville

2/18/91

Unable to deny
Her bonding-place and time,
She turns at last and comes
To one whose early poems
Some twenty years ago
Had touched her being's core.

Tired of some blank sadness,
The sterilized tight void
Where joy's wildflowers should bloom,
She writes him from her room.
Her words like daisies blaze
Brightening more and more.

Woman Mending

after the drawing by Jean-François Millet (1814-1875)

1853

black conté crayon on blue-gray paper

private collection, London

So inward and so near to us the scene
We fear we are intruding just to look
At one intent, yet patient and serene,
Giving herself to work that must be done.

Her practiced fingers, bent, adroitly poised
To use a pitted thimble, needle tip
Pull tight the thread that stitches closed a hole
In a woolen shirt, rumpled in her lap.

A shelf holds piled-up clothes still unrepaired
In the dim, bare room. Scissors hang in reach
From her chair's left stile, ribbon looped through rings,
Blades hidden by her sewing basket's weave.

Such mending never seems to have an end—
The ready fingers, things unraveling . . .
Yet passing through a window just unseen
Light rests like grace and fate on thread and hand.

Arcadian Shepherds

after the painting by Nicolas Poussin (1594-1665)

oil and canvas, 1639

You cannot take your song with you
In the end. Hades and forgetfulness are the same.

Theocritus, *Idyll 1,* The Passion of Daphnis
(translation by Robert Wells)

They happen on a tomb on which no name
Has been inscribed, three shepherds without flocks
Or panpipes, although two of them are wreathed,
For death and art have come to Arcady.

Behind them, straight or leaning, peaks and trees
Seem sentient attendants waiting near.
Low slate and high white cloud-shapes pass and stay
Under a shading sky's cerulean blue.

There, too, a woman, or a goddess, stands,
Her left wrist on her hip, her right hand placed
Upon one shepherd's back, knowledge and calm
Acceptance in her pale gray-yellow face.

The shepherd whom she comforts turns his head
While pointing at block capitals–shocked eyes
Searching the fixed placidity of hers
That look both deep within and far away.

Another shepherd rests against the tomb,
Brooding over a missing chunk of stone,
Still trying to interpret cryptic words:
ET IN ARCADIA EGO–nothing more.

The unwreathed shepherd, bearded, kneels to read,
By sight and touch, each character incised,
His finger tracing a shadow of itself,
Spelling his fate in lettered silhouette.

Who carved this verse, unfinished–without verb?
What mysteries of author, speaker, tense?
Who made this tomb where tombs had never been?
What master practiced here the arts of death?

It was and is Poussin, who, till the end,
Still painted, though with tremors in his hand,

The silence of his Stoic dignity
Like that of her who dominates the scene:

The mother of the Muses—Memory—
Whose shepherds drove their flocks toward piping cries
When Daphnis as a baby lay exposed,
Abandoned in a grove of laurel trees.

The Potter's Epitaph

Inside an urn my strong hands made
Those hands are in their ashes laid,
And I who quickened mother earth
Lie still within the place of birth.

New clay dug up from ancient pools
And fashioned by the timeless rules
Became a pot, conceived, then thrown
Till blended use and beauty shone.

And while it dried I took a knife
To cut blunt words of death and life
In verse that followed, sharply curved,
The potter's field I ruled and served.

Then when the last cone melting fell
In fires of Pentecost and Hell,
The hardened glazes baked and blazed
Black rhymes at which the kiln-gods gazed . . .

"Made both to hide and to expose
My burning flesh in cold repose,
This urn mocks all dark acts of birth,
Holding and yet held by earth."

Charts

Saline, Louisiana, 1957-1959

When I consider thy heavens, the work of thy fingers, the moon and the stars,
which thou hast ordained,
What is man that thou art mindful of him?
Psalm 8:3-4

And there shall be signs in the sun, and in the moon, and in the stars . . .
Luke 21:25

in memory of my maternal grandfather, Henderson Edward Sudduth, 1891-1959

1

You woke just as the sun and moon and stars,
Poised in their constant moving, blended lights,
A moment's single beam in dark and dawn
Spreading along the dense midwinter clouds,
Snow holding till it fell straight down like rain,
Dry shadow-drops in patterns on your bed.

Now sixty-five, finding it harder to rise
For one more day as village banker, mayor,
Church elder, still you did what must be done
Because your word, once given, was for good,
In oath and vow, in pledging the full tithe,
Plighting your troth in civic, private life,
And first to her beside you, dreaming on,
Emma your wife of nearly forty years.

You felt achy and stiff as you sat up,
Leaving the warmth of quilt and comforter,
Legs swinging till your feet touched cold wood floor,
That metal plate like weather in your head.

Unsteady, you shuffled along, room to room,
Turning up each gas heater's pilot light
Or scratching kitchen matches till a flame
Spread port to port behind the radiant grates.

But as you leaned toward burners in the hall,
Your right side deadened, nerves blocked off from brain—
That path between the muscles and the will—
Then you collapsed, half-paralyzed by stroke,
Those sounds that come before and after speech
Rousing a wife untroubled in her sleep
Who found you staring helpless past her eyes.

2

An ambulance soon there from Natchitoches,
Men pushed you on a gurney through the yard,
Immobilized by straps, your mind adrift,
Mixed flocks of birds and leaves on bough and ground,
Your body dotted with crystal hexagons.

And as red flashing sirens cleared the way

Past logging trucks loaded with sand-hill pine—
Their chain-links stressed and strained by dip and crest—
You slipped into another place and time
When medics with a stretcher reached your plane
Shot up by German gunners, limping back
With leaking gas aflame along the wings,
Gliding toward No Man's Land, topographies
Of ink and earth mapped out, their legends read,
The shock of sign and thing at odds and one.

You lived, but with a steel brace in your brow,
The hole in your right cheek a dimple-scar,
Those wounds the medals you would always wear.

Yet now, a harder fall, and you lay still,
Doctors scanning a clipboard by your bed,
Zigzagging needle peak and valley lines,
The heart's cartography, a brain surveyed.

In time you walked, foot-sliding on a cane,
Reason intact but speech a slur of words
Like a toddler's mangled language, though you strove
To grapple back through babble toward a voice
Eluding you ever after, damage done.

3

To let you say what needed to be said
As statement, question, answer, or request,
Your son-in-law, my father, drew a chart
On plywood—a rectangle painted white—
A straight row of numbers, zero to nine,
And two rows curving for the alphabet,
Then underneath YES, NO, HELLO, GOODBYE,
All taken from a talking board, and HELP,
Words ready if you grew too weak to spell.

And so you stayed, with silent dignity,
Hobbling in pain and numbness on the porch,
Your cane-tip tapping out its open code
Between the swing and rocker where you watched
For hours seeing more deeply than before:
Split husks dropping pecans through torn cocoons,
Strung stars and wrens along the winter limbs,
Spring lizards on the warming summer walls,
Sunflowers climbing noons toward noonday sun,
The grains they came from shaken from their heads.

And though at last bedridden, you held on,
Your sleep a kind of waking, waking, sleep,
Mind all but done with measuring the world—
God's copybook of tablet-clay and light—
Prefiguring equations, slated sums,
The ABCs that count the telling names,
The ordinals and cardinals and primes,
Chapter and verse, the tally marks and logs,
Denominators, numerators, lined
And rhyming in the diagrams and schemes
Derived from elemental paradigms,
Spellbound orthographies, broken ground maintained
Until the end of particle and star.

4

And just before you left us for a state
From which there is no waking, that last place
Of sleep and breath, you motioned for the chart
To be brought back once more. Then your good hand,
Guided by magic, science, or providence
Moved like a Ouija planchette, swivel-wheeled,
Fate's heart-shaped indicator prompted at will
Through grammar's fractions, lettered formulae.

And there, where axioms and syntax blend
Like lights above a clouded winter dawn,
You found your way along the road you came
From our first home and lasting habitude,
Those old geographies of soul and mind
Beyond the posted gates, your only toll
A solitary scansion of the land,
The layered tracings, ghostly palimpsests,
That chart and board a Ptolemaic map,
Four corners marked like heaven's windy zones,
A grinning sun, a moon close-lipped, serene,
Two matched pentangle circles, ringed by stars
In a galactic dance, the striking fires,
Bright ciphers of the Nothing and the All
Worded in night and silence, carried across,
Radiant declarations, pilots ablaze
Against a No Man's Land that no one knows,
Direct reflections, certainties unguessed,
One word just like a code-blue button—HELP—
HELLO that only others needed now,
And three for dying: GOODBYE, NO, and YES.

Clockwise

after verse about the hours of the day by Katherine Pyle in Howard Pyle's children's storybook *The Wonder Clock* (1887)

And now at last I lay me down to sleep,
An old man in the winter of his years,
So cold at twilight, taking to his bed,
Well tended by what memory sees and hears.

Upon a hook within the family room
A wall clock marks the hours with its chimes
That comfort me, a widower alone,
Drawn late to other hours in other times.

My wife long gone to ashes, dust and bone,
Our children grown and scattered—I retired
To dwell inside some mellow pensiveness
That took deep hold as my past life expired.

And thus I lie in dark beneath a quilt
My Mary sewed from patches, odds and ends
That match a chronicle of days and ways
My clockwise mind recalls, then sifts and blends:

This stiffened shoulder where each crying child
Would sleep to Mary's baby song I'd sing,
A song she made so simple, sweet, and mild
It was itself the comfort it would bring;

The box of recipes—a wedding gift,
Handwritten cards in script of friend and kin
Long done with needing larder, stove, or board,
Ink fading toward the state their souls are in;

But most, a chest of letters, photographs
That Mary culled and stored before her death,
In scents of pomander and potpourri,
Keepsakes all laced with ribbons and her breath.

Such clockwise thoughts possess me as the hands
Move round a face, a smiling sleepy moon,
Its catalogue of hours my book of time,
More storied nearer midnight than at noon.

And so I know that right here all along
Our common life was not a common thing
But worthy to be praised, like Mary's song,
That only I and silence now can sing.

Test Pattern

It filled the screen from midnight until dawn
After the late show, anthem, station sign
In those brief early days of innocence
When television broadcast black and white.

The pattern was rectangular, abstract,
Made up of wheels and numbers, blocks and lines
To measure shape, proportion, light and dark,
Its soundtrack shrill—the sine wave's monotone.

But centered at the top as pure décor
A chief in profile stared beyond the set
In eagle-feathered headdress, beaded shirt
With cheekbones high and eyes and lips severe.

Penciled in '38 for RCA
The chief looks dignified, and much concerned,
A guardian spirit troubled by his charge,
Fair meadowlands so near where badlands are.

For by the time his image was replaced
With blank plain color bars the episodes
Of which he seemed the genius were no more
Or ran in syndications few would see:

Leave It to Beaver, The Andy Griffith Show
Where fathers talked with sons of right and wrong
Or *Gunsmoke* where Matt shot an outlaw down,
Then said to Chester, "he was just no good."

And now when desperate housewives push aside
June Cleaver, Harriet Nelson, and Aunt Bee
And even primetime viewing is PG
We long for Adam, Hoss, and Little Joe.

*

Today test patterns have no further use
For stations that stay on throughout the night
With infomercials, soft porn, cable news—
No national anthem, sign off, sleep and peace.

And what of the chief? His card was thrown away
In a dumpster when wrecking balls knocked down
The RCA's old factory—then was saved—
Retrieved by one of the demolition crew.

And for a while he stayed—a nightlight shade—
Glowing toward dawn when children safely woke
On cartoon Saturdays as did their folks
Who saw his pattern flicker on the screen.

Many of the nation's television stations used the image of the Indian-head card to be their final image broadcast when they signed off their analog signals for the final time between February 17 and June 12, 2009, as part of the United States digital television transition. . . . It was sold as a night-light from 1997 to 2005.
Wikipedia

Modern Times

1

Goodbye, Dear

How seldom now do you begin with *Dear*,
Both warm and formal (civil) but a mere
First name—"David:"—like a *Sir* or *Madam*
Summons to a wayward child of Adam,
No salutation as in Saint Paul's Letters,
Your curt tone saying one should know his betters
As if you bid a servant or a beast,
And you in all these emails not the least
Aware of such abruptness being rude—
Public, private address grown crass and crude—
And so, in closing, I reply (hit Send)
Goodbye: And let this conversation end.

2

Toll Free

Ire in gehennam!

Reception bad on my cable TV
I punch the 800-number. Technically
Pleasant an artificial female voice
Says "Hi. I'm here to help you. Make a choice:
English? *Español?*" "Latin." "Choose again."
"English." "OK. Now we can start." (I'm in.)
"Let's try to find the problem." "Well . . ." I pause

Wanting to be precise while cause on cause
Is quickly listed for my "Yes" reply
Or cordless button-pushing as I pry
To get more than a word in though the toll
In time and patience, rising, tries the soul
Till "No's," then silence, prompt a change in tone:
"I need my supervisor. Hold the phone
Two minutes." Twenty pass. A curt "Hello"
To which my Latin tells him where to go
As "thanks for calling but we seem unable
To understand the problem with your cable"
And "this call has been monitored . . ." play through,
Reception clear as church bells, ringing true.

Cholesterol

after Robert Herrick (1591-1674), Anglican priest and poet, and author of the poems "His fare-well to Sack" and "The Welcome to Sack"

1

Farewell

My annual checkup and its blood work done
And three weeks' fast to drive high numbers down
I swing by Popeye's for the day's first treat—
A box of spicy thighs, red beans and rice—
Proud of myself as I am every time
Crash dieting to avoid yearlong regimes
To please my doctor who renews those pills
That keep my old heart beating quiet and strong.
But two days later comes the dreaded call,
My G.P. preaching on the "good" and "bad"
Cholesterol—a morality play
Of chemicals with Blood Sludge as the Vice.
So now I run on the treadmill, do dead lifts,
And live on tofu, lettuce, and O'Doul's
Slimming until suspenders must be bought
To hold pants up around new buns of steel
And washboard abs young girls stare at again.
But, Lord, I'm sixty. What's this good health for?
To wander through a nursing home at ninety,
Then curl up like a fetus on the floor?

2

Welcome

And what's the rush? I've got a year of pills
Renewed and I can plead heredity—
My father who ran marathons at fifty
With numbers past two-forty like my own
(My draft number not even half that high!)
Or his own mother who approached the same
Yet died of sheer old age at ninety-five.
And what are my doctor's readings, pray tell,
My dietician's in the checkout line
Stocking up on vodka, cheddar, Boston butt?
So taking one last look at the weird thrill
Of a three-score-year-old body teenage lean
With half a head of hair, a mind half daft,
And wrinkles where old bullied muscles bulge,
I bid farewell to numbers I can't rhyme,
Then go eat in New Orleans at K Paul's—
Welcoming buttered bread, shrimp gumbo, Chardonnay,
Watching abs of iron relax toward abs of flab,
Just grateful I've had sixty years, and sod
This liver and the metabolic gods.

Walking Through Thibodaux

When we came here some forty years ago
I'd jog the bayou road in rain and sun—
Often to jeers, and dodging glass below
When drivers hurled pop bottles just for fun.

But then young doctors set up in the town
And got potbellied patients on a track
Or walking trail to bring their weight back down
And ward off early stroke or heart attack.

So now we greet each other when we meet
At dusk or dawn our headbands dropping sweat
On soaked-through tee shirts, then to quickened feet
That speed us toward our goal of health, and yet . . .

What is the final end toward which we move,
Both sick and well, whether we will or no?
A fate whose nature none of us can prove
But into whose vast trackless realm we go?

May be. Yet still we walk along and gaze
Amazed by dazzling pageants of the skies,
This ordered chaos, star trails set ablaze
Toward which the aster blossoms while it dies.

And so, perhaps, we sojourn after all—
Though worlds like glass may shatter, doubters jeer—
Toward Love, the Great Physician, who will call
Our hearts to health beyond each sweated tear.

Town and Country

Aesop transposed to north and south Louisiana

A city mouse to country come
Picked at his cousin's store:
"How you can dine on rind and crumb,
Root, seed—and little more?

"Here in the north the fare is plain,
Its leavings make no treat,
Taken with rain from leak or drain,
Nothing like what I eat.

"Now visit me, and stay a while,
Down south in New Orleans,
The Quarter, where I live in style
And feast on high cuisines."

The country mouse replied in kind,
"I'm sorry your fine palate
No pleasure finds in bits of rind,
Hock, cracklin, or poke sallet.

"I've been content to have my share
From garden, garbage, table,
Mulch pile, bin, barn—whatever's there.
I live as I am able.

"Yet to return the courtesy
Of your brief visit here,
I'll come, somewhat reluctantly,
To share in your good cheer."

So both mice in a farm truck rolled
From field to river side,
And in a docked boat's cargo hold

They found a place to hide.

"These boxes packed with scuppernong
And peach will have to do
To nibble as we float along
Eluding rat and crew."

So said the town mouse who had tasted
Crawfish etouffee,
Shrimp sauce piquant, Turducken basted,
Bowls of crème brûlée.

"Well, I'm content with well enough,
The wheat seed or the tare,"
His cousin countered–grumpy, gruff,
"I just wish we were there."

And when they were the town mouse led
The way from boat to dock,
Then to his Quarter townhouse sped
Past gate and bar and lock.

And on a table still uncleared
Of silverware and plate
The remnants of a meal appeared.
The mice were not too late.

They tried, with appetites robust,
Broiled oysters on a tray,
Roast lamb with Creole mustard crust,
Then sipped absinthe frappé.

A sound. The cousins, as one mouse,
Pricked ears, and that was that,
Set on by guardians of the house,
Two mastiffs and a cat.

The city mouse took to his hole,
Cramped in a damp moss bed,
While north to a nest of straw and boll
His country cousin fled.

"I'd rather take my chances here,"
The city mouse declared,
"With dog and cat–and trout Meunière–
From rotten parings spared!"

But in the north his cousin fed
On pig ear, tongue, and jowl,

Happy with scraps and moldy bread,
Eye out for hawk and owl.

*

So, north and south, we live and die,
Enjoying, while we can,
Chicken and dumplings, mayhaw pie—
Andouille and boudin—

Though deep in pine flat, cypress slough,
We hear a raptor's call,
Who cooks for me? Who cooks for you?
Who cooks for you a-l-l?

4:00 A.M.

in memory of Philip Larkin (1922-1985)

That was the time you'd claim
And make your own
When dreaming fails and leaves
Us each alone,

No star-crossed lover lost
In sex and sweat
Or Hector braced for dawn
With archers set

Or Lear upon the heath
Raging but this:
An old man in the dark
Groping toward a piss.

The last line echoes Larkin's poem "Sad Steps," line 1.

October Oaks Revisited

of the water oaks at 607 Lafourche Drive, Thibodaux, Louisiana
first written about in my poem "October Oaks" (*The Burning Fields*, 1991)

Now twenty years have gone.
The oaks have gone as well,
Their sawdust on the lawn

Where trunk by trunk they fell

Long after my first verse
That praised them in their prime
Though even then the curse
Of stardust claimed the rhyme

For in that mating ground
Where crickets cried unseen
And shadows without sound
Moved through St. Augustine

The oaks would age and fail,
Pressed hard by flailing wind
In storms that left them frail,
Then given to their end.

The Book of Life

In stock a while, condition–fine,
No typo, blot, creased page, or line
Unjustified,
Its margins wide,
A classic, clean design:

This book of poems–set apart,
The printer's craft, the maker's art–
Was put one day
On layaway,
A dollar down to start.

At last the book became the boy's
Whose Lincoln Logs and Tinker Toys–
Then battle games,
Play's other claims–
Had given up their joys . . .

And at the end of Seven Ages–
Turning years and turning pages–
Working toward dust
As all boys must
He drew Old Adam's wages.

And what of poems so well borne
On pages spotted, browned, and torn–
Wisdom in time
In rhythm, rhyme–

By fingers smudged and worn?

Its crisp dust jacket long since lost,
Its spine's gilt title—foiled, embossed—
Flaking and stained,
Boards warped, joint-strained,
The book was sold at cost.

Yet verse sewn tight in signature
Unthreading now, will still endure—
Columned in print,
A spine unbent—
Taut lines its ligature.

Churches

north Louisiana, the late 1980s

Where nothing can be other than it was
John Finlay, "The Wide Porch," 1984

a thing cannot be other than it is
Aristotle, *Posterior Analytics*

1

In that first place from which the memory
Calls up in words the image of a thing
As what it was, is, ought, and has to be
I see affixed atop a concrete block
By marble graves and gravel parking lot
An old bell without belfry, yoke, or rope,
No longer rung though ghostly echoes toll
Forever for a church that isn't there.

The new church building has its own new bells,
Recorded sounds computer-timed to chime,
Thick red brick walls, low roof, bare windows squared,
Shut tight to trap the regulated air
Of central heat and cooling, no more need
For funeral home fans with winter scenes—
December's Driskill Hill in cresting snow—
Or iron potbellied stoves the deacons stoked
With logs of woodpile oak and hickory.

The worshippers there now seem satisfied,

Their Bibles in the language of the day,
Most sewn in cloth, as always, but a few
With cover angels smiling wing to wing
Or flowers loud in paperback pastels,
The simple hymns, Jehovah's jingling themes,
A happy hopping dot that shows the way
Through verses scrolled on giant projector screens,
The altar call's "Just As I Am," the same,
If lilting toward I Am from Need To Be,
The pews quite different, though, the contoured backs,
The cushioned seats, the smooth white solid pine.

It wasn't always so, for when that bell
Now on the ground rang swinging clean and clear
The pews were straight-backed, slatted, dark-stained, hard,
Their holders fit for glad and solemn psalms
In hymnals filled with Heaven, Hell, and Sin,
No Purgatory but a guilt unpurged
Till soul was born again alone and here
Where star-falls scar the dark with blemished light,
Even their grave elation circumscribed,
Inquisitors suspecting everything—
That self-denial was a kind of pride—
And in rough country hands, soft-leather bound,
Inerrant in its wanderings through tongues,
Pages opaque and silky, strong and thin,
A stately Jacobean Sacred Writ,
Black Bibles that a king had authorized,
Red words a greater king had bled to say.

And there, subsistence farmers, hunger-lean,
Raised up the first church house in those stark years
Between Petersburg's trenches and the Marne's—
The longleaf pine cut down for walls and floor,
Then planed and notched, doors locked with heavy keys,
The rooftree-rafters' sharp-pitched angled arch,
Tall windowpanes, blank gold, green, purple, blue,
A belfry's winding steps and maiden bell.

Inside, before the choir, the pulpit stood,
The holy focal point, and, at its foot,
No altar for high rites of flesh and blood,
Only a modest Table of the Lord,
A place for trays of tiny grape juice cups
And tidbit crackers scattered patternless,
No wine or bread made more with mystery,
And on the table's apron, in relief,
A plain command, the almost fasting feast
They kept: "This do in remembrance of me."

2

And there they felt a steady beckoning
Through seasons of creation and their lives
Drawing them ever onward, pew by pew,
Through north Louisiana when they heard
The tollings and the tellings of the bell.

The back pew first where now and then a child
Would cry to reach beyond the baptistery,
Its waters of the Jordan warm and calm,
The farther shore a mural, Adam's land,
Lambs grazing safe in spring's soft meadow grass,
And all along the cemetery fence
Unbruised magnolia blossoms opening slow
In April when the eastern phoebe leaves.

The older children, restless, further up
Doodling in the Bible coloring books,
Playing footsy under pews as prayers went on,
Girls teasing boys, the giggle-whispering,
Long sermons like eternity to them,
Light-bladed glades outside, their native place,
Looking past John the Baptist to a creek
In which they laughed and splashed through mayhaw days,
The summer herons green along the streams,
Striking quick minnows, stalking almost still.

Then teens and young adults seeing themselves
Slinging the stone that split Goliath's brow
Or dancing like a naked shepherd king
Or in The Song of Songs, their kisses spiced
With camphor, saffron, myrrh, and spikenard,
And in the Dove that seemed a turtledove
Cooing to woo and aching for its mate
Where Jesus rises drenched in sinlessness,
Rose pink so near, unfolding in its rose,
Jays making raucous flocks with mockingbirds,
Male sparrows courting females, feathers preened,
Driving off hawks from eggs in nesting time.

Next, in the middle pews, the middle-aged
Between dependent children, parents, pressed,
Too late to turn back now, so far to go,
Their first and second childhoods distant dreams,
The sun moving up to and through its noon,
Its firestorms flaring west of Galilee,
Kisatchie's asters tossed in autumn wind,
The scarlet ibis climbing toward the Gulf.

And last, in pews near table, pulpit, choir
The old who faintly hear the cries behind
Yet gaze in silent calm beyond the plains
Of Canaan to the Great Sea and their graves,
Torn spider webs hung frosted stone to stone,
Snow egrets over fields of virgin snow,
White berries on the poison mistletoe.

3

And by such pews and bells we come to know
Each season of the body and the soul,
The ways of winter moons and summer suns,
The progress of the far-cast gathered stars
Both wandering and constant by design,
Appearing thus for us, seen as we see,
Our granted vantage point this human pew,
Dear-bought and stained with more than human blood,
The universe a temple, stellar-belled,
Its music fire, its fire a light that sings:
And we who praise are ringers of the things
Just as they were, are, ought, and have to be,
Calling the congregations near and far
To common rites of life, death, peace, and war,
The parts of bells a part of what we are—
The crown, head, shoulder, waist, mouth, lip, and tongue—
Sounding out all our days and nights profound
As does a bell well grounded, stilled for years
Yet tolling in remembrance where we dwell
Forever in a church that's always here.

Calling Down the Birds

in memory of Louisiana naturalist Caroline Dormon (1888-1971)

You saw them just the way they really were,
Those flowers in your gardens and the wild,
Studied, preserved, in earth and paint and words,
The naturalist and artist of one mind.

The red woodbine and orange-yellow phlox,
Greenbrier, blue larkspur, nodding indigo,
The violet oxalis—rainbow names—
A covenant in pastoral catalogue.

You knew the birds as well, the goldfinch, wren,

The swallow, warbler, sparrow and the food
They loved to eat, calling them from the trees
To peck up at your feet the sprinkled seed.

And you would stay at Briarwood—birthplace, home—
Secluded in a wold's uplifted hills,
Your cabin, grounds, a modest green estate
By wisdom and solicitude maintained.

And there some April dawns a pineland quiet
Would draw you on toward spots in partial shade
Good for Celestials, common once, now rare
In north Louisiana's well-drained clays.

Their sky-blue petals graceful on the stem,
They open in midmorning, shrivel at noon,
Then die before their first and only day
Darkens toward far-off clusters of the stars.

And you remembered how their meadowlands
Once flowered around Old Shreveport to its edge,
Now ringed with plants and neighborhood escapes
Lying like slabs above the dusty bulbs.

*

I came from Shreveport often as a boy
To visit kin close by you, in Saline,
And I would ask to share your solitude
By following and watching for a day.

You taught me birds you named by sight and song
And let me smell new cuttings taking root,
Species at threat that you would propagate,
Their wildness spared and thriving in your care.

And once, when I brought down those early poems
You read and complimented, being kind,
Sensing how I was trying to say my way
Back home to that same place you never left,

You had me stand apart, yet almost near,
Then called the autumn birds from bough and sky
To come to earth and eat Celestial seeds,
This time from open hands you lifted up

Toward feathers cloudy-black and iris-bright,
A kingdom needing peace, a saving grace,
A mixed flock growing larger by your love,
Still trusting that first promise you had made.

Porches

The Village of Saline, Bienville Parish, North Louisiana
at My Late Maternal Grandparents' House

The sand and gravel road, smooth asphalt now,
Passes beside the church and sunken stones
Of kin both dead and living yet awhile
In memories of one who left and stayed.

I slow down for those fields recalled and seen—
The cultivated, fallow, undisturbed—
Shift my old standard into neutral gear,
Then quietly glide toward stillness and the drive.

Others have owned this house for sixty years,
And though my home is here in every sense,
Possessing and possessed I cannot step
At will upon a transferred property.

So rolling down the window I look out
Binding in mind what's gone with what remains,
Then walk up to a gatepost where I wait
For shades to gather thin in autumn air.

And there, in seasons blending without end—
The bloom and fruit, oxalis and pecan—
On that deep porch between the hall and yard
I see myself and listen, man and child,

To voices long conversant with a world
Made up of things that have their place and ways
In calendar and catalogue and rhyme,
The holy days of ordinary time:

Spring's golden corydalis, white-topped sedge,
The yellow evening primrose, yellow worts—
St. Peter's and St. John's—in summer dusk,
Wisteria in thickets by the streams,

The sprawling moss verbena—purple, rose—
By early August done, October's frost-
And chain-leaf asters, winter possum haw,
And dandelion puffballs at winter's end.

And where these thrive and die without a sound
Pine warblers nest unseen in tallest pines,
Their high-pitched trill forever coming down
While from the last few open longleaf groves

Now passing with the passing hillside farms
Lark-sparrows sing in elegy and leave
Stump fields of their unsettled breeding-place,
Searching in other woods for native ground.

Such things I take to heart and keep in mind,
Beholding and beholden, in their gift,
Each one a porch—a station and a way,
The inward and the outward reconciled,

The fathomed patterns matching, world and word,
Like mockingbirds whose mimicking in spring
Sweetens into a single autumn song,
By Choctaws called "the bird of many tongues."

And so I leave the gatepost and the drive
In treetop light from afternoon's low sun
That blinds me in the rear-view mirror's glass,
The future now reflected in the past

Along this sand hill road where crest to crest
Pines rise sky-high in colonnades of fire.

Fairgrounds

Louisiana State Fair, Shreveport, October 1961

after Philip Larkin's "Show Saturday"

Late morning and the first cars roll up,
Motioned into their parking spots by staff
Who point down a roped way toward ticket booths
Either side of the clicking turnstile bars.

The children go through first, racing ahead
Into a place where fantasies come true;
The parents listen for the rising pitch
Of barkers holding toys out from their stalls.

But it's too soon for that and carnies still
Stay busy picking up last night's debris:
Matted cotton candy, deflated balloons,
Popcorn scattered like seed, crushed Dixie cups.

And so, to start, the Ag-Show, on its own,
A harvest festival of crops and stock,
Now set apart from midway games and rides

Long since the main attractions of the fair.

The parish champions are on display,
A town of temporary tent-barns, pens,
Black Hereford and Angus—bull and cow—
State winners with blue ribbons garlanded.

Some city boys and girls in shorts and T's
Printed with Mickey Mouse or Donald Duck
Marvel at beasts both magical and real
Serenely chewing cud above the dung.

Off by themselves, under a bigger tent,
New tractors gleam, posed like showroom cars.
Pamphlets are given out by salesmen dressed
In Caterpillar yellow, John Deere green.

They nod toward a corner where an angled fence
Rails off a nineteenth century wooden plow,
Its iron blade dulled and rusted, handles, smooth,
Worn down to fit a single pair of hands.

The children, hungry, tug at their parents' arms.
They're restless, and it's getting well past noon.
Concession stands entice them with the smells
Of corndogs, burgers, onion rings, and fries.

And now they're ready for the carousel,
Holding tight to the ponies on their posts
Going up and down and round and round
And that's enough: it's time to go back home.

Soon afternoon and twilight bring the teens,
Older ones driving, younger ones dropped off
By fathers, who'll return for them at ten.
The carnival and night grow bright and loud.

And everywhere thrill after thrill draws crowds,
The Teacups spinning and the Tilt-A-Whirl,
Bumper Cars, the Wipeout, and the Whip,
The Wild Mouse with its unbanked hairpin curves,

Playing with gravity, jolting space and time,
The riders still dazed as they find their way
Down platform stairs onto the firm flat ground,
Some whooing, giddy, others, throwing up.

The line is slow outside the House of Mirrors,
(An even flow so panic doesn't start),

A maze of see-through panes, reflecting glass,
And doorless frames that seem to lead nowhere

Then suddenly confront one with a form
Known, yet unfamiliar, bending out or in,
Frightening and laughable—the mixing tears—
Torso collapsed, a bulging wide-stretched mouth.

The carousel outgrown, not wanting to leave
Just yet the revelers head for the Ferris wheel,
Couples among them snuggling in the seats
Spoke rods lift north, each stopping at the top.

And when the gentle back-and-forth is stilled
They look down at the midway, up toward stars,
The wheeling lights and music, in their spheres,
The fairs of earth and heaven almost one.

But then a slow descent to the exit ramp,
The long way round to reach the parking lot,
To make it last, the couples hand in hand.
And as they pass the Ag-Show tents and pens

They see the cows asleep on hay and sand,
At home and whole where others once had been,
The winners with blue ribbons garlanded,
A childhood memory come back again.

Let all this be forever as it is.

Biographer: A Life

in memory of Mark Royden Winchell (1948-2008),
author of biographies of Donald Davidson and Cleanth Brooks

Leaning through silence to a dead man's mind
Dick Davis

He sits amid the facts he's gathered in
From interviews, books, archives, scattered prose
Mastered at last so recollection's pen
Can resurrect the dead by what he knows.

He minds the many pitfalls of his art,
Wary of how some storytellers err
In idolizing, tearing men apart,
Iconoclast or hagiographer.

He must engage, yet shuns the quick surmise,
With passion for those cool exactitudes
He isolates from hearsay, myths, and lies,
Tactful and tentative as he intrudes.

And when the work of long hard years is done
As chapters of his life in holograph,
He'll rest with each dead man whose race he's run,
Their hours enshrined in timeless epitaph.

Lee in Darkness

Lee, "a public nuisance"

Not marble nor the gilded monuments . . .
Shakespeare, Sonnet 55

It is history that teaches us to hope.
Robert E. Lee

A century and more he stood alone
Atop his column, elevated, grave,
Arms folded, in full military dress,
Looking hard north from where "those people" came.

Now workers come, in bulletproof vests and masks,
Lifted up toward his feet by a yellow crane,
Lashing him with blue straps, straining to turn
Tight bolts that held him steady in his place.

And soon the crew would hoist, then bring him down
Where civil war had broken out again—
Our own Fire-Eaters, Abolitionists
Shouting half-truths, flags clashing at the base.

Such wars displace old statues, raise up new,
Which will themselves be toppled, shattered, ground
Into the very dust to which the dead
Like columns that exalt them must return.

Lee was no "marble man," no man of bronze,
And would have been dismayed to find himself
Set on so high a pillar, so revered
By some as almost saint or demigod.

And yet how few have characters less flawed:

This man whom Lincoln offered the command
Of a whole army to subdue the South
(His statue raised for that inside the Dome!),

This sinner who not far from a black man knelt
There at the rail while other whites held back
Until by his example shamed and led
To join him at the Table of the Lord.

The public is not ready for the truth,
So cautioned Lee when southern flags were furled,
This man who did his duty, kept his faith
That time might soften fury into love:

Old soldiers reenacting Pickett's Charge—
The Jubilee of Gettysburg that fell
The year before the Great War—graybeards all,
Rebs crossing blood-sown ground toward Yankee tears and hugs.

But, Lee, "a public nuisance," is removed
By politicians, men in vests and masks,
From civic space to city warehouse hauled,
Consigned for now to darkness not his own.

Yet on that pillar where so long he stood
There still remains the measure of the man,
A presence some can sense and none disturb
Sculpted in tempered memories and words.

The War Between the Dreams

Old slave and planter graves a flight apart
For thrushes eating seeds of grass and yew,
The unmarked plots and plots with dates and names
Too weatherworn to trace and know in stone,
Bones sinking toward a spring no well can reach,
600,000 dead for whom the War
Has long since ended and will never end,
The blue and gray at peace beneath the green,
The Deep South vultures riding updrafts north,
Smelling the human meat two states away—
Cold Harbor in the rank and columned air—
Flocking to open feasts of bowel and blood,
Blacks joining their red cousins, circling high,
Then swooping and alighting, plucking eyes
From bloated bodies hissing in their gore,
Confederate and Federal the same,
Cain slaying Abel, Abel slaying Cain,

The first fruits and the last of staff and scythe,
Of muskets and repeaters, bayonets,
The wounded paralyzed between the lines,
Crows tugging at their guts as they looked down,
The cries for "Mother!" heard and yet unheard,
Prophetic epitaphs in diaries
Of the dead: "June 3. Cold Harbor. I was killed."
Pride and compassion clashing through a truce,
The colors of both armies on the ground,
The Stars and Stripes beside the Southern Cross,
The standard-bearers leading, first picked off,
And somewhere in a clearing hidden still
From this new restless unaccustomed mind
That cannot now remember or forget,
Among a people neither lost nor found,
Each year the older birds, the winter scouts,
Come back to claim familiar nesting sites
Beside the sisters—beans and squash and corn—
The planted standards neither flown nor furled
But steadfast in the time of egg and seed,
Gourd poles, for the purple martins, hung with gourds.

The Turning of the Cannon

They gleam there wheel to wheel on that last ridge,
Keeping us from the valleys of our birth
From which we have been driven, field by field,
Leaving dead kin to hold our native earth.
And yet like shades dissolving dark in dawn
Those people seem as abstract as their maps
That simplify our tale to their idea—
This barn we built, that chapel where we wed,
Each family plot railed off by spike and yew—
Just dots or patches hatched, not real and true.

Now fault lines cross and part on common ground—
Matter made absolute in chattel slaves
Chained to the land or urban sleights of hand
That pay in scrip of rhetoric and debt—
But in the heat of battle such cold facts
Are lost in fumes, confusion, civil war
Though not on us, hunkered in great live oaks
Whose limbs in wind conduct night's silent fires,
Old monotones of star-scored earth and sky,
Grand anthems of the essence and the bone.

And though these stately measures fade away
When shot tears hot through smoke that will not clear,

And we are cast as cast-out demons in
Simplistic allegories of our foe,
We'll charge once more their shifting lines and guns
With bayonet and clan-yell fixed, then raised,
Our muzzleloaders taking down whole crews
That man those massed Napoleons we'll turn
To drive them one fine April from the ridge
That slopes toward the Old Republic's Washington.

The Voyage of Pytheas

in memory of Allen Tate (1899-1979)

We thought we saw some distant citadel
On those sheer cliffs of Thule where we sailed,
First mapping craggy coasts of Cornwall, Wales,
Then north into uncharted deeper seas.

Ice-crusted bluffs broke up from breaking spray,
Their bottom rocks thrust downward toward the core,
And on bleak heights white birds we could not name
Left eggs in crevices where blizzards roar.

And we, who, from the south, knew how its noon
Soaked orchards ripe with olives, grapes, and figs,
Now stared on barest stone that blocked the stars
Whose light dripped salt from glazing oars and rigs.

And when slow polar swells raised up our ship
Between night's sunward sea and seaward sun
We glimpsed the final limit of the world
As fire fell curled and frozen from those walls

Where we had flung it. Then, terrified, we turned
Our prow around, bore toward the middle sea,
By Thule's winds brought home to Thule here–
Late hoarfrost on the tender lemon trees!

In the Beggar's Palace

after passages in Books XXI and XXII of *The Odyssey*

Like a singer long familiar with his lyre
Who loops the twisted sheep gut, bound at tail and bar,
Turning a new peg until it tunes the cord,

He strung the great bow, bending its limbs with ease,
The test-pluck sounding high like flights of swallow song,
The shaft zinging clean through twelve ax-handle eyes.

A beggar no more, aiming true with measured rage,
He targeted at will each uninvited guest
Who swilled his wine, gulped food, bedded his ready maids
All night, while his pressed queen drew the slowly woven strands,
Saved by a web's deceit, but then betrayed, undone
Till bronze-tipped arrows threading the air sped home.

Soon those who had given themselves to would-be kings
Unwillingly scrubbed blood from upset tables, chairs
And dragged slain lovers off, their corpses trailing gore,
Then after were hemmed in hard by yard and wall,
Like thicket-birds come to roost, trapped in a net,
Thrushes and doves flushed toward another kind of sleep.

And there, pulling plied cable, taut from post to dome,
Set high enough so a barely lifted foot
Could just brush its shadow moving on the ground,
Telemachus had them bow to a noose's loop
That tightened until they writhed (though not for long),
Snapped neck-bones, muscles convulsed . . . in stillness limp.

Then Odysseus' old nurse, who knew him by the scar,
Brought purifying sulfur, torches dipped in tar,
Blue flames from the yellow crystals melting red
In trays along the fumigated hall, the dead
Suitors finished, a body of work made so
By a crafty king who strung a poet's bow.

Testament of the Elder Son

Now his elder son was in the field . . .
Luke 15: 25

for the Southern Agrarians

The twilight spreads through barley, wheat, and rye
Bending in winds that never stay the same
While I, a posted ghost who raised them high
Still hear the swaying grasses say my name.

I bear the ancient burden of the earth
As steward of the corn and egg and seed
And understand what bulging barns are worth
When famine sows the land with fearful need.

And here I stood some forty years ago
Still winnowing the tares from bearded wheat
At nightfall when there rose up from below
Wild music for the prance of dancing feet.

Then leaving these high terraces I found
My father's house aroused by wine and song,
My grain-fed calf spit-roasted, turning round,
My younger brother robed among the throng.

I shunned that unjust feast but sent in word
Which drew my father out while I complained,
Though he, in his warm mercy, barely heard,
So flush with lush forgiveness unrestrained.

He said again that all he had was mine—
As if it could be otherwise by law—
Although a third was gone among the swine
Whose latest feeder's new gold ring I saw.

Strong drink, the dice, the whores, the foreign gods,
Then famine in the land—he told his tale
That ended in a wallow's carob-pods
And in a revelry more fit for Baal.

Years passed, my father died, and I became
Sole owner of estates where I was born
Whose harvests long had granted me the same
Great stores of wine and cattle-flesh and corn.

A man of substance taking stock I paid
My wealthy sonless neighbor's bridal-fee
To have as mother of my sons a maid
Erotic in her comely modesty.

Together we grew middle-aged, then old,
With sons enough to work a fertile land
Now doubled as my prudence had foretold
And daughters married well as I had planned.

And what of him for whom the calf was slain,
A rioter welcomed home with riotous dance?
He soon sought that far country once again,
His contrite heart no more than circumstance.

And when at last word came that he had died
Of drunkenness, disease, and poverty
I placed him with his father, side by side
In shallow graves beneath a carob tree.

The Hay Wain

after the painting by John Constable (1776-1837)

1821

oil on canvas

Midsummer noon: a tributary stream
Glides slowly by warm meadows toward the Stour,
And there, fording the shallows set agleam

By cloud-light rippling in the shaded hour
A hay wain stops to cool its wheels' iron bands
Before a place the bankside trees embower.

The wain will round this spong toward pasturelands
Where distant figures, bending, rake the hay
Later to stack and bale with practiced hands

While deep in reeds, his pole and line in play,
An angler stands as mated ducks glide near,
All waiting for the fish that swim their way.

Almost unchanged, Lott's Cottage is still here
Just as it was three hundred years ago,
And from its porch, extending like a pier,

A woman stoops where currents coldly flow,
Filling her jug as chimney smoke drifts white
Far from a pot hearth-logs smolder below.

The watered team will move on, bearing right,
But now the driver rests against the wain's
Slats added to low boards for space and height;

Meanwhile, a younger helper, rising, strains
His voice and arm to hail a dog that turns
Toward him alone under the coming rains.

Above, a brown cloud none as yet discerns
Moves down over the windrows winds explore,
Leaving wet stalks to dry when noonday burns.

Unseen—because the painter stood before—
His father's mill, grinding the wheat to flour,
The family business John chose to ignore

Though want forced him to render, tense and dour,
Those country-gentry portraits he could sell

When few would buy his landscapes of the Stour,

A realm at peace in which his mind might dwell,
No church or castle anywhere in sight,
Only a pastoral world he loved so well

That here at last he got it wholly right,
No restless, fretted strokes but things serene,
Unmannered in the equalizing light.

Bringing Home Cows After Eden

north Louisiana

Through cover crops of winter oats and rye
Along a trail first cut by buffalo
A farmer leads his milk cows from the fields
After a day let loose in stubble hay.

The cattle egrets stay to dig up grubs
Under a shallow frost-line cows disturb
Grazing by sun and moon and by the light
From stars that died a billion years ago.

The starlight brightens deep in eventide
As creatures move along the ancient way
Until the man discerns familiar shapes
Of gate, trough, well, coop, wallow, pen, and barn.

The cows bed down and sleep in bovine peace,
Not yet gone dry and tagged for the slaughter-chute
While on a hayloft rafter talons clutch
A barn owl waits for rustling in the hay.

Shepherdess with Her Flock and Dog

after the painting by Jean-François Millet (1814-1875)

1863-1865

black conté crayon and pastel with pen and black ink on beige laid paper

"Make more idylls," his Paris dealer said,
Poor Alfred Sensier, caught in between
The artist and a public he had shocked:

That grim *Man with a Hoe* the year before . . .

And thus you read the classics once again,
Your Île de France absorbing as its own
Theocritus' green Sicily and Cos
And Virgil's island-hearted Arcady:

These sheep at peace, still huddled as they graze,
A dog alert yet easy in its stance,
A shepherdess, so comely and serene,
Head bent to tell her threadings as she works

Her needles though her staff is now at rest
As if she dreamed of Saturn's Golden Age,
Nor is she far from Eve who calmly led
The first sheep out of Eden when she fell—

This human muse—both simple and profound,
Where longing and belonging dwell as one
With forest, plain, and field, near Barbizon,
What Vincent saw and called your "holy ground."

To Her Who Bears These Verses

Goddess, fertile and waiting,
Maker of our creating,
Coming to me in slumber
Deeper than name and number:
I waken to our mating.

My need become your need,
You draw my words like seed
Till blooming white with aster
Against the stars' disaster
Your womb bears out my creed

That *word-thing* is the kenning
Uncoupled by a sinning
When like from like first wandered
And poets only pondered
The hyphen's quiet unpinning.

Yet when in wakeful dreaming
So seamlessly beseeming
You answer me unbidden
Revealing what is hidden
I feel a love redeeming

Each cloven metaphor
Where breakers mark the shore
Of time and space upwelling
In rhymes made more compelling,
More telling than before.

Infinitives

do it for ancient love
Gloucester to the Old Man in *King Lear*

most modern English usage guides have dropped the objections to the split infinitive
Wikipedia

in memory of H.J. Sachs (1904-1983)

You never tired of telling us again
That story, when, in 1932,
Hearing the atom had been split at last,
You slowly walked the English building halls
Dreading a bomb's apocalypse to come,
Then glimpsed as you passed an open classroom door
A colleague lecturing freshmen on the split
Infinitive, still going by the book,
An old-guard battle-ax grammarian
On separating particle and verb.

Years later, in the '60s Sturm und Drang
We read through *Lear* with you as wandering guide,
Chain smoking Kents, injecting politics,
And we, like Kent, attentive to a king,
Some of us on the front row with a light
And cigarettes to offer should you draw
The last ash to its filter and be out,
Rapt by the situation's irony,
A split infinitive, the atom split,
That colleague whose priorities you mocked.

For, after Hiroshima, you would ask,
Why care about a verb kept from its sign
Or study Keats' "To Autumn" while the fields
Hide silos ripe with warhead mega-bombs,
Each one a key click from a blast beyond
Fat Man's and Little Boy's a thousand times,
A fatal knowledge we cannot unknow,
Forever undisarmed, these latter days

Always October 1962,
Kennedy grim on black and white TV.

And you would pace like Lear upon the heath
In storms of atoms and the atmosphere—
Particles, stars, all forced from centering rings—
Then hold up hanged Cordelia to arraign
High "Justicers" enthroned above their laws,
Impassive while the showerheads spread gas
Not far from ovens fed with human flesh
Till evening when the camp guards cleaned their pipes
Under a lamp's soft glow, neat whiskey near,
And Mozart on the crackling radio.

Yet history still may be a tale well told,
A wedding, not a funeral, at its end,
The timeless twining in and out of time
Sewing the book of hours of things and tongues
Where *was* and *is* and *will be* make one tense
Beyond all tenses, every part of speech
Incisive and precise, if bravely placed,
The ethicist and rhetor standing firm
In testament before a firing squad
They bless with prayers and crossings by the wall.

But then, on 9/11, when the planes
Flew into towers that fell into themselves,
Firebirds consumed with shearing wings aflame
And only ashes rising from their ash,
The word came down to let our classes go
If the stunned students felt they could not bear
To try to learn with terror in their heads—
Jumpers to streets a hundred floors below—
And yet I walked the halls past empty rooms
To hold my class in writing poetry.

And as I went along I thought of you
Who many years before had overheard
That exacting grammarian and judged
A solecism something trivial . . .
So when I reached the desktop podium,
Opening the worn handbook to a page
Turned down at our last meeting, I looked up,
Then told those who had come that they could leave
For family, priest, friend, counselor, smoke or drink
Though I would teach if even one remained.

I quoted Auden on the death of Yeats,
The poet's role to pity, heal, and praise,

Mastering the craft and going by the book,
And though they all were shaken, lost for words,
No one rose to go as I stressed again
That rules of verse can set a poet free—
Caesura, line break, meter, rhyme, and stave—
Significance bound up in space and time
Like particled infinitives unsplit
In atom, grammar, host, the maker's art.

And while I spoke I felt you standing there,
Your love for "unaccommodated man"
An "ancient love" like blinded Gloucester saw,
Still fixed in syntax and its hierarchies,
Those old subordinations, phrase and clause,
Philology, the chain of being, wed,
Though we would ask, "Is this the promised end?"
"Or image of that horror?" "Fall and cease!"
If words should fail and language come to harm
When dying kings hold daughters in their arms.

Ordinations

priest, poet

Receive this Bible as a sign . . .
The Book of Common Prayer (1979), 534

Younger than I by nearly forty years,
He stands for examination, then kneels,
The bishop laying hands upon the head
Of one who prays for strength to rise again,
Holding on tight to a Bible, the gift
A bishop gives to all whom God has called
To preach the Word and offer bread and wine.

Here in the pews, near three score years and ten,
I see myself—and not—in that young man,
For I was also called, ordained, my gift
Not given by a bishop but a voice
That left me with the silence of the page
And language from a common lexicon,
The Holy Spirit blessing *grape* and *grain*.

An Exmoor Tale

Toward dawn he made his way by bay and cliff
Into the Brendon Hills, journeying west
On through the Quantocks to collect a debt
From one who had ignored his many bills.

In town he had a shop with staple goods
And out of town a farm whose meats and greens
He sold with flour sifted from his grains
All native to a world he loved and knew.

And so he rode across the summer moors
With heather, ling, and whortleberry decked,
Glimpsing the elusive roe deer and the red
At daybreak in the distant hillside mist.

He knew the birds as well, by habit, name,
The scrub's grasshopper warbler, bred in heath,
Redpolls that nest on moorland edges deep
In sessile oaks, and, by the channel bays,
Snow buntings, ospreys, egrets, harriers
All fishing while long swells salted the caves.

And pushing on till dusk mile after mile
For hours intent on justice, recompense,
Fair dealing, and the holding to one's word
He reached at last an isolated farm,
Ill-tended, where his debtor could be heard
Behind that door on which the traveler knocked.

Slowly the door was opened and he gazed
Upon a face angelic yet distressed,
With eyes like wells of light but in a haze,
Skin pale against the dark brown feathery hair.

The man who came would enter a strange room
The other kept in twilight–candles, faint,
Illumining a pen, chair, table, page,
An empty glass still smelling of strong drink
And something else, some flavoring spice, or drug.

The two men spoke alone an hour or more,
Yet still the bills remained, though credit stopped,
And he who traveled far to balance books
Gave up on one he could not understand . . .

Then tiring far from town as night wore on
He headed for his farmstead closer by,

And there, as he had left them—hives and pens,
The bees and cows, and, in the heeded fields,
Green wheat just turning golden toward the fall.

The next day he wrote off the unpaid sum
And lived on toiling as he always had
In intimate blood kinship with the land.

Years later, someone showed him that small book
In which the debtor blamed him for a poem
Whose birth he'd interrupted with his knock.

And there he read of things he could not know
Except by correlation to a world
He nurtured as its substance nurtured him:
A holy river like the river Exe
Rising at Exe Head, flowing south through shale,
Unmeasured caverns Bristol bays' deep caves
Below Great Hangman Cliff, an eastern mount
Dunkery Beacon, mystic honey-milk
Those hives and cows he tended long before
He'd be The Man from Porlock evermore.

Peasant Leaning on a Pitchfork

after the drawing by Jean-François Millet (1814-1875)

ca. 1848-1850 (Paris and Barbizon)

black conté crayon on paper

private collection, Europe

Midmorning, and the autumn harvest done,
Stubble burned, a young man rests a moment,
Leaning against his pitchfork as he dreams,
His head turned well away from waiting fields.

A slight smile, half-closed eyes tell of longing
For Paris and his story's happy end—
An artist painting pleasing country scenes—
O surely there in all those years to come!

But dumped beside him now, a pile of dung
The cowherds bring, his work to work it in
Until the soil stinks, ready for new seed,
This ground where men by human need are bound.

Not far, two older peasants, long resigned,
Toil on, their heads bent down toward spread manure,
Thinking of noon's brief sleep while line by line
Trees reach to brush the light in light brown sky.

The young man would not dream of being them
And cannot know as yet that there will be
No turning from this turning of the dung,
Bucolic in his urban fantasies.

Noonday Rest

after the pastel drawing by Jean-François Millet (1814-1875)

1866

pastel and black conté crayon on buff wove paper

High August noon and skies are cloudy-bright
Over young lovers sleeping in the shade
Of a huge rick their daylong labor made
Between the twilight hours of moon and sun.

The woman's cheek rests on her folded arms,
Smooth skin the wrinkling heat leaves cracked and dry.
The man's brow sweat is cooled by a tilted hat.
Their faces turn like wheat a tawny bronze.

Far off, cattle browse at a cart's tall wheels
Worn by the many rounds from plain to barn.
Nearby—one blade upon the other laid—
Two sickles, from the Iron Age come down.

The reapers gather grain-heads in a fist,
Then cut back toward themselves, the curving edge
Of tool and weapon wielded in the fields,
This battle of the harvest marked by Cain.

Their provenance—Millet's own history,
Early and late, the shady grove and glade,
The nymph and hero naked in the bays,
Embedded here almost too deep to see.

Peasant Woman Watering Her Cow

after the picture by Jean-François Millet (1814-1875)

ca. 1863

oil paint and black conté crayon on pink prepared canvas

dessin peint

Fall skies glow pink and golden on a ground
Prepared and worked—the canvas and the land—
Black bones of crayon drafts left showing through
These watercolor washes drawn in oils.

Late afternoon still lingers as it fades,
The sun's north rim descending to eclipse,
And all that moves or stays on Chailly Plain
Is blended in one dimming silhouette.

Along horizon lines of mind and earth,
Crossing a rise just on perception's edge,
A shepherd leads his straggling hollow flock
From scanty pastures home to feed on sleep.

And where the shades stain scrub a deeper green
Dead stunted trunks angle toward light and rain.
A woman walks on stones beside a pond,
Watching her cow drink water from the stars.

Lapped ripples crest and spread near skin-tight ribs,
Gaunt haunches, udders giving little milk.
A head's reflection noses toward the air.
From a full barn's loft-window no bale falls.

The moon protracts a single lighted claw.

The Stubble Burner

after the painting by Jean-François Millet (1814-1875)

ca. 1860

oil on canvas

Tired reapers gone to thresh and winnow seed,
A stubble burner comes, her task to light

Stalk-stumps cut down, then raked up into piles,
The fall's last harvest, given to the fire.

Some heaps are smoldering, smoke rising white
Toward buff-white clouds wheat golden in the sun.
The burner watches hard, her pitchfork tines
Ready to toss more straw on ash and spark.

She stokes black centers growing wide and low,
Bringing to flames the air they eat and breathe,
This Chailly peasant—but her profile Greek—
Her straight lips set beyond a frown or smile.

Her world is as she finds it, undisturbed
By dream or longing, fretting or regret,
And yet she seems Athene, looking on
As plumes spread west from Troy to Barbizon.

The turning year, her years, stay what they are
As season blends with season, flesh and earth,
The Sower and the Reaper soon to come,
The night a stubble field of scattered stars.

The Threshing Floor

in honor and in memory of Jean-François Millet (1814-1875)

Late autumn and the reaping, binding done,
Spent carters bring more sheaves to a threshing floor
Where flailers wait, long hours of work before,
As days grow short under the year's low sun.

The floor is stone—smoothed on the bedrock's head.
The flail is helve and swipple, clasp, and ring.
Each beater walks on stalks, his downward swing
Cracking the chaff whose grain is ground for bread.

Some seed, the best, is sown among the crows,
Cast out upon the fatal earth again
Where it will sink—till raised by warming rain—
Under the stubble-ash and winter snows.

*

And so the year for years went on and on
From season unto season toward the day
Machines were made to shake the seed away
From chaff no longer split by flail and stone.

Now thrashing cracks the atom to its core,
The mind a weapon flailing its own self,
While deep below the continental shelf
The Thresher stays unraised forevermore.

Yet here and there a weathered floor remains
Tilted, exposed to take the rain and wind,
Where, dead and ready, given to their end,
Winnowers toss aloft the ancient grains.

First Steps

after preliminary sketches, the finished drawing, and the "pasteled" drawing
by Jean-François Millet (1814-1875)

1858-1866

with quotations translated from letters written by Millet to his art dealer in Paris

Washed linens draped along a picket fence
Running beside the garden, house, and yard
Dry white against the greens of shrub and tree
Whose shades are conté gray on thread and board.

The garden has its own fence—like a toy—
A line of tiny sticks that barely stand,
A marker, not a barrier, a sign
For any who step over or around.

The autumn plants have wintered into spring—
Sprouts rising toward a light on melting snow—
Maturing, then dug up, a poor man's food,
Potatoes, carrots, turnips, cabbage, beets.

Nearby, a mother, bending from behind,
Steadies a little daughter set to walk,
While almost too far off for her to reach
The father kneels, his rough soiled hands stretched out.

And there, upon the edge of letting go,
The toddler takes a first step on her own,
Uncertain . . . fall after fall to come,
Making her way toward strong uplifting arms.

*

How long Millet would take to get this right,
Sketch after sketch to shape and place, and then,
The finished drawing, monochrome, composed
In "calm" he sought "to stop the rush of time."

And so the scene would "concentrate itself"
On "real essentials"—"catch the intimate"—
In these our common lives . . . a trusting child
Who like us all must learn to walk alone.

But in the 1850s few would buy
Such drawings—peasant life too stark and hard
To hang on paneled walls, near port, cigars,
In Paris, Boston, London, or New York.

And so, to stave off poverty and please
His dealer, Sensier, Millet "enhanced"
A picture he thought done in neutral tones,
Coloring in the lines with soft pastels.

Yet "First Steps" as he sold it, heightened, bright,
Depends on the perspective coming down
Draft after draft—black chalk across white sheets—
The father, mother, daughter, unenhanced,

Drawn closer to each other and their ground.

Reading Lesson

after the drawing by Jean-François Millet (1814-1875)

ca. 1860

black conté crayon on wove paper

*

St. Anne Teaching the Virgin to Read (1839, oil on canvas, current location unknown)

Cold light brightens the panes it passes through
Into a room where mother, daughter, sit,
The teacher in a chair, child on a bench,
Dawn sun illuminating face and page.

Around the figures warmly dressed in wool
Are crayon shades—sleep, waking, work, and play:
A made bed, sheet turned back, a pillow fluffed,

A feather duster hooked high on a wall,

A shelf with jars and bowls yet higher still,
A basket near the mother, raveled clothes,
And on the window ledge a propped-up doll
Blanketed, kissed, and left at lesson time.

The mother tilts a primer in her lap,
Inclining toward her child who leans to see
Each letter by a pointer singled out,
The ABCs of words and verses learned.

Millet, too, learned, in 1839,
His first submission—turned down by the Salon,
A painting in a drawing lost and found,
Bound pages in an artist's Book of Hours,

Color intoned, well grounded, hymning limned,
A story weaving in and out of time,
Psalters of Nazareth and Normandy,
St. Anne teaching the Virgin how to read.

Of Root and Bloom

for my daughter, Anna

The second word you ever said was flower
That autumn when the purple pansies blew,
Time waking every season in its hour
Till reason's seed found fertile ground in you.

For eighteen years you germinated here,
Louisiana-rooted, marsh and hill—
From buckled bluffs the Red carves stark and sheer
To swamps where the Mississippi has its will—

And as you grew you came to see and know
Moist meadow beauties, goat's-rue, greenbrier strung
By pinewood bogs, cold holly-oaks in snow,
And lyre-leaf sage whose song is never sung.

But now Sewanee's mountain is your home
Where other flowers surround you and you bloom
By rock and trail and hollow when you roam
On foot or bike or look out from your room:

The meadow rue and rue anemone,
A Carolina allspice picked for Joe,
The fall's grass-of-Parnassus left to me,
Forget-me-nots I'll scatter as you go

Down from the mountain to a world you bring
Seeds blossoming from each rich fall and spring.

The Scholar

His mindful eyes take in the poem he reads
Again and yet again until it lives
Inside of him suspended while he gives
As gloss whatever help a student needs.

He knows in depth the author and his time,
The history of the text and of its form,
Alert to variations from the norm
In stanza, line, caesura, foot, and rhyme.

He works with grace, intent and yet serene,
Not twisting sense to serve a will to power
That pays off in the academic bower
But saying what the words most likely mean.

And so he writes brief notes with modest pride,
All pointing toward the poem they lie beside.

Headmaster, Mother, Son

A mother and the tired headmaster sat
Relaxing in his office while her son
Was being interviewed, but then their chat
Grew tense once her hard questions had begun.

The mother said, "Headmaster, let's be clear.
This prep school is elite and rigorous,
Expensive, too, so if our son comes here
What's in it in the end for him and us?

Will he succeed in business, politics,
Make good connections, have his name put down
Before some flashy whiz kid's from the sticks
For Princeton, Harvard, Yale, Cornell, or Brown?"

"Yes, Madam, if your boy is bright enough
To be admitted, works hard, he'll do well
Because our old curriculum is tough,
But that is not an end on which we dwell."

"Then what," quipped she, "is your primary goal?"
(Miffed and bewildered, letting out her breath);
And he, "To tend to body, mind, and soul
And to prepare him, in a word, for death."

Headmaster Leaving

The snowflakes on the oaks have stayed the same
Through all the changing winters of the years
As every boy's bright face has since I came
To make pressed lips articulate with tears.

The scrums, the prep-times, first loves, chapel prayers,
The Founders' Days, the war dead etched on brass,
Strict prefects calling *lights out* from the stairs—
These were the holy texts in memory's mass.

And though I bore the headship and its stress—
Hirings, firings, urging Old Boys to give
And give again, yet doing more with less,
My life a death through which a school might live—

This classroom was my own, oak-paneled, small,
Unfitted with those terminals and screens
New colleagues have to have all down the hall,
Their chalkboards not on walls but in machines.

And here each year a dwindling remnant read
That first and greatest tale of rage and lust,
Dreaming of Helen's breasts and Hector dead,
Troy's battlements collapsed in burning dust.

Yet now at last I leave this room for good
Where ghosts still whisper Greek attentively
While twilight blooms through panes in Gothic wood
And snow in oaks falls silent over me.

Two Poems on Quietude

1. Old Office, in Retirement

Five long hard years away
To be department chair
I'm back at last to stay
And breathe a calmer air,
No timelines to compel,
No problem personnel,

Reports, bad budget news,
Evaluations, pleas
For grades, tense interviews,
Administrationese
In which too much I've sung
And not the mother tongue.

And thus I'm here again
Where music, books, and tea,
Blank paper and this pen
Will be enough for me,
Familiars of a soul
By quietude made whole.

2. Familiars

They haunt these rooms and halls, their native place,
Attendants that will gather by the side
Of all come home for good to private space
Where inwardness and quietude abide.

A child's milk-bottle nipple split with age,
A confirmation Bible's tattered spine,
An old love-letter's fading yellow page,
A farewell poem that lacks its final line–

Such things dismissed as sentiment, cliché
Are guarded night and day by spirits blest,
Driving cool analytic mind away
From reminiscences the heart knows best,

Those images so luminous, discrete,
Connected till a life is made complete.

Peasant Girl Day-Dreaming

after the painting by Jean-François Millet (1814-1875)

1848

oil on panel

i

The distaff on her lap, the spindle dangling
Between her knees from a limp left arm,
The fingers all but ready to let go,
She cools bare feet on earth still undisturbed.

This is her special place to think and dream,
A settled talus boulder for her seat,
A wall of rocks moldering though it holds
The steady weight of elbow, hand, and chin.

Twin trees behind her long have taken root,
Their branches interweaving as they rise
Above green seedlings that can only grow
Stunted between the canopy and ground.

The woman is a shepherdess, her flock
Grazing somewhere nearby yet out of sight.
Her gaze is toward the one she would become.
The woolen threads she'll spin tell what she is.

Beyond the rocks, against a slate blue sky
A sun, pale as the clouds, is almost gone
Leaving behind a face still lost in light,
Not solar, but the dream-like light of dreams.

And there she stays, both other and the same,
Suspended in a soft and fluid glow,
Floating past resignation and regret
Toward husband, children, Paris, riches, fame

Then back, a warp and woof of fancy, fact,
No willowy figure with a low-cut blouse
Tight-corseted but a sturdy girl whose dress
Is loosely fitted, flowing like a robe.

ii

Her world is not Watteau's nor yet Millet's

Where gleaners gather up the fatal grain
But one in which her yearning still belongs
With distaff, spindle, sheepdog, staff, and sheep.

Her pensive sadness holds her, holds Millet,
Far from the clash of citizen and king,
The masses, troops, and bloody barricades,
That Paris he had fled for Barbizon.

And there, in fear, ill health, and poverty—
Rheumatic pain migrating joint to joint—
He came home to a place he'd never seen,
Painting a light whose source is not the sun

But cheeks that bloom as the smooth brushstrokes dry
On panel made of heartwood by a man
Who like the girl through dreams could wander free
Or flower in the ruins of Arcady.

As Far As Light Remains

All alone in twilight a cold crow is calling
Out of the leafless tree while near and far away
As far as light remains a ghostly snow is falling.

So, when dying thinkers over-vexed with galling
Enigmas of the mind cry out for one more day
All alone in twilight a cold crow is calling.

And the poets, lost in dream, wordlessly recalling
Images of Eden find that words can only say
As far as light remains a ghostly snow is falling.

Even theologians who strain to hear enthralling
Yet silent choirs of angels fear that every day
All alone in twilight a cold crow is calling.

Physicists, too, who'd think it too appalling
If Love were our First Cause are simply left to say
As far as light remains a ghostly snow is falling.

Yet where these others falter, silent lovers sprawling
In love's sweet after-sadness say best in their own way
All alone in twilight a cold crow is calling
As far as light remains a ghostly snow is falling.

On Recovering the Use of His Eyes

after the Latin verse of Samuel Johnson (1709-1784)

Universal Lord, who tempers the rife
Vicissitudes of everything in life,
Who bids the night, gloomy in icy cold,
Be changed into the limpid morning gold,
Who willed it that, by humid clouds obscured,
Puffed up by stinging blood, my eyes be cured:
Where pleasing day but heightened my dark fright
You brought me health and gave me back to light.
Lord, how can I attend in prayer and praise?
A student of the Bible all my days,
O may I ever, rightly, in my station,
Honor you with useful application:
For, Father, proper thanks to you are given
By him who uses well the gifts of heaven.

Wells

In Norse legend, Odin had to tear out and sacrifice his right eye in exchange for a drink from Mimir's well—The Well of Wisdom. The waters of this well held the knowledge not only of what things were but why things had to be. Mimir took Odin's eye and threw it into the well where it is said to shine forever.

A round wall made of native clay and lime
Put up to stop a dreamer just in time
Or warn a king thirsty for something more
Than water from the well's deep flowing floor.

Beside the wall, a statue—lichened, worn—
Its head struck off, a green man long foresworn
Or Mimir, Odin's "wise rememberer,"
Who knew not only what but why things were . . .

One polished coin was all I had to show,
Its head an Indian chief, tail, buffalo,
So with a wish I flipped it in the well
But whether heads came up I could not tell

And my wish thus be granted for the ground
Under the spring that fed the well, though sound,
Rose from a place where shadows go before
And after things that gleam then gleam no more.

Yet, heads or tails, my wish might still come true
For none know how and why some wishes do
Once made upon whatever What or Who
May be in wells we peer at now, not through.

The ravens on the crank-rope, bucket lip,
Drinking from rain and well-spring, drop and sip,
The green man's body splotched with yellow-green,
His brow above the grass, his face unseen:

Are such things surfaces that nothing delves,
Literal symbols given to themselves,
Or were they, at the core, as good as one
Till *is* first twined with *like* and came undone?

All things are wells. A Digger dug them, left,
And left us under-diggers in the cleft
Where, that long noon, still shoveling at the base,
We saw, through welling dark, the stars in place.

Then climbing step by step we heard, below,
Groundwater swelling, quickening its flow
Both from and toward a fountain at the source,
Time out of mind in time its only course.

There, coins, like wishing stars, still twinkle, fall,
But whether calling heads has helped at all
And which side faces up we no more know
Than water's mirroring windows blindly show.

Yet at a depth we once could reach and mark
A Sioux's head and a bison lie in dark
Not far from Odin's eye, the price of sight,
Reflecting in the unreflected light.

Shepherdess and Flock at Sunset

after the picture by Jean-François Millet (1814-1875)

ca. 1868-1870

pastel and black conté crayon on wove paper

He loved the twilight dimming into dusk
Through which a peasant walked his donkey on
From long days pitching wheat in summer fields,
No Joseph going home to Bethlehem . . .

But here, for once, a blinding sunset bursts
So bright the sun itself is lost in light
Whose white core sets the lower air aflame
And spreads along a thread of plain and sky.

The plain is featureless, no crumbled wall
Or tower's rubble-stone, just grass and gorse
Where sheep as brown as earth nibble the ground
And one small boulder where a shepherdess

Sits knitting with her back against the blaze,
Weaving her destined threads while sinking rays
That soon will flare at dusk to die in night
Still faintly paint a sky with Mary's blue.

Vigils

a north Louisianian looks south

January 6, Epiphany and the first day of Mardi Gras

The quiet alone is holy and enough
So long as night still darkens into dawn
And fallen starlight rises from a lawn
Whose snowflakes twinkle deep in matter's stuff.

And on this night when hope and fear grew calm
The Wise Men knelt where Child and Mother were
With gifts of gold and frankincense and myrrh
For king and god, for soul and body's balm.

And as the words of Matthew draw me in
Once more to where the heart and mind are one
Though history and myth have come undone
In these late days when faith itself is sin

I think how many winters just the same
Revels of music, food, drink, dance, and sex
Have ruled with Orpheus, Comus, Bacchus, Rex–
Those passing kings great crowds loudly acclaim.

Now stars of Hollywood outshine the Star
With glittering gifts all wise men would disdain
Though thousands wait for throws in dark and rain,
Not Gaspar, Melchior, and Balthazar.

And so Old Adam still will have his day

As celebrant at feasts some people keep
For flesh and blood that never wake from sleep,
This bread and wine of human show and play.

Yet now and then forever in the fields
Of space and time whose carnivals will end
Shepherds abide through night to watch and tend
Till Wise Men come to know and knowledge yields.

The Break-In

> How strange seeing your poems in a book . . .
> I once could feel the pathos of those nights
> About them still in hottest Baton Rouge,
> Black coffee, poverty, the sweated line!
>
> John Finlay (1941-1991), "To a Friend on His First Book,"
> *Between the Gulfs* (1986)

Some forty years ago . . . yet in my mind
From time to time I see those rooms again—
That spare unshared apartment where you lived,
Earning the Ph.D. at LSU—
A bed half-made, a nightstand with its lamp,
Ash tray, and cigarettes, and on the floor
A stack of books you read, then underscored,
Engaging every text, intently fixed,
Your very being seemingly at stake,
Choragos in tense dialogue with kings,
From Holy Writ and Plato's Socrates
To Thomas, Dante, and the troubled reigns
Of Nietzsche, Freud, Tate, Kafka, Winters, James,
All actors in the drama of a soul
You strove to save from tragic turn and fall.

Your place had little more—a single pan
To heat up coffee-water on the stove,
A black typewriter with its sticky keys,
Long yellow pads for drafts of verse and prose,
Scenes from your struggles with the Gnostic gods
Then foreign to an Alabama farm
Whose seasons of the church and earth were one.

And there you'd dwelt among the things that tell—
Spring dogwoods, Easter lilies, hyacinths,
Late summer's morning glories, white and blue,
The fall's frost-aster petals on the ground,
And Christmas holly weaving winter peace
For mantel, yard, grave, chancel, garden, door,

Or pastures you would cross to reach a slope
With sisters watching as you called and traced
Between the primum mobile and pond
The northern constellations, name by name—
The Hunter and the Dragon and the Lyre—
Job's Coffin held aloft by dark and stars.

Sometimes that realm could seem so far away
And yet be near "in hottest Baton Rouge"
Where you walked back one night to quiet rooms
From wine and conversation, new work shared
Through dinner with likeminded poet friends
To spy a door ajar, a window prized
By thieves who'd broken in but then had found
Nothing worth stealing—old clothes, older books,
A manual Underwood, fair-copies typed,
Ashes of finished cigarettes and thoughts,
No TV, radio, hi-fi, or cash—
And so fled empty-handed, cursing God.

And when you saw that all you had was there—
The cinder-block bookshelves' unpainted boards
Still holding Shakespeare, Milton undisturbed—
A poor man dancing past the robber band,
You knew you had been faithful to a gift
The Holy Ghost as Muse bestowed at birth,
Plowing by mind and hand down lines and rows,
True to the ancient sanctions of the land.

And though in your own way you'd come to drink
Like Socrates the poison of the age—
Narcissus leaning breathless to the pool,
Sherlock aroused for Moriarty's kiss—
You wrote late poems and essays to be whole,
Returning to that place where you were born,
Full harvests of a Blood Moon in the fields
As you stayed up all night, suffering AIDS
A decade while completing those two books,
Your story left for others who would strive
For mind's integrity, which, years ago,
A break-in had confirmed, exemplified,
As did your final moment's final breath
When from your deathbed halfway rising up,
With blinded eyes you looked beyond and said
"Plato?" to one now sent to take you home
To that last, great symposium of Love
At which the conversation never ends.

SELECTED NEW, UNCOLLECTED, AND PREVIOUSLY UNPUBLISHED POEMS

(1973-2023)

Reliquiae

summer 1974

for John Finlay

We walked at dusk from Canterbury close,
An image of Saint Thomas slumped in blood
Soon shut within the dark of mind and door.
A tide of shadow shrouded eastern walls,
Enfolding in its crests the crumbled graves
Where parting words had struggled from the stone.
With clumsy steps we moved among the dead,
Respectful of the rites that led them there
To threaten desolation with their faith.
Beyond the sunken dust the stars remained,
Ancestral lights no homage can allure,
Our wandering fathers careless of their kind.
At evensong survivors sang and prayed.
We turned aside to perish with the saved.

Earth and Stars

1975

Light that makes all things seen, makes some things invisible. The greatest mystery of Religion is expressed by adumbration.
Sir Thomas Browne

Its face of dust behind a mask of light,
The moon begins the cycle of the dark.
Like some rare mind it clarifies the stars,
The ancient constellations in their cars,
Composed of mortal light and emptiness.
Their radiance progresses through the night
Until the morning sun's despotic blaze
Annihilates the legends in its glare.
Those distant solar bodies, unassailed,
Once circled earth in celebrated mode,
The absolute horizon of the will:
The moonflower's wakened blossom softly arched
To open under Aries in the dark.
But now, as then, like windfall seeds the stars
Must wither in the cold, deposed at last
By some obscure encroachment on design.
Along the east horizon threats of dawn
Begin to wash the Houses of the south.

The mind withdraws, attentive to the earth,
That, driven from the center of its sphere,
Demands no less the old fidelity.
The wasted moon floats toward its death of light
As morning burns toward isolated stars.

Narcissus in Death

Persuaded by illusion to the true, I breathe
The water's face, crowned by the wreathing sprays of curls
Pulled down by the sinking brain. Locks of clouted gold,
Unwinding, serpentine, spoil of the ruffling waves
Collapsing over me in death: the shallow wraith
Who peers reflects what you emblaze, the heartsick mind
Defaced, compelled to meet the phantom it disdains.
Beyond the famous pain, bewildered by a kiss,
I drift in the soundless swells of sleep, through panic
Into bliss, silent and darkening to a dream of thought,
Dimmed image of my own apostasy. Whose mind
Contains the beauty that I saw, so singular
And still, enlightened wake of perfect countenance
I gazed upon and fell?
                                        Betrayed by breath I find
These rippling visages, elusive and divine,
Glimmering, in the distant presence of the sun,
Lost aureoles, ever-widening, out of reach.

The Sirens

"You will return, but all your men will drown":
Tiresias' blood-loosed words possessed me still!
What need had I of moly or the bough
Who gathered from the dead such prophecy?
Within these arms, enchanted by my power,
She whispered of a song beyond all sounds
Indigenous to earth, immune to charm
Or fixed heroic will, save Orpheus'
Alone: "Red fingers tore the tones from strings
Silent and deafening, Plutonian
Modulations, airs stained with fame and blood."
Bewitched by innocence, I plied the wind
That pushed us from Aeaea toward their isle.
Serene with pride, sedate in intellect,
Eager to know these chords the rhapsode matched
Fearing to hear yet never overcame,
I ordered them to bind me to the mast.

Within their ears—wax sweet with honey drops
Still clinging in the cells made soft as earth
By Helios Hyperionides, my lord.

Drifting in the west, as noon passed on to night,
We neared the Sirens' Isle. Old tricks of wit
And cleverness beguiled, I thought of dusk
In Ilium, of music, faintly heard,
As Trojan shadows burned on rubblestone,
Apollo's strains untuning in the fires.
Puffed up with swills of wind, the sails
Tilted against the sun, wheeling down away
Beyond the Gates. Then, from Troy, by Circe blown,
Apeliota stilled. In rhythms keenly tuned
With skilled technique and cunning of their craft,
The crew pulled through the calm. Dried in the sun
And polished watertight, long pinewood oars
Declined. Sliced, in translucent sheets, froth-lights,
Dispersed in brine, slid thinly from the blades.
Locked oarsmen dipped and spanned.
The Sirens sang.
I heard the song, measured above the deep.
What Orpheus, in fearful art, drowned out
From noonday air, I knew, swooning awake
From all I was, impermanent as mind.
My virtue led where virtue cannot go,
Essential night no science can divine.
The world I'd known—spume blown from Chronos' lips
Murmuring time in interlunar sleep.

Seduced by purity, past wiles I cried
For final silence after final song.
Blue-toned in Helios' sinking arms, eyes stared
Unfixed on anything I saw. New gusts
Screeched through mouths of corpses beached in marl.
Black plectrums plucked the strings of lyres, driftwood
Taut with flesh stripped twitching from the drowned.
Bees tilted and sucked the purple irises.
In asphodels, Leucosia called me home:
Unshrouded wisdom glinting on a face
Beyond torn rocks, red with anemone.
Bones glistened on the reef, lifted breakers moaned,
Far starlights wandered shoreward on the foam.
Sprays burst apart and fell in salty veils.
Deaf sailors rowed their king beyond the pale.

The Watchman

> not a word of all we have said about the universe
> could have been said if we had not seen
> the stars and the sun and the moon
> Plato, the *Timaeus*

Working hard near midnight on the sense
Of some Egyptian scholiast of Plato,
I'm suddenly brought back from the Nile's thick mists
Swirling into the fetid breath of Toby,
My blind, arthritic mutt, who's nuzzling me
To take her out to piss. So folding my
Timaeus into its gloss, I go outside
To wait as she wanders through the yard
Brushing the new-sprung asters—her eyes
Milky and unfocussed—trying to find
Vague traces of a world she used to know.
And there as my own eyes dilate and gaze,
Adjusting to the depths of dark and light,
I see within the blackest gaps of space
Appointed stars that shone in Homer's mind
And round the flowering throne of Dante's Rose.

High priests and mediators of the One,
Star-martyrs, burned for being, signal suns
Torched by the pallid watchmen, peak to peak,
Theirs is the one, the prime and final tale
Of cindered parapets in utmost Troy.

Late brother of such dust, twinkling with mind,
I too would be a watchman, though like my dog
I search a Milky Way spread out in space
Inscrutable and true, a glozing stream
Foamed from the deep and elevated caves,
The blazoned *res* at which old Plato gazed
Flowing on Helicon's starlit Ilissus.

The Wicked Steward

> Then the steward said within himself, What shall I do?
> Luke 16:3

For centuries my family managed the land,
Generations of stewards, responsible
For stable, orchard, field, accountable
To a master whose favored line persisted

As our own. For years I watched my father
Driving the day laborers, advising
The master, checking the granary's ample stores—
Jars of April barley, summer grapes and wine,
And oil from olives ripe in latest fall—
Moderate yields sufficient to our need,
And when my father died I took his place
Embraced by his old master, now my own.
All through the early rains we broadcast seed,
Then raked it deep into the terraced soil,
And when the winter rains grew warm in spring
I walked the risen rows of headed grain
Bowing in the breezes, thanking God.
How pleased my master was to tell me there
That he would go to pray alone in Baca
Leaving me in possession for a time.

At first I worked as I had always done
Sowing, tending, harvesting our crops
Grown in loam kept fecund by mild demands.
At evening I would rest beneath the palm
That shades the master's porch, although in time
Distracted from the fixed stars' steady flames
My eyes were often caught by the reveler's torch,
A shifting fire that called me to the town.
One day I set another in my place
And left a wife with child for other things.
My factor sent new money quickly made
Too densely planting overburdened soil
Drained by the speeded yields of golden grain.
Meanwhile, in half-lit rooms richly censed, I drank
Expensive vintages, foreign wines, sank back
In purple robes, and watched the naked dancers
Ease the way with oily breasts and buttocks.
Coins flashed in the harlot's palm that raised
My manhood up to yield its seed to lips
Or to the sterile, oft-aborted womb.

At last, I went back home, disturbed by dreams
Of locusts, blight, white hail, and desert storms,
And where the milk and honey once had flowed
I saw parched hives, dried udders, withered figs,
Cereal seared, bleak sheaves of the rotted crop.
I passed abandoned shrines of harvest gods
Erected in my absence, mud effigies
Baked and cracked by Jehovah's noonday sun.
Then in the airless granary underground,
Beside the ransacked amphoras, I came
Upon my factor, slain by his own starved hinds,
Climbing outside I hastened to the graves

That held the master's family and my own,
And there by my father's long untended plot
I found my buried wife and infant son.
I prayed in vain that Adam's double curse
Might somehow still be lifted.
Then I heard
Rising at a distance from the dust
The happy salutations of my master
Returning from the desert to my trust.

In Due Season

Mark 11:12-14;
Ecclesiastes 3:1-2

Five thousand years ago in Paradise
When Eve and Adam sinned and had to gaze
On nakedness they'd cover with my green,
They fell, and I fell too, by time defined:
These leaves bright, single, hairy, deeply lobed,
Branches twisting, wider than I am tall,
My weak wood apt to rot away within,
Bee-dusted seeds and flowers inside the fruit,
My roots the dresser digs around and dungs
So that, cut to the ground, they'll sprout again,
A trunk whose fluids suffer in the sun,
And shoots that grow to bring a tempering shade
Till flesh is ready, bending on the limb.

And then one greenest spring in Palestine,
My twigs not weighed down yet with summer yields,
A hungry man passed by from Bethany,
The House of Unripe Figs its language-name,
And cursed me for my fruitless vernal boughs
He withered at a word, but with what reason,
For how could I bear fruit but in due season?—
His anger at the moneychangers changed
To wrath against a thing his saying made.
Yet if my flourishing across this land
One day will mean his kingdom is at hand
And Israel a fig in fullest leaf,
When time is ripe, he might remember me.

Holy Saturday

> There is no celebration of the Eucharist on this day.
> *The Book of Common Prayer* (1979)

The altar stripped, the cross wrapped dark in gauze,
The service brief, sad, stark on that one day
We cannot take the body and the blood
Of one who lies beyond us in the tomb,
We listen to the readings—Job's iron pen
Graving in rock how flowers blaze and fade,
The psalmist's watchman marking from his tower
Stars that burn down the houses of the night
Toward Christ who stays a stronghold, castle, crag
For all now crowned in culminating love.

And yet past these set texts the mind will drift,
Blighted by the Enlightenment's bright-blind ways
That led it out of error partly home
To stumble where the heart goes on before
With darkness its companion, on their own
Through valleys whose commended spirits pass
Toward hands that hold love's genesis and end,
Washed with the spices Nicodemus bore,
The yellow aloe's stiff and bitter flesh,
Myrrh flowing from the manger to the tomb.

But on that second day did He descend
Into the Pit of those suspended souls
From Adam to a thief by faith made whole
Or did He lie decaying on the stone,
His napkined face forever breathless there?—
Not far from which a gardener then seen
By women as an angel or the Lord
Tended a plant whose story told their own:
An olive stump with new shoots rising green.
Joanna's tears agleam on stump and stone.

Lines in Advent

Through ordinary time we come again
To Advent and the waiting on a sign,
Kneeling in pews, then trying to prepare,
A burdened heart, the body of our sin
Brought low by our own choices, by design,
Our wonder in an attitude of prayer.

Night's watch fires burn far up above us there,
Appointed, named, and numbered sending beams
Down through the eons to a chancel wall
Whose colored glass, now cold in autumn air,
The pieces held in place by leaden seams,
Depicts a Christ beyond the cross and gall.

One hand has bread, the other wine for all
Who pray the prayer He taught us—heart and mind
Together and our will "Thy will be done"—
Redeemed at last from Adam and his fall,
The Way the only way for humankind,
The very blood and body of the Son.

And yet . . . before Communion has begun
The Words of Institution give me pause,
The mystery of *is*—like "Let there *be*"
And Christ the Vine, the Shepherd—coming undone,
The metaphors of being and their cause,
The snake's disastrous *as* a part of me.

Outside, the stars keep burning, as they must,
Illumining the stained-glass grape and grain,
Shapes of the elements we take on trust
Though I trust too in lines of grace and pain
In which alone I feel at one with Him,
My cross to bear, my Star of Bethlehem.

Doubter at the Rail

The cup and paten set on cloth and stone,
Red wine dilute with water and a bread
That does not rise—pressed grape, the wheat's ground head—
No place in which a mind can come to rest
If it would bear its cross of consciousness
Not toward Skull Hill but out of Plato's cave,
And these things left—railed off—that cannot save
A man who would drink hemlock at the end
Like Socrates and choose not to pretend
That long ago a single newborn Star
Led Wise Men to a wisdom "from afar"
Nor think this bread and wine are any more
Or less than what he took them for before,
Death's elements, the only fruit of earth,
A body's sustenance, its mortal worth,
This common meal we all must eat alone.

Compline

Faint fires thin toward the stars
Arrayed with bristling spears,
Encircled in their cars
By night's resistant fears.

To final prayers the soul
Compels its twilight form
Till all the heart withholds
Desires the ancient norm.

The compline torches dim
Their service and the world.
Who long can think on Him
In timeless darkness hurled?

The untolled hour comes.
Earth sleeps in winter will,
Benighted as the Nones
When God's own tongue was still.

Reading the Bible

At first, a simple bedtime picture book,
The garden with no snake seen in the tree,
Dry manger-wood, not cross-wood bleeding free,
A lion and lamb beside their shepherd's crook;

Later, the stately phrasings of King James
Fathers would read each morning at the table,
Bacon and grits at one with Cain and Abel,
The soul and body fed by things and names;

Held, too, by pulpits crowned with a pastor's frown,
Centered between the people and the choir,
The Good Book pounded till it sparked hellfire,
And altar calls, not altars, brought them down;

Then after, those long years of foreign balm,
Aurelius on the Danube, Plato's shades,
Valentinus craving light in matter's glades,
The Gnostic or the Stoic's hollow calm;

Yet in good time, at last, a change of heart,
The Bible taken back down from the shelf,
Read every day gathering a broken self

That it might thus be mended part by part

By that old storybook whose tale redeems
When fathers read to children like a child,
Not shepherds lost but loving, meek and mild,
Bringing their flocks back home to Eden's streams.

The Seven Virtues: A Lenten Meditation

Three thousand years have left us this
Précis of health and sober bliss:
Temperance, the broad firm base,
The drink refused with quiet grace;
Prudence, rich at folly's expense,
The interest of common sense;
Justice, blind in the balanced scales,
The weak man freed from strong men's jails;
Fortitude, outfacing dread,
The great poem done as the cancer spread.
Such natural virtues well defined
By Greece and Rome, the classic mind,
Prepare us for the higher three,
Faith, *Hope*, and *Love* called *Charity*:
Faith, the flower of reason's seed,
Rooted deep in fear and need;
Hope, the craving of the soul
That cannot think itself the whole;
Love, by which we know the One
Who loves us as He loves His Son;
And, to these antidotes to vice,
Gentlefolk will add the spice
Of *Courtesy* to sweeten up
The virtues' sometimes bitter cup
As John once stood apart, yet near,
In honor of the Virgin's tears.

Appearances

but then, face to face
St. Paul, 1 Corinthians: 13:12

We saw them best in winter, bright and whole,
The constellations moving through their spheres,
Arcing across the darkness of the pole,
Marking the skies with cold and fiery tears.

But now in orbit underneath the moon
A satellite's thick lenses make us gaze
Through Pegasus, the Lyre at midnight noon
Further into a blurring cosmic haze.

And there we watch a romance of the stars—
Red Giants, White Dwarfs, Dark Matter's Black-Hole Tomb—
All come from one Ur-Atom nothing bars,
Exploding, then ballooning to its doom.

Yet though Ptolemy's optics seem undone
To rubble by the Hubble's piercing stare,
We know that stare's too fierce to be the one
That finds in time this given world we share.

For when we love we love not well away
Nor dwelling bone-in-bone but with a space
Between us set like stars that prance and play,
Apparent, there, and aching face to face.

Death of a Modern Platonist

My eyelids close, as nightfall drapes a cave,
Faint starlight glowing in the blue-veined skin
Too weakened now to open once again,
This darkened flesh no flesh can ever save.

The world has proved illusion after all,
Its solids dissipating through the grades
Of liquids, gases, elemental shades—
Oblivion's images that so appall!

Yet in my youth I too would feel the sway
Of matter's fey attractions, rounded hips,
Soft breasts whose hardened nipples sought my lips,
Warm seed drawn out in loving's fertile play.

And though in middle years a shadow came
Between the mind and matter, there were days
The flesh could still seem sacred in its ways,
And where it tended mind would tend the same.

But then as muscle shrank from skin and bone,
The mind, grown keen in wrinklings of the brain,
Awakened to the trappings of its reign,
Sad Jacobite in exile on its throne.

Sheer gauze of quartz or lead's translucent veil,
The sun at noon as but a kind of dark,
And night itself a light dark stars demark–
Such constant aberrations tell the tale:

The body dies, and none of us returns,
The universe burns out in final cold,
Its ashes settle in a place untold,
And where the mind is left no mind discerns.

The Glowing Door: After Reading the Poetry of Jones Very, Unitarian and Mystic (1813-1880)

> Jones Very stood alone, within a circle which no other
> of mortal race could enter, nor himself escape from.
> Nathaniel Hawthorne, "The Hall of Fantasy"

It shone within a wall of blackened stone
Whose layers were compressed into a dense
And all but absolute consistency.
How often we had glanced at that bleak sheen
Wondering who could cut through such a rock
And with what primal adamantine tool.
And yet the door was there, its golden hinges
Glimmering in the bolted underplanes.

As far as we could tell the door would move
Although its knob, made strange by lunar heat
And solar cold, was hard for us to grasp.
No master key had ever worked the lock
Whose hidden parts would grind each time we tried
The most delicate motion left and right
Listening for a clicking as we pressed
Against a grain that glints but never gives.

And there we stand as always in the rays
Emitted blind and shining from a source
That touches us although we cannot breach
By human will the plane that holds the door.
And yet perhaps for now it is enough
To know a way remains, though sealed in light,
Through this thick wall on which we have to gaze
At faces untransfigured in its glaze.

The Jaded Socratic

They love me for my questions, don't you know?
I who gave up real teaching long ago,
Nodding at wild opinions spouted out,
Saying "Perhaps, perhaps" without a doubt.
The relative to them is absolute,
Odd postulate my logic could confute
Were they not all such products of an age
From which so few can ever disengage.
Yet should I try to tell them that, they'd scoff:
Brains with whole layers of consciousness sheered off!
I give them what they ask: a dream returned.
And who am I to tell them they're unlearned?

The Golden Years

Through middle age we heard a Siren song,
The Golden Years that drew us all along
Toward slow Greek island cruises, bingo nights,
Golf in the gated villages, delights
Of that blue pill for which her good eye twinkles
When his limp member rises from its wrinkles.

But soon time broke on rocks in salty spray
And wax that stopped deaf ears crumbled away,
And by the bone-strewn meadow's golden shore
We heard what others heard who'd gone before
In shells the Sirens filled with our last breath:
Tiredness, illness, forgetfulness, and death.

First of the Final Things

How often do we try to turn away
From facing it: the plain, blank, simple fact
That none of us forgets—our own one death—
Even in sleep or some heroic act
That takes the breath away.

What lies beyond this world we cannot know
Though we may think, hope, yearn, surmise, and dream
This side as to the other side of death—
If such is even there—where *be* and *seem*
Might be both *like* and *so.*

And what could follow–Judgment, Heaven, Hell?
Waters of uncreation, pool and tide?
An endless nothingness past life and death?
Pishon in Lethe flowing deep and wide
Forever from the Well?

The stone no angel's hand has rolled away,
Fire-shadows on the wall of Plato's cave—
Things flickering and fixed, all stayed by death—
The screening images we make and crave
Have yet to show The Way.

An Order for Evening

> This order . . . is appropriate also for use in private houses.
> *The Book of Common Prayer* (1979), 108

> Ps. 39: 13-15; 88:19

1.

The dusk moves through its deeper later grays
When I can barely read by natural light
The psalter in the prayer book Cranmer made.

And with the sky not dark enough for stars
Whose rays will glimmer late upon the page
I have a small white candle burning low.

The Psalmist sings of night and day as one,
The sun and moon created, set in place
To know their coming up and going down

And we could see their faces and could hear
Choired voices far beyond a fatal tree's
Stark chronicles of death's long history. . . .

But then, in time, there came a nameless star
Followed by knowledge into wisdom's cave,
Light strong enough to touch a baby's face

At midnight and a man's at midnight noon,
Then filling with its glow an empty tomb
Where Easter candles took the primal flame.

2.

This is "the greatest story ever told"
Of faith and hope and love and of the Word
Who made them the beginning, middle, end. . . .

And yet I hold back—wonder, ponder, ask
If questions are the answers they would find
In sentences too tentative to stop

At faith and hope—or disbelief, despair—
And I in Stoic resignation left
To try to love my neighbor as myself

(If love of self can be a selfless love),
Trusting *humanitas* will still endure
Till city wall and garden wall are one,

With all the gates unlocked, and moon and sun
Send down a single beam to light the way,
The human mind an owl among the ruins,

Awakened by a wound from waking sleep
To find its home an Eden full of tombs,
An angel now, entangled in a brain,

Making the tools that fashion what it finds,
Yet meant to hear the tales of dark and star
Told in a language older than themselves,

The Gladsome Light staving off ghost and bone,
The wonted hymn, the undefilèd tongue,
A *Nunc dimittis* fit for Simeon.

Yet from its stub my private Paschal flame
Flares over waters there before *there* was,
A faceless place, the elemental ground,

The warp and woof of space and time entwined,
The black and white to which all colors come,
That canvas where I make my chalky scrawls,

Cave paintings on the walls of nothingness.

Abstract of the Common Kingdom

It is a given world we share by grace,
Dependent stewards gazing from our place
Upon the strata'd taxa's likened things,
Those woven tropes of gold creation sings
Against the dread accessions of the mere.
These chains of food and being linked by need
Are love's necessities, matter's iron creed,
Beholden holy orders that declare
Earth's Christendom of water, fire, and air.

As Dante saw ascending, such things appear
In analogue, ghostly at the core,
Each one a trenchant instance, something more
Than to itself it is, as we shall be
That day our kindest seraph, by decree,
Comes down as Hermes drawing from above
Those bonded correspondences of love.

"That Heavenly Country"

Its mountains rise before us like a dream
So real our lives become what they envision,
Those blazoned elevations, Zion's skies,
Blue on blue, serene in true seclusion.

And there in time we gaze upon the faces
Of those sheer cliffs where only laurel grows
Or drink from springs that gather in the passes
Flowing from older sources on below

To where we crave, as natives of the base,
These gleaming peaks, archaic in array.

*

Inside them lie the valleys with their graves
Of our most ancient fathers, tilted stones
Worn smooth of name and number in the shade
Of ash and bay entangled there alone.

And here, on dateless clay, our scribes engrave
Reprises of the timeless validations
Scried by those mad fabulists who died
In that last pass before we reached our station

Dreaming of things revealed, not merely made,
Of Aristotle's rock and Plato's glade.

*

And though we sniff the brazen fragrances
Of consciousness and history and time,
Whiffs drifted from an apple's seedy core,
We breathe the vibrant silence of a clime

Confirming sounded ground whose root-words bloom
Out of those blest essences we sense
When shepherds pipe in time their timeless rhymes
On heights whose echoes beckon, as before,

Both Moses and Elijah to converse
With one who is the Word our words implore.

The Waters of the Garden

in memory of Edgar Bowers (1924-2000)

They foam upon those cups our hands create
That we might drink at evening while the stars
Awaken ancient cravings for a state
Marked by the empyrean's fiery bars.

Along the waters' edge unwithered figs
Teeming over the sedge in sweet oblation
Hide migrant swallows resting in the sprigs,
So tentative of purpose and of station

Until a music calls them down to drink
In twinkling streams by which we pipe in bliss
Attuned to Eden's reeds upon a brink
Whose winds are moving still in windlessness.

Body, Mind, and Soul

Body: Black matter is the mother of my flesh,
My father what my mother's webs enmesh.

Mind: The glow toward which I rose has always shown,
The one thing that is mine and mine alone.

Body: Food, sleep, and sex—these are my prime delight.
They keep me fat and happy through the night.

Mind: I love the valid pathways where I move
Approving everything that I can prove.

Body: I fear sudden weight loss, lumps, a short pained breath,
Heart beating rapidly out of time. Death.

Mind: I crave yet fear to know from whence I came
Or whitherto I go, and who's to blame.

Body: The mind is where my senses coalesce
Beneath the bleak abstractions they distress.

Mind: The body is a beast I strive to rule,
Domestic, playful, compulsive, and a fool.

Body: And am I then not free, as I suspect,
But some crude tool of will and intellect?

Mind: And I, am I the master when I strain
Within these oily coilings of the brain?

Soul: O mortal mind and body, you must try
To love each other's nature lest you die
Outside those old dependencies that free
All bodies, minds, and souls and let them be.

Thoughts After Anselm

A spoof. A hoax.
One of His jokes.

He spoke it drunk.
The punch line stunk.

A rip-off. Goof.
A galley proof.

Divine Idea.
Diarrhea.

Monkeyshines.
An off rhyme.

A wound. A riddle.

Distributed middle.

A single poppy.
Carbon copy.

Auto da fé.
Shadows' play.

An interlude.
Nothing brewed.

Revelation.
Or duration.

One long curse.
Or the reverse.

A call. A word.
Being heard.

Ens and means.
Opening scenes.

A peek. A hint.
A sacrament.

Aseity
It may not be.

But the universe
Could be worse.

A Defendant Speaks

Dyads of depth and silence,
Informers who betray
Yourselves in all your clients,
Arch counsels who convey
Unanimous decision,
Determining our days
In prison and recision:
We bring to you our case.
Our sin was but our nature,
Our nature but the cause
Made present in a creature
Who did not make its laws.
Great justicers who sentence

Transgressors of the Word,
Outcasts beyond repentance
Whose pleas no silence heard:
Our justice is your sin
Traduced by our appeals.
What holy dark begins
Enlightenment anneals.
Dim ghosts we one time were,
You offer clemency
For crimes we but infer
From your delinquency.
So distant, near, we grieve.
The world is all we find.
Our crime our sole reprieve:
Apostasy of mind.

Nightmares

We wake to sweat and heartbeats uncontrolled,
Disoriented like a patient wheeled
From surgery, still half-anesthetized,
Then struggle to resume a troubled reign
Over black depths, the primal under-mind,
Sheer terror and unguardedness combined.

We watch until the dawn and world return,
Familiar walls and pictures, windows, chairs,
Our native shades, each fixed in its own place
Against those twisted images that rose
Like wild Leviathans to break and sound
Out of oblivion's gulfs and range unbound.

Good sense and senses gathered once again,
Stark dread now sunk back down to its dark source,
We censor or dismiss the horrid scenes,
Long kisses from a hated face we crave,
Beloved kin we murder unawares,
Doors opening on depthless shadow-stairs.

Yet though we say we live in modern times
Unhaunted but in play at Halloween,
We still know nightmares, waking or asleep,
New holocausts, the broken, last taboos,
Good Doctors Faust and Frankenstein who call
At every house with black bags that appall.

The Progress of the Moon

> Victor Hanson understands the intimacy that should exist between men and land . . . it is not only humanity that needs his words, the planet does
>
> James Dickey, jacket comment for Victor Davis Hanson's book *Fields Without Dreams: Defending the Agrarian Idea* (1996)

Through woods the moon moves deep and high in night
Over the winter limbs of oak and elm,
Old groves of frosted mistletoe and light,
The magic facts of matter's elder realm:

Above, great constellations, placed and found,
Chaos and order, one, in wild control,
The burning wing and tongue, the well-turned ground
Of Pegasus and Draco round the pole;

Below, this world of star-drawn mist and cloud,
Of hills and seas far eons shape and waste,
Sublunar runes long chiseled in the shroud
Of bough and bone, by nothing laced and braced;

And in between, an arcing sphere whose course
Had once kept heaven fixed above earth's crust,
No more a verger marking the divorce
Of realms that mix telluric, stellar dust.

Midwinter Spring

prélude a la fin de siècle

When dandelions as yellow as the sun
Spring from the winter grass's paler blades,
The warming South's calm January days
Restore a mind abstracted by its act
Between December frost and April balm.

Tired by the bleak repletions of the fall,
The gathered fruits of Saturn and the Mass,
Weary of feasts, epiphanies, and gifts,
The body and the spirit's wracked embrace--
The fasting mind would fasten on a text

As on the ur-text, text of text itself,
Beginning of beginning unconceived.
Tracing the racinations of the Word
Back to the root of Eden's double-trees,

Such mind exhausts the virtue of its soil,

Where, as the Logos' sinking nether-tip
Enters the ebon bedrock of the loam,
Dark pride is twined in its own blazing veils,
Screened by pure self-knowledge, self-deceit,
From what must be unseen and must be here.

Aroma of the known invisible
Donnée! most fragrant of abrasions! drift
Down from the frigid poles of Ought and All
That in midwinter spring your winds may bend
The bitter, mortal mind to its sweet end.

God's Commons

from a barrier island off the Louisiana coast

Across the night's high pastures where they graze
Beneath a blue occlusion that exudes
From utter nothing, the herded stars
Crop grass grown black beside the undug wells.
Two roots of light and darkness flowering down
Out of the spreading crevices of the said
Entwine in pliant bindings that decline
Through musings to the massive habitudes.
Beyond the founded mountains' rolling slopes
Breakers of chaos burst in gurgling caves,
Thundering undersongs of the fluid
Ruminations, littorals scrolled in foam,
The singing things ineffable in essence
Ranging through the changeless laws of change.

Glad matter's florid tropes grown bright with life
Trellising into presence through my
Night-rooted eyes, these bloomed illuminations
Are protrusions of the true, not gutted
Tufts of nothing science spies but Eden
Gone to seed, the milk and honeyed planes
That Canaan claimed from Zion in its prime.

A posted guard who watches as he walks
Across the marred foundations darkly starred,
I see God's commons blossoming in time
Where shepherds turn their dirges into psalms
Whose telling names and numbers still rejoice
In vital pipings calling to the fold

Things lost like lambkins crying from the cold
Till drawn by love that knows each bleating voice.

Full Moon

The moon is moving high and deep in night,
Orbiting earth, its disc now rounding out,
As full, and fully there, as it can be
Journeying on through time's eternity.

And we? What do we see? Just rock and dust?
An arbitrary sign we correlate
To chastity, change, madness, death, or lust,
No more than what we make of it ourselves?

Or is there something else, in crust and core,
Something we once belonged to long ago
When cold reflected light first brought the mind
From shadows toward a fire that came before?

The moon is moving from and toward its source,
No longer circling round a centered ground,
Its plenitude remembered, understood,
Elliptical of earth as earth of sun.

Of Tragic Pastoral

Such verse would seem to go against the grain
Although its sweet catastrophe could be
To pluck from those most innocent descriptions
First-fruits of earth's rejected sacrifice,
The leavings of a tragic act rooted
In ancient lands layered with implication.
Its theme would be the blessings of its curse
Mouthed out in vivid diction, strictest rhyme,
And rhythms heightened and tightened till the lines
Might cry in their own strained voice against a world
Our greatest works can praise but not contain.
And yet, that uncontainable world, this poem,
In the brotherhood of otherness would be,
Between themselves, no less than metaphors
Lashing all those word/things slashed apart
When Abel's fluent blood cried out from the ground
Near which, bent down in the bending grain, Cain,
Scyther of life, queried the Word itself,

Becoming the first false rhetor among men,
The ears of emmer-wheat left deafened in his sin.

Moon, with Sun and Stars

Come from the dark
To die in light
Moon's changing arc
And aspect mark
Sublunar night.

Yet from that night
The daystar's fire
Will pluck its light
Till noon makes bright
Apollo's lyre.

And long that lyre
Pours forth its strains
In songs of fire
Till twilight's choir
Of crickets reigns.

And while it reigns
Black wings grown stark
Play Chaos' strains
Whose close contains
All stars in dark.

Late Summer Psalm

Outside the study window flaxen grass
Matted above the pale late summer blades
Draws grackles to bewildered moths that pass
Forever from the new-mown under-glades.

And there by cooling roots the crickets' shrill
Cries rise from rubbing vibrant wing on wing,
Males sensing ready females and the chill
Of autumn frost in night's dread lengthening.

And where the yard climbs up the bayou-side
A live oak weighed with acorns twinkles gold
While star-and-firefly galaxies abide
In swaying limbs the mortal heavens hold.

Meanwhile, inside, faint moonbeams gloss a page
Whose words emerge from fiber marked with gall,
The speaking leaves of Eden that assuage
A fallen world that cries their silent fall.

Yet here on oaken shelves mere wood and ink
Preserve a cosmos pressed on heart and mind,
A turning world-tree burning on the brink
Where love composed with light the dark we find.

Of Hearth and Stars

The winter evening deepens in a yard
Speckled with stars so cold in sky and grass
Between which V's of great blue herons pass
From home to home, tired migrants, flying hard.

And in this old abode of birth and death
Where midwife, doctor, undertaker come
And preachers read King James with ribboned thumb
To mark a first or final human breath

I rock in my grandfather's rocking chair
Beside a hearthstone flecked with ash and fire
That chimney-winds draw up as they aspire,
Then drift in smoky flow through dark's charred air.

And in that flow both hearth and stars are home
To farers on the heavens' earthly track
Housed by the plotted bone and zodiac,
These radiant graves of angels where we roam.

Things

after Psalm 19: 3-4

We live among them here and partly are
What they have ever been and still will be
When soul from flesh is sheared along the scar
That marks the stitching-place as soul breaks free.

Yet if we hold them wholly in the mind
To take apart and savor, then let go,
The essence of our senses but the rind

Of some rich fruit we taste but hardly know—

The bare pecan whose trunk is simply there,
Its winter limbs against a winter sky,
The squirrel that brings the nut through dusk's dim air,
Just doing what it must to live and die—

Such things in turn may be more than they seem
In matter's shadowland of squirrels and trees:
Creatures who'd wake with us in that first dream,
Time's common tongues in timeless colloquies.

August into Autumn

North Louisiana

It happens every year almost the same
And always late in August when we pause
Just long enough to see what time has done,
Sly changes nearly imperceptible
Moment to moment holding us at last
While molting birds gone quiet watch the stars
As summer moves to its appointed end.

The mated dragonflies, whose months are years,
Their eggs already floating in the reeds,
Now glide more slowly over lake and blade,
The great blue skimmer, eastern amber-wing
Still hunting for mosquitoes, dusk and dawn,
But farther off as the dense swarms grow thin
And crickets call all night through cooling trees.

2021

The Regnant Moon

Late moon of Lent and winter, you emerge
Gaunt in dented silver on the verge
Of daybreak's bleak suffusion, a bright
Stone martyr drawn and quartered by the light.

Tiared by stars, robed in the essent sun,
You rule the strata'd blackness of the One
Probing fecund dregs your beams consign
To Hecate, Diana, Proserpine.

A liege man of the night, I find you here
Throned in the mind as in your ancient sphere,
Coursing relic zones once held in festive sway,
The ghostly queen of stasis and decay.

Lonely, serene, placed in the vested whole,
You glow in space as in the spacious soul.

Oxalis

South Louisiana

Midwinter here gives way to early spring
With February just begun,
The last freeze all but done,
And pink oxalis close to blossoming.

It likes the morning sun, then filtered shade
Warm afternoons, each leaflet-stem
Wilting till light grows dim,
Unwrinkling when the petals fold and fade.

Great swathes spread wild on open pineland floors;
Clumps mound in lines by garden walls
Or where a pathway falls
Between the garden-gate- and threshold-doors.

In meadows, yards, it seeds the windy grass,
Long stalks soon flowering everywhere,
Thriving in earth and air—
Invasive beauty!—come to stay, then pass . . .

For hardy as it is, at times a pest
Attacks it: powdery mildew rots;
Smut, rust, and fungus-spots,
Leaf miners, spidery mites plague, infest.

And if the plant escapes insects, disease,
Late summer still will wither, bleach
Dark leaves as petals reach
Their end in autumn frost or winter freeze.

All this we know, as flowers cannot do,
And so we praise them while they stay,
Hoping till our last day
That seeing things in time will see us through.

Song

In brush when snowflakes cling
The winter wren will sing,
The burden of its song
How long, how long?

Come earliest in spring,
To dead oaks martins bring
The burden of their song,
How long, how long?

Mockingbirds in summer trees
Sing lifted melodies,
The burden of all song
How long, how long?

In fall, no more is heard . . .
Wren, martin, mockingbird
Unburdened of my song
How long, how long, how long?

From the Footbridge over Bayou Lafourche, Thibodaux, Louisiana

Stained planks of pine arc bank to bank at dawn
Over the river's long abandoned bed,
This southwest forking bayou flowing on
From northern springs the melting winters fed.

And here where cold blue realms of whites and grays
Are lost within a dense primeval green,
Bent willows trail their leaves in golden rays
Whose blades sink into depths that move unseen.

Two mallards paddling upstream through their V's
Widening out behind them near the planks
Dabble in duckweed floating to the lees
Of winds urging these waters past their banks

To that great shelf of silt, mud, shell, and sand
Below this pinewood bridge which verges on
Tropics far from the tundra's treeless land
Whose snow geese seek our snowless winter dawn.

Bird Watching

for Don Stanford (1913-1998)

O learn to open the creatures
Richard Baxter

i.

You held those birds so firmly in your mind
Setting them free in song, in poems that defined

A chasm too profound ever to cross:
You marked the abyss as gain, accepted loss.

And yet how well you knew them all the same,
Your "oriole's thin dividing flame,"

Your thrush weaving through the woods' deepening green,
Your sea gull storm-blown out of the sunlight's sheen,

Abstractions from the senses that became
The symbols that were latent in each name.

ii.

This spring in a quiet turn in the garden path
I put out elderberries and a bath

Attracting to my daughter's great delight
Some local birds that came to trust the site.

Now mockingbirds, grackles, and one mad jay
Gathering scattered seeds then flying away

Grace our feeding-station where they wing
Quick-eyed with purpose, alighting to sing

Across the noted chasm to a mind
So different in degree, so like in kind.

Home: A Farm Wife's Daybook

I consider the days of old;
I remember the years long past;
I commune with my heart in the night;
I ponder and search my mind.
Ps. 77:5-6

Today I sugared and sealed the last preserves,
Blueberries plucked in deep July outside,
Cooked down for hours till time itself conserves
Sweet essences where flesh and mind abide.

*

I read my Bible far into the night
By moonbeams bright as limelight on a bed
In which my husband dreams of harvest, blight,
A mystery play he stages in his head.

*

The morning psalms all tell of Lebanon,
Its hills that peak in cedars, windblown wheat;
Outside, ice-crackling fields slope up and on
Toward dogwoods white in Easter's late white sleet.

*

Near dusk I rock before the hearth and sew
By stone and wood turned up in well-turned land
These cotton threads I stained dark indigo,
Stark strands strained tight by native heart and hand.

*

The hall's grandfather clock goes *tick* and *tock*,
Stark makers of its well-read book of hours,
Its turning moons grown ripe like sheaf and shock,
Time's gathered aftermath of scattered flowers.

*

His muzzle on cold paws beside the fire,
Our bloodhound, far in winter, warms old bones,
Eyes fluttering back once more in dream's desire,
Hares chased through snowy ash by the hearth's pawed stones.

*

The weather in the window takes its time,
Late winter dandelions, mid-August cries
Of crickets doomed to mate, then die in rime
When fall's shrill winds exhale their icy sighs.

*

From speechless dreams I wake before the day,
The Bears and Hunter coursing round the pole,
While like its owl night's silence seems to say
This world is more than matter, mind, and soul.

*

I made a simple soup from stalks and heads
Of those last plants the winter garden yields,
Shallots and cabbage, finished in dead beds,
Their mulch a pulp to feed green Easter fields.

*

Our moon-drenched village square's a golden glade
For a medicine show's snake oil and midnight ramble;
At home, for cure, I raise a yellowed shade
On shrikes whose lizards writhe on thorny bramble.

*

What must be done draws me through predawn cold
To this black hole, its starless pit of lime;
I sit and let necessity take hold,
Soul humbled in the wrenching stench of time.

*

Outside, by night and day, the solar years
Move through their seasoned eons, holy tones
Of equinox and solstice, centered spheres,
Slow quarter notes of quartered skies and zones.

*

Inside, the wound grandfather clock ticks on,
Diurnal and eternal in its chimes,
Its face of changing moons sounded by one
Great lunar noon that ranges through its rhymes.

*

Bought needles knit spun threads of yellow flax
Dyed by the essence drained from indigo,
Our local colors stained, then placed on racks,
Taut mind and matter twined for use and show.

*

Waiting on yeast to foam, the well-worked dough
To rise as wheat stalks rose to give us flour,
Loaves baking in their spells, then cooling slow—
All things in God's good time since time's ninth hour.

*

From fields where cows graze deep in winter hay
Manure and mulch enrich and cover roots
Till tender stems, engendered by the day,
Make green our pale March garden with their shoots.

*

My husband sows deep furrows with his salt
Dropped on seed-crop grains, pushing his plow
Through ready earth till sundown brings a halt,
Then supper, bed, a fertile wife's *now, now.*

*

As words give way in moaning's wordless kiss,
Held by his dark fixed eyes and lowered tone,
My many *no's* become one *yes* with his
Warm wet shaft nudging under the quim-bone.

*

Midwinter spring and one lorn butterfly
Is born into a world of ice and doom;
Soon time will tell great blood-moons prophesy
When blood is held inside this lunar womb.

*

Each spring leaf-blades curl aching from the waste
Of sludge-ice melting brown into the wild
Whose verdant urgencies surge up in chaste
Passions that wed to make a man, a child.

*

He sucks my milky nipples by the fire,
My newborn son whose name is carved upon
Gray headstones of his grand- and great-grandsire,
His own head tender still by embered stone.

*

Some wonder why I chose to stay at home,
A shallow question fathomed best by this:
Why would I be unsexed?—a bubble in foam
Adrift on the stillest depths of *hers* and *his?*

*

Beyond the hilltop twilight flares, then fades
From wrought-iron fence and tilted marking-stones,
My kindred's dust and souls among the shades,
Spare Vulgate psalms above their common bones.

*

First flakes that melting dwell in winter veins
Of fall's red leaves the brittle ice-winds stir,
Azalea-springs in February rains,
Green summers quelled when autumn crickets chirr . . .

*

A century of lines and this lined face
Almost a centenarian's, I close
My daybook now, this cedar chest the place
For words close-pressed by rosary and rose.

Twilight in Saline

July, 1961

in memory of my maternal grandmother, "Muzzie" (d. July 15, 1962)

The dawn spread up through darkness to the moon
Whose silver disc persisted in those beams
That cleared the hilltop pines of midnight mist.
A breeze still cool with evening and its dew
Brought scents of the wild azalea to a sill
Whose window box of portulaca stayed

Unstirred until its heads of showy blooms
Unfolded in a radiant crest of sun.

The cricket-cries grew quiet in the light
That warmed me toward awakening once more,
A boy of twelve, in childhood's twilight time,
Spending vacation weeks in country peace
With you, Grandmother Muzzie, whom I heard
Singing a psalm at daybreak in your garden
There in the last full summer of your life
And in the last full summer of my own.

Your hands moved through the staked tomato-vines
Pinching off leaves beneath each yellow flower
And picking reddened fruit from bending stems.
Then scattering corn to lure the chickens out
You took two snug brown eggs from empty coops
And went into the kitchen while I dressed.
Fried bacon, cheese, tomatoes in an omelet
Soon sizzled in the skillet's bacon grease.

The pan and dishes sudsed up, rinsed, and dried,
You watered with your tilted watering can
Each window box and bed and flowerpot–
Pale pink impatiens, yellow marigolds,
Blue periwinkles, rosy spiderworts–
And gathered mint where shaded faucets leaked
Cold water droplets drawn from purest springs
Straining through sand and clay below the well.

This done, you sat and rested on the porch,
Still living out unairconditioned times,
Fanning fast with a stick-and-cardboard fan
Compliments of Greenbriar Funeral Home:
Its front, Saline in winter, magnolias
In the snow, the reverse, a calendar
To help us number all our mortal days,
Your last twelve months, the years of my short life.

But hardly knowing then as I know now
How soon you would be gone, I left the porch
To spend the long warm morning lost in play,
An aging child-ghost haunting its own dream.
I hung the woodpile lizards from my ears
And let the black grasshoppers grown so large
Crawl all across my sandbox-buried legs,
Then swung on my old rope-swing toward the sun.

And hearing pots clang as you fixed our lunch

I ran through the melon fields to Diddywah,
An Indian pond well hidden in its glade.
Cattails, ferns, and lily pads, the fallen
Cypress logs drifting with glider turtles—
I stripped and swam like a son that Adam
Might have had in Eden, my darkened crotch
Still innocently breaking from the waves.

Noon raining light and heat into a sheen
Of sunshine floating cold upon the waters,
My hunger honed to sharpness like the bell
You rang to bring me home to homegrown fare:
The buttered corncobs picked that very day,
String beans tied up with toothpicked bacon strips,
Crisp drumsticks from a grain-fed barnyard hen,
And gravy-brown potatoes in their cream.

Famished from the morning, I ate and ate
Nourishing body, mind, and soul as one,
Then gave in with reluctance to your need
For bed rest in the torrid afternoon.
Air drawn in deep to feed your failing heart
You seemed a breathing corpse beneath the sheets,
Your rising chest upsetting my toy wars,
Dead Rebs and Yanks all silent by your side.

Thus offered up the freedom of the house
I went from room to room on progress through
A child-heir's pledged domain until I found
The button box whose buttons told their tales
In metal, leather, cloth, a chronicle
Fleshed out in blouses, gloves, a wedding dress
Placed in the cedar chest's dry scented dark
With quilts, lace christening gowns, and other lace.

Outside, midafternoon's relentless reign:
Mace-headed stickers waiting in the blades,
Fast cardinals pulling earthworms from the earth,
A thrush fanning up bugs from grass and dust,
A shrike-speared lizard writhing on the thorn,
And me, in your employ, swatting on the porch
At houseflies (one cent each), horseflies (a nickel),
Your laissez-faire young capitalist in his prime.

Then tiring in the twilight I would sit
Legs kicking from the rotted front-porch boards
As you snapped pole beans and cut up yellow squash
Humming the hymn I'd sing next when you died,
"The Old Rugged Cross," while in the yard and sky
Where the pecan grew one with Yggdrasil

Fireflies and constellations twinkled on,
Bright works both wrought and wrested from the night.

Our supper, cold fried chicken, hot cornbread
And buttermilk, we ate outside at evening
Hearing a slow wind moaning in the gourds
Hung hollow from the low limbs of the tree,
Feeders for wrens in flight from northern ice,
Or else we gazed across those sandy fields
Of watermelons, ghostly oblong globes
That ripen through July's high midnight moons.

And so I went to bed although you stayed
Until I prayed the Lord my soul to keep
("If I should die before I wake" still there)
Though it was I who'd waken to a day
One brief year hence to hear you'd passed in sleep
Into the peaceable kingdom of the heart,
Those parishes that bear toward paradise
Where shrikes and lizards tend each other's young.

Jogging Through Thibodaux

4:00 A.M., August 1997

Rolling out of the bed at 4:00 A.M.–
The rested brain come back again from sleep
With images and rhythms for a poem–
At 48, I'm still content to jog
My same nine miles, a mile for every muse.

And so, dressed out, I walk up to the road,
Breathe deeply and then do what must be done
When mortal flesh is nearer death than birth–
Slow deliberate stretching till the pains
In muscle, nerve, and bone seem somewhat eased
Within the measured flow of breath and blood.
Then going up on tiptoes, hands held high
Like some Arcadian waving at the stars
I start off working through the creaky knees,
Bruised heels, and aching tendons that the miles
Now bring as trophies fit for middle age.

From Len to Young then left on Ridgefield Road
I pace myself while bleary eyes adjust
To darkness and stiff feet to uneven ground
Until a natural rhythm settles in

And I can flow along in silent rhymes
Of soul and bone and flesh and blood and mind.

Then speeding up as much as time allows
I turn on 8th St. taking in sweet scents
Of Frost's new lumber stacked beyond a fence
Up which the purple morning-glories climb
To blossom in the lengths of coiling barbs.

Not far beyond, the Twelve Apostles stand,
Great antebellum oaks that shade the dead
Including General Nicholls, C.S.A.,
Buried beside high Anglican St. John's
Whose north Louisiana priest maintains
The catholic faith in this apostate age.

Then, when created night grows most intense
Against resistant stars' coeval rays
I turn up Jackson St. and reach the bridge
Below whose clanging grates gray pigeons stay
Until my passing scares them and they rise
Flapping over the duckweed by the banks
Where I dodge smashed bottles sticky with the dregs
Of last night's beer and breathe in stale air spread
Like incense out of Rox's and Rene's.
But now the bars are silent as I stride
On up the bayou side toward Audubon
Then over the bridge to LA 308
Whose shoulders leave me room enough to run.

And there along a slight incline that crests
A mile ahead beneath a clump of trees,
Hard ground I always cross as "Pickett's Charge,"
I gingerly sidestep in a changed pace
As though treading in dread through uncreation
Dead dogs and armadillos, shattered glass,
Hubcaps and rubber spun from cars that pass
Breaking the limit not two feet away
From where I slowly go toward other ends.

And yet at last, though tired, I make those oaks
Whose wreathing leaves brush curls across my brow
If I don't flinch and duck, a brief sweet crowning
Outside the general store and that home stretch
Whose finish line is Laurel Valley's cane.
And there above the sugar-fields the dawn
Reveals a tattered V of migrant geese
Laboring through creation on their way
By instinct to the brink of all they crave.

Below them, flush with sweat and runner's blood,
I stop and clap my hands in heart's elation,
Breathe in and out and in to the lungs' stretched depths,
Wring out my soaked headband and fast-walk back
At peace within the flesh's predilections
And in the mind's most valid habitudes
Toward which I keep on going though I creak
Through every foot of every mile and line,
Like some too weary goose behind the wedge,
Making its way with music through the skies
Toward Hermes of the lyre and wingéd shoe.

Old Bird on a Telephone Pole, Old Man Watching

With black wings pressed against his sides he stays
High-perched alone while younger birds untold
That sought mosquito hawks warm summer days
Are far in flight from northern night and cold.

Below the twilight grays of cloud and sky
The bird is fixed on nothing as he stares
Beyond the downcast eyes of passersby
All caught in a bewilderment he shares.

Behind the dimming clouds a full moon glows,
Mere symbol of itself as it would seem
To one who fears the little that he knows
Is like a bird's eye darkening agleam.

He stands with hands in pockets deeply pressed,
His form grown blacker now as night grows old
Like that lone bird whose essence he had guessed
Was ghostly as his own in polar cold.

Along the Bayou Side

for C.S.B.

The winter morning waiting in its night,
I wake and walk along the bayou side
In thoughtful solitude, my fifty years
Demanding now this constitutional.
No longer young and starry-eyed with life
I watch the glittering distances again

Yet not for mythic emblems drawn from fire,
The Herdsman and the Hunter and the Cross,
Or houses vanished with their guardian ghosts
In zones mapped out by telescope and probe
But as themselves, an open mystery
Inanimate and grand, a vividness
Against some blank, divine, and primal ground,
Old subjects of an undivided realm,
Sojourners on the stream of space and time
As I through town along this bayou side
Where starlit waters flow through banks and mind.

Windsor Ruins

built, 1861 burned, 1890

Port Gibson, Mississippi

for George Core, editor of *The Sewanee Review* in which this poem first appeared

In a land so green and old the heart beats near
Its ancient range of innocence and fear,
Bare on drained embankments Windsor lies,
Columns holding fast to evanescent skies.
Risen with his fever Windsor came to seem
Its master's last delusion, a forest dream
That left him free of consciousness and good,
An Indian asleep in virgin wood.
He died in time, a mortal cotton god,
Buried dark in earth beyond his white facade.
Yet soon Vicksburg winds straining the Grecian frieze
Drew blue smoke bleeding southward through the trees,
But he knew nothing, Clio's favored son,
Dead of natural causes, 1861.
Now, where New England artisans confined
In local wood broad shapes of Attic mind,
Mocked by the elements' apostasy,
In ruin alone is Windsor's beauty free—
Cores of slave-made brick inside their plaster case,
Lichen grown gold against the northern face—
Pillars even Davis guided by at last
To a modern South abandoning its past
While Windsor burned, escaped from Yankee rage,
Fired by a cigarette in the Gilded Age.
Since then, although a century has tried
To evade what crumbled Windsor cannot hide,
Its blackened capitals of iron acanthus
Still raise their rusted trays of ash and dust,

Corinthian remains whose ivy pours
On rooms where bees have spread their clover floors.
So chastened by defeat, the Trojan soul can sound,
In Windsor's seasoned glade, Virgilian ground,
Mild berries sweetening in the columns' ripened shade,
Bobwhites calling through the fluted colonnade.

Upon the Cover of *The Fugitive Poets: Modern Southern Poetry in Perspective* 1965; William Pratt, editor; Paul Davis, artist

The cover holds us from the poems within,
This young Confederate Davis captured here,
A private guarding gates at two removes,
This painting of a statue of a man.

Yet all we see is something like a bust
And so we must imagine in his hand
A loaded musket, sharpened bayonet,
His hard feet planted firm on rocky ground.

The granite head and kepi, Rebel gray,
Targets of war and weather, pitted, flecked,
Stand out against a background without cloud,
A sky, cerulean, not Yankee, blue.

A crack through cap and temple, cheek and jaw,
Has scarred his face, making it seem a mask
That might be chiseled off to get inside
At sins his countenance must surely hide.

Three climbing vines bring flowers from the earth,
The blood-red petals circling dusty gold,
With lance-tip leaves, to nestle and caress
This man of stone to whom they try to cling.

The soldier stares far off yet deep within,
Haunted by all that cannot be undone,
Still resolute and stoic, sternly calm,
Unconquered by defeat, or victory.

His burden is to know in vein and bone
The Cornfield, Bloody Angle, Sunken Road,
Peach Orchard, Wheatfield, Crater, Hornet's Nest,
Arms stacked at Appomattox, going home.

Home to what little pillage, arson left,
Ashes of barn and farmhouse, slaughtered stock,

And Reconstruction that went on and on
For one who owned no mansion and no slave.

In time his history became our myth
With Butcher Grant and Lee the Cavalier,
The Lost Cause, General Order No. 9
We knew by heart, our Gettysburg Address.

And we erected statues in the squares
And gave our streets and children heroes' names,
Preserving what was best in what they were,
An "Other" that modernity abhors.

And those same years we bore, alone, apart
The consequences of a world we shared,
The northern slave ships bound for Africa
With rum that built those fine Rhode Island homes.

And now iconoclasts deface, destroy
Whatever threatens them, complexities
They could not stand to find inside themselves,
New Puritans whose world is black and white.

All this is there in that young Rebel face
Paul Davis painted—steadfast, fugitive—
With memories of a past the future holds,
The War that never seems to have an end.

And in this book his granite statue guards
Are poems redoubtable, in well-plowed rows,
Ransom and Warren, Davidson and Tate,
A new New South much older than the Old.

And in those poems, and others of their kind,
Beyond destruction, lies a pastoral land
Where black and white might blend in weathered gray
When gates unlatch and flowering vines entwine,

The clinging green, red, gold—cerulean blue—
All heralding a realm not far behind
This painting of a statue of a man.
We know, without the saying, where it is.

The Statue in the Glade

> Only such men could tell what once could be,
> Hear what we hear, see what we see.
>
> Donald Davidson, "Late Answer: A Civil War Seminar"

The wind is all but silent in the pines
Around a glade whose light comes down from fire,
Not filtered or aslant through needle, cone,
A heightened brightness passing as it stays.

And there, alone, a ghostly statue stands
Through which both beams and shadows make their way
From morning until evening, and at night
Stars twinkle down, then up, from sky and blade.

The statue is a private, dressed in gray,
Coat, musket, powder horn as though of stone,
Feet wrapped in rags, the very ground his base,
His piercing gaze fixed like a bayonet.

Now palpable in recollection's flesh,
A solid wraith, the boy can never be
Defaced or toppled, scorched, or spat upon.
Flung paint would splatter only earth and air.

A legend on a plaque no fingers trace
Is like a graven shade, the wording worn
And in a language hard to understand
Except by those who heard it at their birth.

Beside this hidden glade the woods are still,
The trees the last of old growth longleaf pine,
Their birds those birds that winter in the South
Or stay year round in this their native place:

Rare pinewood sparrows perched on topmost limbs
Where quiet and a breeze bring them to sing,
Pine warblers sending down their liquid trills,
Nuthatches who will never leave their trees.

Who shaped a statue made of words in air?
What story does its silence have to tell?
Who now can speak the long-forgotten tongue?
Who passes through a woodland's public square?

The soldier knows humility, defeat,
Intricacies of history and its myths,
Given to inwardness while others judge
Him guilty who will never judge themselves.

He did his duty, held the line, and saw
That his condition is the state of man,
Its "Ye shall be as gods" the fatal choice
That all men make and thus should understand

Those boys who charged up Cemetery Ridge,
Then fell back with their chests toward Yankee fire
So not to be thought cowards shot from behind—
Picked off by quick repeaters on the crest.

And one slain there no bullet now tears through,
A marble specter, in and out of time,
Who gave his country all he had to give,
This boy, who knew he had not long to live,

Who died before his love became a crime.

Pickets

> Watch ye, stand fast in the faith, quit you like men, be strong.
> 1 Corinthians 16:13

The stars around us gleam like bayonets
As though another foe had gathered there
To bear down on our army long dispersed
Behind us in the cold and smokeless air.

But word of that last order and parole
Arrived too late at this remotest post
Where we will stay forever on alert
In one thin line unbroken ghost to ghost.

Our mission was to be keen eyes and ears
Detecting all about our dwindling corps
Great movements of the northern men and guns
In numbers we had never seen before.

We slowed them down with skirmish and melee,
Sharpshooters targeting the brigadier,
Battery captain, bolder NCO,
Our crossfire rebel yells heard far and near.

At other times we felt a brotherhood
When pickets on both sides would sing the same
Old songs of mothers, sweethearts, peace, and home
Along the Rappahannock and the James.

And we would trade tobacco, coffee grounds
On tiny sailboats drifting with the wind
And in our common tongue whisper debates
On how the war had started and would end.

Yet on this line fighting has never ceased
Though arms were stacked and swords made shares again
For we must hold the earth that holds our bones
Under the winter snow and summer rain.

So now we load new Enfields of the air
With bullet points for sermon, parley, speech,
And in this war of words our aim is true:
The enemy is never out of reach.

And while we keep our watch we wait on those
Who one day may see what and as we see,
Then take their stand beside us to resist
The abolitionists of history.

We are not statues, names of schools and streets,
But guardians of memory and myth,
Gray wraiths that will not rest until our own
Confederate reckonings are reckoned with.

For only then will constellations gleam
Like distant campfires where two armies are
And we will see at last through twinkling tears
Star Spangled Banners bright with Stars and Bars.

The Buried Dixie Cup

Saline, Bienville Parish, 1961-2021,
in a field not far from my maternal grandparents' house

So many years and still that paper cup
Stays buried in my mind as in the ground
Though memory and will would dig it up
And spill a boyhood's treasures all around:

Two soldiers locked in combat, blue and gray,
A Yankee and a Rebel bayonet
Crossing in some unchronicled melee
Where long lost brother toys are fighting yet.

Beside them, coins—a penny, nickel, dime—
A wheat-back Lincoln, chief and buffalo,
Liberty winged, each struck by place and time,
And one gold curl I cut to go below.

I scooped out sand where rows of corn once grew,
A Caddoan "old field" cleared of girdled trees

On wolds whose rippling hills were shaped anew
For ages by the tides of inland seas.

Then gently working the cup down in grains
Until pure sand gave way to sandy loam
I made a grave in Eden for remains
Of legends that had now become my own.

Years passed, and country kin, their house was sold,
And yet the cup would haunt me, sunken deep,
A story with an ending unforetold
Whose words would draw me on in waking sleep.

And so I took a road I knew so well
Through north Louisiana where it leads
To memory's grave and grave goods that compel,
The land and mind one map an old man reads.

The field was there, but by thick brush reclaimed,
Yet still I found the resting-place I made,
Wild corn stalks tall near things no marker named,
Tasseled like flags waved in the cannonade.

My splotched hands sifted sand from piles built up
Till in my palm I held them once again,
My soldiers, coins, discolored, but no cup,
Its elements dissolved by sun and rain,

Or curl whose strands had spiraled out of time
Like history itself, which in the end
Brings all that was and is to one full rhyme
As *Dixie* brims when all its meanings blend.

The Dixie Cup was invented by a Boston lawyer, was named after dolls made in New York City, was originally manufactured in Pennsylvania, and is now owned by Georgia-Pacific, an American pulp and paper company headquartered in Atlanta.

Beyond These Earthly Bonds: Reading the Southern Quarterlies

Come steaming from the shower into towels
I pat my pink skin dry then grope about
For tissue to clean my lenses and the glass
In which as sweating palms dispel thick mist
I feel again that periodic shock
When recognition lags behind the years

Till what one is and was seem disengaged.
The man inside the mirror looks at me
And I at him each gazing on a late
Submergence of identity in kin
Come back to flesh again in my own age—
My proud grandfather's jowls, a reddened face
And beer belly from uncles once despised,
My father's golden curls now frayed and gray,
Glints of a mother's country-gentry eye.
Such ghostly hosts transfigure present time
Beyond the moment and the momentous self,
Dull governors of this most craven age
With all its bitter ideologies
Abstracted by the will from sheer desire.
These musings soon suffused in the mirror's mist,
I slip into my robe and highbacked rocker
In which for years my father slowly died
And sip Earl Grey, the tea my mother loved,
Flipping through the southern quarterlies,
These autumn leaves imprinted rich and deep,
Looking for some rare poem reaching beyond
The drift of sense and sentiment in time
To touch the vivid givenness of things.
Such glinting hints Jacques Maritain proclaimed
The radiance of the ontic mystery:
Primal light made blatant in creation,
True beauty mimed in meter, silence, rhyme,
The valid spare abstractions, right and wrong,
A rhetor's voice declaiming public things,
The laden details' grave and happy access
To one who dwells beyond these earthly bonds
Disclosing those unshadowed habitudes
Now unconcealed, emblazoned in poiesis,
As when we see beyond the imaged glass
Some trace of that true self that always was
Hidden within each wrinkle, blotch, and scar
Or glimpse within the daybreak's natal glades
An unworn path to that still open gate,
God's postern by the Pishon's gleaming stream
Flowing below those laurels, oaks, and bays
That lead us into Eden when we come.

The Final Citadel

The mountains wait,
I said, in the long beat and rattle of siege
At cratered Petersburg. Too late
We sought the mountains and those people came.

> And Lee is in mountains now, beyond Appomattox,
> Listening long for voices that will never speak
> Again[.]
>
> "Lee in the Mountains," Donald Davidson

The Appomattox flows through Petersburg
East from the Piedmont and its fountainhead,
Joining the James to empty into the Bay,
Its blooded water salt and ocean blue.

The river moves through history as well,
By primal rock, shell fossil, Indian trail,
The corn patch and tobacco, cotton field,
The smoked-out stacks of cabin, plant, and mill.

The sun goes toward the Piedmont from the sea,
Then on above the Cumberland Plateau,
Its westward light declining where a man
Corrected, brought good order, page by page.

He edited his quarterly alone
For over forty years: a general
With troops positioned in the groves and fields
Of Academe—reports sent back and forth

Between his citadel and a frontline
Pressed yet holding, pickets driven in,
Defenders behind parapets, entrenched,
Veterans of the mine and mortar shell.

And he endured, like Lee at Petersburg,
Long under siege—attacked from north and south—
The Yankee left always flanking down
His thin gray line the blue waves rolled and broke.

So in the end he had nowhere to go
West of the mountains and that stormed plateau,
His citadel in ruins from torch and ball—
His Turnbull House—by total war destroyed.

And just as Lee rode Traveller alone
Into the hills outside of Lexington
He walked across that campus with his dog
By cindered stronghold to the resting-place

Of generals and bishops, lettered men—
Remains of Andrew Lytle, Allen Tate—
Graves graced each spring by a tiny Southern Cross
To mark Confederate Remembrance Day.

And of the generals long buried there
I call to mind Edmund Kirby Smith,
Late to surrender—June of '65—
In Galveston, with two republics dead,

Who had Dick Taylor fighting on the Red,
Keeping the Yankees out of my hometown—
Shreveport—through which no Appomattox flowed,
Last capital where the last flag came down.

Erasers

North Louisiana, 1959

They come back now from sixty years ago,
Not wholly on their own or by my will,
These memories that change yet stay the same,
All but effaced, though I can see them still . . .

The building was already decades old
When I went there to learn the elements,
A grade school that had been a high school once
For Cedar Grove when cedar trees grew dense.

But then the river city spread up hills
Absorbing crossroad, hamlet, village, town,
Some schools, like mine, repurposed and renamed,
And every one-room schoolhouse taken down.

So *Fairfield* would survive, its limestone, brick
Creating space for coolness, warmth, and light—
Tall windows, taller ceilings—ceiling fans
And coiled gas heaters keeping the air just right.

*

Each classroom had a blackboard made of slate
And underneath a finished pinewood tray
Where stubby chalk sticks lay in their own dust,
By hand and mind worn down till worn away.

There, too, were felt erasers, used and left
By teachers and their pupils being done
With sentences and problems, diagrams
Of knowledge and its one long proof begun.

My desk held other tools that grade by grade

Helped me to measure, read, write, make, construe—
A pencil, newsprint, compass, ruler, book,
Construction paper, crayons, scissors, glue.

And every year my latest teacher saw
How I worked best when doing so alone,
A quiet child, content with inwardness,
A boy to trust outside and on his own.

*

So in the hour before the final bell
Midafternoon I pushed back in my chair
Whenever I was called to gather up
Erasers white with dust from board and air.

I walked the long main hallway end to end,
Then passed through an arched side entrance under BOYS,
The ribbed erasers held against my chest,
And stepped down to a playground without noise.

Backstops and swings, hoops, monkey bars, a field
For racing, a knightly piggyback fight,
Or Smear where we would chase the outcast 'It'—
Yet not a child except for me in sight.

And there with absence and its solitudes
I made my way where I had gone before
Bringing the blocks of matted wool across
Mown grass that once had been a forest floor.

*

At last I reached the trees, two first-growth pines
Spared by the builders when they cleared the ground
And laid a school's foundation, leveled earth
By those tall trunks with sun and silence crowned.

Then one by one I beat the erasers hard,
Clouds rising from the bark and grooves and gum,
A ghostly image left on flaking plates,
Rectangles of a powdered calcium.

My duty done, I paused, then went straight back
And placed the cleaned erasers on their tray,
Ready below a blackboard once again
To lie in dust and wipe the dust away.

All this was long ago . . . a story told
When memories connect, as by design,

White chalk across a board of shale and clay,
Motes floating gold in light from pine to pine.

Of Literature and Life

for a mother whose son died at the age of twelve

But when my mind remembers, unamused
It pictures Korczak going with his children
Through Warsaw to the too substantial train.
Edgar Bowers, "In Defense of Poetry"

And round that early-laurelled head
Will flock to gaze the strengthless dead,
And find unwithered on its curls
The garland briefer than a girl's.
A.E. Housman, "To An Athlete Dying Young"

How moved you must have been to come to me
When the spring term was over, not to complain—
You knew you'd make a B—but wanting to say
In person what you could not say before.

The course was Understanding Poetry,
Offered to sophomores not in liberal arts
To satisfy the core curriculum:
Exposure—brief—to the Humanities.

Most students sat through class resigned and bored,
Willing to serve their time for sixteen weeks,
Cellmates with dreaming poets, eager to leave
For "the *real* world" with their B.S. degrees.

So I, to try to free them from themselves,
Assigned a two-part paper, "Lit. & Life,"
The students' task, to analyze a poem,
Then link it to a story of their own.

And you chose "To an Athlete Dying Young,"
An elegy and epitaph combined,
About a runner taken in his prime,
Not lingering till fame had turned to dust.

Your story made a sadder parallel.
It was about your son, a player skilled
At hitting fastballs hard against the wall,
Running the bases, sliding safely home.

But on an early summer afternoon,
Driving him from the game, the shoulder-ride
And trophy his to tell about and show,
You eased through a left-turn green light, seen too late

By a honking eighteen-wheeler skidding ahead,
Its swinging trailer smashing through the door,
Crushing a boy who died before your eyes,
Gone before you or he could say a word.

How long you searched for words, pleading with God
To give you understanding and a peace
Not found in years of therapy and prayer,
A consolation deeper than your grief.

Then, in good time, something would draw you here,
Not chance or fate alone but common grace
That led you to another like your son
Who died and lived again in Housman's verse.

And having said at last just how that poem
And paper had the power to touch and heal,
You left in tears, yet strengthened, not by me,
But by the virtue found in poetry.

I never saw or heard from you again
Though memory brings back from time to time
The image of a mother who returned
In gratitude for "literature and life."

And though I know that you were not alone
In writing on a poem you made your own,
Of all who might have come to tell me so
You were the only one who ever did.

~

Coda

Your story is from thirty years ago,
And I am long retired with the times
In which the kind of paper I assigned
Let likeness bring "relationship and love."

Now more and more a cored curriculum
In place of broad surveys of English verse
Tempts sophomores with some narrow "topics" class—
"Comic Book Zombies—The Apocalypse!"

And there, old canon poems, the living dead,

Dissected as *topoi*—mere rhetoric
Of politics and sex—are tagged with "trigger
Warnings" for those traumatized by fact:

Unflinching Homer fixed on severed heads
Whose lips still begged for mercy in the dust,
Apollo chasing Daphne into a tree,
Bull-raped Europa under the god's white thighs,

A floating dagger pointing toward the king,
Or lashed Fedallah gazing from the whale,
From this and more—hard givens of our myth—
The tenderhearted mind would turn away.

But you, who had no time to turn away,
Who had no warning—saw split-second death—
Took courage from consoling recompense
In lines about an athlete dying young.

To the Descended Muse

When I was young and prayed
Your image would descend
In eros without end
To the fertile verse I made,
You glimmered on the skin.
And when you let me in
Your rhythms would repeat
In ur-words indiscrete
Epiphanies of sense
Our poems would evidence.
But now that I am old
And the withered blood runs cold,
Sometimes I only see
Great Plato's shadow-hell,
Gray matter in its shell,
The atomized debris.
Then goddess I disown,
I would you were a fire
To burn away the bone,
Possess the mind alone
And ravish it entire
With knowledge, not desire.
Yet when I hear the hush
Of beauty in its rush,
Night-birds in the migrant air,
Willets prancing the sheen
On shallowed strands, the green

Ditches of wild aster,
I come to love again
Your dark incarnate skin
Whose sacrament I crave,
Tongued flesh in the shaded cave.

The Rear Guard's Report

What I am engaged in is a rear-guard action
R.L. Barth, 1983

We made them pay for every inch of ground
Battling in the capital street by street,
Their officers picked off as round by round
Our sniper fire postponed that last retreat

Where swarming in elation's disarray
They pressed but could not break our old formation
Or counter classic tactics of delay
Directed by that vet whose terse oration

Rallied us in these mountains where we lie
Waiting like fate while one by one they file
Through passes strait as at Thermopylae
Toward bayonets fixed, no quarter, final trial.

The Linker

in memory of Wilmer Hastings Mills (1969-2011),
fellow Louisiana poet, who called the poet a "linker"

Night deepens till the stars begin to gleam,
Then brighten one by one as by design,
All wandering yet fixed, all unaware
Of how they came to be or what they are,
Angels who bear the message of themselves
Beyond affection, hate, indifference,
Old torches tarred with dark, lit peak to peak
To flame out on the plains of nothingness.

Yet here, between a study's one dim lamp
And mansions blazed by heaven's blinding fires,
A poet's odes will glisten in the skies,
Aglow with every glowing star they praise
Till dawn will hold them all in that first light

The Linker on his porch looks up to find
When pages strung with lines have strung The Lyre:
Likemindedness between the mind and Mind.

My Father's Shop

'Has my lord dallied with poetry among the roses?'
Queen Guinevere

The king's poet ached with belated verse;
he took part against himself

of Taliesin, whose name means 'radiant brow'
Charles Williams, *The Region of the Summer Stars* (1944)

So many years . . . yet still I find you there
Pushing the pedal of your potter's wheel,
Shaping wet clay for the kiln's burning air–
Old elements that you could see and feel.

And from a lump well-turned arose a bowl
Or column, balanced, set, by thumb and palm,
Then bisque-fired, glazed, glaze-fired, and so made whole
By paint and flames that harden into calm.

You built that shop yourself–from slab to roof–
Detached from the house, your own place apart
Where you could dream, engaged, and yet aloof
As who and what you were emerged in art.

From boyhood through my teens at times I came
To watch you work till hand and eye would bind
Imagination, intellect–the same,
And you would sing the song of heart and mind.

Then in good time, I too sang, in my room,
Like Arthur's bard, of white knights, black despair
In adolescent poems of gloom and doom
And courtly love for blushing maidens fair.

And one such knight a well-born maiden wed
But in that bed where ice would glaze desire
Her passion took the form of formless dread,
His hands unskilled at bringing clay to fire.

And by my own rhyme broken I soon sought

A place where goodness, truth, and beauty met
In hands through which the whole man thought and wrought
And you, my father, shaping, singing yet.

You spoke, though hesitant, to your grown son
In that repressive Baptist atmosphere
About the art of love, and what is done,
The secrets of a craft at last made clear.

The craft was learned too late. The maiden fled,
Her cutting words a blessing and a curse,
The knight who bled forever on their bed
Nursing a wound whose healing made it worse.

Yet in that knight and bed a shaper lay
Who rose to work his verse through bisque and glaze,
Each deep-cut word steel-penned in tablet-clay,
His mind a kiln, his ways a potter's ways.

And like a potter when the wheel has turned
And kiln-doors open to a cooling shelf
With column, bowl, cracked or intact, he learned
That verse well-turned may turn against itself.

*

Father, your shop was torn down years ago—
And you long dead, and I not long to stay—
Yet both near Taliesin, brows aglow,
God's potters singing from and of the clay.

Bringing Home the Calf Born in the Fields

after the painting by Jean François Millet (1814-1875)

oil on canvas

1864

They know their way along the stony path
Worn down between the meadow and the barn,
Two peasants, holding poles level and low,
Bearing a newborn calf on golden straw.

Through tangled dark green canopies of trees
The distant pasture grass is barely seen,
Its soft young blades unhardened by the sun.

The mother cow, her udder full of milk,

Licks clean her calf still wet with afterbirth.
A woman tending to them looks away
From care that stays, while on a threshold stone
Two little girls, her daughters, watch and wait,

As still as they can be. The elder hugs
The younger from behind. They see the calf
As not unlike themselves, the nursing cow
As something kin to what they may become.

The two men take the newborn past a wall,
Their hats wide-brimmed, their heads in shadow bowed,
Their faces grave, their working clothes like robes,
Their rough hands clasping staves as they process.

They carry life at home with mysteries,
An ark with tablets, rod, and manna pot,
A maiden giving milk. her manger child
By animals beheld, by love sustained.

And from that place a calf looks out at us
Who see before, beyond it, deep within,
A creature's wonder meeting with our own
As each perceives the only world that is.

The Shepherdess

after the picture by Jean-François Millet (1814-1875)

c. 1870-74

black conté crayon and pastel on gray paper

Late in the day he drew them all as shades,
Shepherdess, flock, and dog on Chailly Plain,
This one last time rethought and rearranged,
Their twilight waiting just beyond the sun.

Then came the toned-down colors, dark pastels,
Except for her whose bearing is a prayer,
Head bowed and fingers counting, thread by thread,
Undimming as the earth and heavens fade.

The dog stays in the middle ground, apart,
His long watch into evening near an end.

Ewes gathered to the ram still feed in peace,
Tasting green blades they see as gray and brown.

The girl is fixed on work now well in hand,
Wool knitted from the very sheep she leads,
Yet has no shepherd's staff, for day is done,
And nothing there need ever move again.

This is an *Angelus* beyond the bells,
A girl shadowed by fire that dies away,
Unearthly in some palpable design
These shades of light and dark we comprehend.

Shepherdess Sitting at the Edge of the Forest

after the painting by Jean-François Millet (1814-1875)

ca. 1848-49

oil on canvas

No soul in all his work is more alone
Than this young girl here at the forest's edge,
Lost in rough clothing–cape, scarf, dress–head capped,
Her right hand close beside her, empty, still,

Her left holding a staff against her breast.
Before her lies a portion of a road
But where it goes and comes from, like the girl,
Remains unknown. Behind her, thick trunks seem

Too dense for even wind to penetrate.
The girl is staring down yet far away.
With no fold, sheep, or sheepdog, unaware.
This is the only painting Millet sent

To the Salon in 1849,
Not like his Captive Jews in Babylon
The year before, no epic Bible scene
Or pastoral dream from Fragonard, Watteau,

But this, just two hands high, so far beyond
The Paris Revolution he would leave,
A human muse who waited for him there
Beside the Fontainebleau near Barbizon.

Forest with Shepherdess and Sheep

after the painting by Jean-François Millet (1814-1875)

1849-50

oil on panel

Mornings he worked his garden row by row,
So near the Fontainebleau and Chailly Plain,
True use and beauty mingling when he sowed
Tomato seeds with seeds of marigold

That drives away the whiteflies with its scent.
Long afternoons he painted things he'd seen
By light that made his art and garden thrive—
Minders of herds and flocks from plain and wood

Or *potagers*—their soil in oils alive.
Then, when the light would fail at last, he'd go
Gathering scenes like seeds to plant and tend,
And once on such a walk he found a girl,

Her staff and body blending in the trees
Through which her sheep went straying as they grazed
Toward mushrooms in a damp and ample shade,
Some ground from which all arts and gardens come.

Shepherdess Knitting, Outside the Village of Barbizon

after the painting by Jean-François Millet (1814-1875)

ca. 1860-62

pastel over black conté crayon on laid paper

For years he put aside his bright pastels
That brought to mind rococo fantasies
Long ago abandoned—the slippered feet
Of Shepherd-Ladies kicking up above

Their filleted straw hats and petticoats
That ruffled as they swung in fragrant glades
Or danced with gamboling lambkins kept as pets.
Yet now that he had drawn them as they were,

Not dallying with beaux or crowned with flowers

But prodding flocks through twilight into night
He called his pastels back to paint this scene:
A girl below a boulder wreathed in leaves,

Lavender dress, blue cloak, and salmon cap,
Brown work shoes, staff, thick-knitted winter sock,
Her black sheepdog who'll turn away from sheep
Browsing under a moldering green bank

Toward those whose gaze intrudes on life and art,
A wall of beeches past the close-cropped grass,
And, in between, her red-roofed Barbizon,
The forest, village, plain a world apart.

Departure for Work

after the picture by Jean-François Millet (1814-1875)

ca. 1857-58

black conté crayon with pastel on cream paper

The dawn's last star is lost in morning light
Above a couple bound for tended land,
Taking a path worn down by clog and hoof,
Their dress and shirt a homespun peasant blue.

The woman rides sidesaddle, ladylike
But on a plodding donkey, reins relaxed,
A beast with burdens—basket, flesh, *panniers*—
Its head just turned along the well-known way.

The husband, armed for labor, walks behind,
Pitchfork on his right shoulder, at the hip
A short draw-hoe, hooked by his elbow crook,
His left hand in an empty pocket cupped.

They have what earth provides, a water jug,
And for their noonday meal potato-cakes
Or bread kneaded from stalks gleaned after yields—
Like bedding straw, when their first child is born.

Their faces stay expressionless and fixed,
As if the here and now were far away.
They know there is no flight and no return
Forever in this Egypt of the fields.

The Gust of Wind

after the painting by Jean-François Millet (1814-1875)

1871-73

oil on canvas

We keep our heads down as we have to do
Because this picture does, for thus Millet
Has kept things in perspective, made us safe . . .
What dominates the painting is unseen.

A wind-throw oak half torn from a blasted crest
Sends pulled roots searching upward for the earth.
One clump, unpulled, is reaching toward its tree
Buffeted by the gusting northerlies.

The storm leaves frothy ruffles in a stream
That flows before and under dip and rise,
Its jutting rocks forever worn away
By currents of the water and the air.

The oak holds on though leaning toward a man
Chased by a snapped branch clutching with its twigs.
The shepherd falters on toward scattering sheep.
His dog and crook are nowhere to be found.

Near distant rippling swells of autumn wheat
The dawn-fires wash stone houses, pens, and barns.
A spreading light turns orange on the ground.
The earth and sky are clouded and aflame.

Wind-bent, the shepherd bows before the sun,
Planting his feet in fear—then driven on.
The tree, too, seems aware and terrified.
We hear the primal waters in its leaves.

And in that rushing sound our heads stay down
Here in this world whose roots have been exposed
By atoms blasted outward, gust on gust,
Prevailing winds no painter can compose.

The Old Wall

after the painting by Jean-François Millet (1814-1875)

1862

oil on canvas

September in the later afternoon
A stag peers out through shadows in a breach
Where hunters pulled down sandstones from their wall
Between the ancient forest and the plain.

Atop the wall some browning ferns send roots
Probing the cool dry air for warmth and rain.
Antlers tilt back as smells are taken in.
The angling sunlight gleams on point and stone.

Not far beyond the gap, on open ground,
Come from reaped fields between the scythe and fire
A tuft of wheat-grass bends with spikelet seeds.
The harvest's last cut stalks are still ungleaned.

The buck is hesitant to leave the trees,
Old hardwood stands of locust, birch, and oak.
He knows the pathless ways to that safe place
Where does will bear his fawns in meadow-glades.

The forest floor was once the floor of seas,
Its sand through centuries washed white and fine.
Below, a Celtic city of the dead
With auroch horns among the human bones.

The stag lives in the moment and deep time,
Antlered Cernunnos hidden in a deer.
The wall, long weathered now, is cloudy gray.
Bared inner stones stay orange in the sun.

He needs to eat. The golden grain lies near.
The breach and wall both hold him. Ears are pricked.
He listens for snapped twigs, a trigger-click.
The scent of ready does is in the air.

Autumn Landscape with a Flock of Turkeys

after the painting by Jean-François Millet (1814-1875)

1872-73

oil on canvas

1

We see them all at once, then one by one:
The woman faced away—dress, cape, and hood
Darker than clouds backlit by a dropping sun,
Her long dry switch lopped clean from sessile-wood:

The hock cart left on ground ready to plow,
Wheat sheaves piled high and golden turning brown,
The lattice-gate still holding up for now
Against deadweight, tied bundles tumbling down:

A rocky hillock swelling toward its crest
Beyond which lie a cottage and what seems
A massive chimneystack whose smoke spreads west,
Pluming between drawn clouds and sinking beams:

A dwindling turkey flock where older droves
Once numbered in the hundreds and a girl
Would urge them on through upland sessile groves
To look for acorns when the leaves first curl:

And from those groves, the one tree that remains,
Its gnarled and scraggly branches stilled within,
So far from fruit and bloom and summer rains,
The winter solstice soon to come again.

2

The tree's last leaves are carried in the air
Before white birds caught up in cloud and light,
A mottled flock above Chailly-en-Bière,
Sublunar migrants bound toward moonless night.

The birds had perched on crenelated stone
Moments before—that chimneystack a tower—
Some rubble crumbling under when they'd flown
High away from abandoned keep and bower.

It was an open furnace for the town,

Stubble and durmast burning in the hall
Where spark and flake and ash all mingle down
Under those stars that wander till they fall.

The woman looks ahead toward deeper cold.
Her turkeys peck and scratch with beak and toe,
These New World birds at home within the Old,
Brought back by Jesuits from Mexico.

And who is she who drives them with a switch
Toward winter and an end that stays the same?
Death? Fate? Ourselves? All of these? Which is which?
This face unturned, this one we cannot name.

End of the Day

after the drawing by Jean-François Millet (1814-1875)

ca. 1852-54

black conté crayon with white highlights on blue-gray laid paper

The sun gone down too far for him to see
Through shadows on an easel he would walk
Among his subjects, all drawn home by dark,
Done for the day with work that's never done.

Potato diggers—husband, wife—still fixed
On separate tasks, he, putting on his coat,
His pitchfork thrust in loam, she, tying a sack
To heave into their donkey's grass *panniers*,

A shepherd on the hillcrest, flock and dog,
Gray wraiths rubbed in by a crayon's black stub,
Heading toward woods too dense for grove or glade:
Such fixed solemnities would hold Millet,

The rounding hours and seasons of the earth
Marking the end of day and all our days
On ground we till, manure, sow, tend, and reap,
Then burn and till again for dung and seed

Before the sunset deepens into dusk
Beyond which dawns the first and last of stars
Glowing toward Egypt's fields while dying bright
Both into and against the coming night.

After Rembrandt's *Philosophe en méditation*

1632

A pensive man sits near a table placed
Against a window-ledge, now gazing down
Upon the blank stone floor, turning away
To ponder questions prompted by his book.

Across the room a woman, bent, intense,
Shifts wood with tongs to stoke a hearth's low flames,
Bringing back heat needed for warmth and food.
Between the two a staircase spirals high,

Steps rising into dark at their first turn,
Then further steps seen only from below.
Above the book, in golden light aglow
Plain glass, far from the hearth, is stained bright cold.

The old philosopher has paused, perplexed,
Mind winding like bare stairs up into night,
Longing for Plato's sun yet ever held
To earth by a fire's clasping iron tongs.

Lecturer in Old Age

The Teacher is no longer the Sage on the Stage
But the Guide by Their Side
a modem educationalist

I shuffle now where once I briskly strode
From classroom door to lectern there to place
A tattered textbook three editions old
With yellowed notes to match each yellowed page.

Above desk-chairs all etched with lovers' names
Rapt faces fix aglow on laptop screens,
Fingers raised up, ready to tap out notes
And scroll whole epics down in their machines.

Outside my class they're "paperless," they say,
Their libraries held in flash-driven microchips,
Blackboard to them a system, not a place
Where chalk sticks shed bright dust in waiting trays.

They see me chained, a shade in Plato's cave,
A prisoner not yet come into the sun,

A troglodyte who scrawls on lightless walls
So far from PowerPoint's transparencies.

Yet sacred wood survives, the Logos' ghost
Ingrained for good and ever in the mesh
Of hand and spine and page where words root deep,
Their essence fleshed where no hard drive can fail.

I do not let them break out in small groups
Or bring by essay-drafts for free critique,
My red pen always ready, full of ink
For in-class themes that make them sweat and think.

And so behind this lectern like a priest
With pulpit Bible open to the verse
His sermon drives hard home till hearers shiver
I stick to my old dictum: *stand and deliver.*

Epigrams and Briefer Lyrics

Coda

What is this knowledge one
Cannot elect to know?
The eternal washing and
Unwashing of the soul.

No unsuspected flood
Within the coral mind,
Enlacements alkaline
Engulfing dark with blood.

Inviolable this grief:
Experience that breaks
And breaks upon belief,
The breakers on the reef.

*

Skydiving over Acadie

Spread-eagle in a rush of high thin air
Suffused with sun, suspended in descent
She feels so free of what awaits her there,
An ancient ground that draws her though a tent

As silken as the flesh between her thighs

Will end this dream in which she still is caught
Thrilling over Gaea in Jove's bright skies
Till fear weds prudence and the string's pulled taut.

*

Husbandman: Of the Pastoral Poet

for Harry Duncan, Poet and Bookmaker

Green seedlings set in these
Rich beds well turned and tended
By one whose craft has mended
Matter and mind's divorce
Now flower from the source
Of mystery and presence,
The gathered scents of essence,
Pressed blooms from Eden's trees.

*

Of Water and of Fire

Thales or Heraclitus–who was right, or close enough?
Whose element could be the groundless ground, the primal stuff?
Or was it something other, or was nothing to be found
Beyond Hercules' Pillars (both a portal and a bound)
In twilights of Ionia at Ocean's endless bars,
Suns going down in flames below the waters of the stars.

*

Reading *John 1* by Twilight

The day is done, the opened verses heard
Faintly by one now failing in old age
When moons, not suns, illuminate the Word,
A cold pure light prevailing on the page.

*

In Advent: For John Finlay

From *A Garland for John Finlay* (1990)

You know the flesh and soul's profoundest night
Marked out by that Thomistic intellect
Whose terms, now as ever, lead you to expect
To find in utter darkness utmost light.

*

In Extremis

"in the farthest reaches"

Where word and thing, enwoven, are as one,
From grain to angel spoken into place
In radiant scales of grace notes by a Grace
Whose Word will come to nothing and declare
That symphonies of Mind-and-bone are done,
All raveling in the silent light and air.

*

History of an Idea

after J.V. Cunningham

"I Am That I Am" God said to Moses;
But nowadays all anyone knows is
"I gotta be me," as Me proposes.

*

After Etienne Gilson

1. For the Thomists

God made us out of nothing, it is true,
But, tell me, did He make the nothing, too?
And if He made the nothing, as you say,
What ever did He make it of, I pray?

2. Nocturne

O fallen stars, returning to a night
So wholly cold, the old and holy mere,
What darkness ever vanished into light
Or kissed the golden fissures of your tears?

*

God the Father

Authentic absolute of perfect will,
Lost immanence of all that we disdain:
Now you have gone, your image drains to nil
Till mind alone is sacred and profane.

*

Midwinter Stars

Enlighteners, who plot your long divorce
From one whose will divines its own demise:
What undersong, untuning at the source,
Evades your bright design beyond devise?

*

Plotinus on Dying

As body founders, merging with its night,
The mind, enmeshed in blind consistencies
Of flesh, distends, aground in surgent seas,
Flaring in underplains of actless light.

*

Pieta

So long bemused, and afterwards aware,
Beyond intent, I countenanced your face.
The line that shapes my intellect, your grace:
It is the lord, Agape, whom we bear.

St. Peter's, Rome, 1968

*

To the Father

Even here, even now, in this distress
Of seeking and not seeking you I find
Your absence takes the image of a mind
In wordless shade, the matter you express.

*

S.J., i.m.

God's Holy Word, good sense, the classic past—
These molded your devotions to the last.

The Complete Christian

after Samuel Johnson's Latin poem *Christianus Perfectus*

Whoever in a holy way would find
Himself brought back to Christ's compelling mind
Should try to wipe away the world's deep stain
Neither grasping at fleshly delights in vain
Nor being swollen up with pride past his degree,
But standing always on what's yet to be
And plucking thorns of terror from the heart
Should take all God's kind will may yet impart.
Then, too, no one should ever be to blame
For loving the world if that love is the same
Unlimited enclosure of devotion,
Most holy, always ready to endure affliction,
Eager to pardons acts that go amiss,
Delighting in forgiveness; and, for this,
Consecrated flames should glow within the soul
That life may be made sacred and made whole.
God, first and last, he ought to please, not offend,
That the course of such a life might never end.
And though, a sinner in time, he feels oppressed
By madness and self-hatred, in his breast
He'll find a place both safe and right for him.
And he should never waver or for a whim
Go off at times in this or that direction
Nor doubt the Lord, but in faith's recollection
Give up to Christ his heart and mind entire
Despising mortal things for one desire.
He ought ever to fear and take good care
Never to be like the common crowds who dare
Sever themselves from laws they should obey,
Laws which lazy souls let slide away
Fitting necks to easy yokes, as though insane,
To avoid faith's full work that's only done with pain.
God wants nothing great to fall out of its place
But asks by right for all He gave in grace.
So, at last, straining high, the Christian aspires
Perpetually with that help he now requires
To keep straight on and clearly understand,
Sensing within each act God's kind command.
Thus, by degrees, good habits will reform
His life and mind, according to the norm,
And he will be, as far as it is given,
Like God and leave the things of earth for heaven.

Taking Down the Tree

some sixty years ago

We put up this year's tree on Christmas Eve,
Anglicans now, waiting on Advent's end,
The four wreath candles, violet and rose,
Guttering under wicks too short to trim.

*

The tree was from the north, a balsam fir,
Cut off above the stump, then shipped down south
To live a while in milder winter air,
Stacked in a lot till bought and taken home
To be a fragrant twelve-day Yuletide sign,
Held steady in the old stand's metal bowl,
By pointed blade and twisted screw secured.

We watered it from time to time, and yet
Needles still dried and fell among the gifts,
Browning on boxes yellow, red, and gold
With ribbons curled and knotted into bows.

White lights were strung around uplifted limbs,
Spiraling down below the treetop star
Through bubble candles, crocheted flakes of snow,
Icicle strands cascading toward glass balls
A great-grandmother painted, just three left
Unshattered by a careless brush or drop.

*

The children gone to bed, though not to sleep,
Watching a clock whose hands are nearly still,
Their mother, all her work done, under quilts,
Guarded in dream by her own helper elves,
I stay awake and put out unwrapped gifts
From one in whom the youngest still believes.
Then fill the stockings up with jelly rings,
Peppermint bark, and twisted candy sticks.

*

The fire is out below the stocking-hooks
Although a log is smoldering aglow,
And there I stop, looking up at the tree.

*

And not just at a tree but at a world,
From water at the bottom to a star
And in between a galaxy of lights
On branches with their people, beasts, and things,
A caroler, a church mouse, and a horn,
A crèche of woven straw where angels sing.

These images in mind I go to bed
Till wakened by the children half-past four.

Their mother makes them wait till prayers are said.

Then in no time at all toys, books, and games
And other gifts are claimed: an Alamo
And a Civil War playset for the boys,
Jewelry stands and girl-bikes for the girls,
Hardbacks of the Hardy Boys and Nancy Drew,
Monopoly for them all to grow into,
Scrabble and Clue, for words and mysteries.

The children find and lose themselves in play.
But day has peaked at dawn. Elation fades
Through morning and the long slow afternoon,
With naptime, weighing heavy, just fought off,
Then early bed, and making up lost sleep.

*

The wrapping paper, ribbons, paperboard
All bagged and thrown away, we leave the fir
Still decorated, still lit up at night
For twelve more days, waiting on three more gifts,
The Wise Men's gold, and frankincense, and myrrh
For one who had been born to be a gift
Not under but upon another tree,
The king of earth and heaven, and of death.

*

Then time at last for taking down our tree,
The ornaments in tissue gently laid,
The caroler, the church mouse, and the horn,
Their box the box they came in years ago,
Its corners torn, its snowflakes worn away,
Victorian glass balls unbroken still,
Brought up the attic ladder to a dark
Where they will stay unseen and out of mind

Though glowing yet awhile in children's dreams.

Then checking limbs for anything we've missed,
Its stand removed, we drag the shedding tree
Out to the roadside where it slowly dies
Without its roots or water, unadorned,
A symbol now of nothing but itself.

*

And all down the street we see the other firs
Put out from other houses where a truck
Will stack them flat and take them to the dump.

*

But through deep nights of this Epiphany,
Anglicans who would liken thing to thing,
We look up at the sky as at a tree,
Its taproot, top, at either end of time,
Old oceans both above it and below,
Its branches strung with stars, the icy trails
Of comets, and the moons and planets hung
To hook around their paths around a sun,
The spinning balls of water, gas, and rock,
Galactic candles wheeling in their wreathes.

*

And with the naked eye, or telescope,
We try to understand as best we may
The only gift but one the Maker gave,
The mystery of creation, birth and death,
And of our being here to be and see,
Reaching like balsam firs toward Northern Lights
And past their solar flares to a fixed North Star,
Wondering as we ponder how a night
Will come at last as it was meant to come,
With all the decorations put away,
When time is right for taking down The Tree.

Nunc Dimittis: Two Experimental Poems (2018-2020)

More Than Words Can Say

written after doing a program on poetry and music for the Thibodaux Music Club in the Parish Hall of St. John's Episcopal Church, October 10, 2018

These fragments I have shored against my ruins
T.S. Eliot

I have made a heap of all that I could find.
David Jones, translating from Nennius' *Historia Brittonum*

All things are twofold, one opposite the other, and he has made nothing incomplete. One confirms the good things of the other . . .
Ecclesiasticus 42: 24-25

1

Late winter nights he reads his book of stars
By light that casts bright shadows on the page,
The captured flattened depths, the gleaming sheen,
World pictures in a single picture framed,
Bringing him word of things unseen before,
Grounded abstractions glimpsed in the misty grain,
Unburied skeletons of ghost and bone,
Their last remains immortal on the shore.

2

He holds creation open in his hands,
The color photographs of galaxies,
Pixels of atoms and their atmospheres,
Ptolemaic correlations, coming round,
Elliptical and wayward as they stay,
Swayed by the uncorroborated gods,
Epics of ice and fire, of rock and dust,
Old chronicles beyond interpreters,
A world of worlds inscribed in nothingness,
Spontaneous proposals, free as fate,
The given, the un-given, and the found,
Sojourners moving to and from their home,
The point of everything their starting point,
Inerrant in their plotted wanderings,
Strangers in some strange fellowship akin,
Adopted and abandoned, kept apart,

The matter of apocalyptic psalms,
Their parallels balancing clause by clause—
The Serpent, Virgin—Libra in between,
The golden discs and chains, the Maker's Scales—
Verses reversed, reflections of themselves,
Turned and returning, cycling line to line,
Beginnings inconceivably complete,
Repeating with original response,
Unlisted catalogues of goodly stuff,
The one thing done the only thing undone,
Said lyrics for the music of the spheres,
A language "understanded," of the tongue,
The hand of Cranmer steady in the flame,
The Norman, Saxon, Latin all transposed,
Made plain in stately rhythm, simple phrase,
Vernaculars archaic, obsolete,
Current through eons, coinage of the realm,
The grammar of creation fitted, fit,
The sentence going on beyond its end,
Inscriptions scored, incisive and precise,
Case, number, tense, and person making sense,
The telling prefix, suffix, stem, and root,
Eternal chapters finished just in time,
The cursive flourishings of *ur-* and *ens,*
The starlight in the window on the page
From stars that died the moment they were born,
Brought down by Hubble arcing round and round—
A silence ringing true in stellar bells,
Their changes ranging constant as the hours—
By Voyager sent back while sailing on
Toward some most distant Ithaca no man knows,
The final island where each flowering vine
Is native and invasive and at home
By towers whose walls are burning on the shore
Beyond the planets and their pebble moons,
Beyond the bubble of the heliosphere,
Beyond the domination of the sun,
O how he learns to grasp them, weigh and praise!
Saved by a late revival of the eyes.

3

He moves his index finger word by word
Under the captioned photographs and charts,
A radiance translated from the page,
The Deep itself upwelling, mired in fire,
The lordly correlations, ranked and named,
Doves hovering above the governed tongues

Sworn to an ancient liberty they restrain,
Not even Einstein, Ptolemy at odds,
Wayfarers on the way to here and there
Where what is known is never wholly known,
The mysteries of fact and common sense,
The sheer unlikely likelihood of things,
God's *That* and *What* obligatory gifts,
The lettered essences from A to Z,
Lections no editor can rectify,
The toppled columns at the ledgers' edge,
The pastured stars still grazing in their flames,
Fall slaughtering in houses, holes, and zones,
The Farmer making night-rounds, field and yard,
Digging up boundary-stones where none were laid,
Exploring shores beyond the reach of seas,
Glaciers in the hayfields, fossil-shells
Imprinted on the inland mountaintops,
Washed up by tides still ebbing as they swell,
(Way stations on the only way to go),
The weathervane and road sign pointing on,
The astral tabulations graved in fire,
The scattered patternings that loose and bind,
Findings beyond judgment, verdicts unconfirmed,
The bitter hemlock, vinegar, one cup,
Socrates and his questions on the cross,
Christ dead in Athens, finished with his friends,
Peter's rooster, a cock for Asclepius,
Torn pages from the star book's book of hours.

4

The mind inhabits its own world, this world,
Knowing itself by what it can perceive,
Perceiving what itself alone can know,
Peering far off through telescope or probe,
Scanning deep space for measure, stave, and rhyme,
Sojourning toward a home it never left,
A place strangely familiar, all but named,
A grammar school of atoms parsed apart,
Elements only numbers diagram,
Foundations quaking under their own ground,
The turbulent universals, battered facts,
The given that the mind would give a voice,
The deafening proclamations' faintest strains,
Things that would sing of things their state declares,
Telling the story they were made to tell,
This book of stars the stars themselves compose,
Epiphanies midwinter clarifies,

Their matter scored for elegiac lyres,
Word music of the music of the spheres
For Lyra rising, star beams yet unstrung,
As taut and haunted as they always are
When poets write and read the selfsame text
Whose telic metaphors would show the way
Should "like as unto" be the likely end
And words be something more than words can say.

*

Evensongs

> At evensong survivors sang and prayed.
> We turned aside to perish with the saved.
> "Reliquiae," 1974

i.

Grown old, and growing older, not caring
As one should care, hardly able to care,
Familiar things held dear now passing strange,
Enticing in their rapt indifference,
A universe come out of nouns and verbs,
The dying birth cry, snow dust on the bud,
Sojourning clouds staying unshaped, untouched
By our interpretations–matter detached,
Waves breaking on the rocks they wash away.
Those pitiless pietàs without tears.

ii.

Harps in the trees, the fiddle on the wall,
Old waters calmed by words troubled once more,
Incarnate nothing's uncreated face,
The silence letting language have its say,
Translation's seeds plowed under, line by line,
Soon rooting deep and flowering in time,
Tautology and paradox at one,
A there that was not there before it was,
The ground always moving under our feet
As we look around, both up and down, at
Oblivion's star-point epiphanies.

iii.

The mystery remains, a presence felt
Until the senses weaken and the mind
Is ready to hold on to letting go,
Odysseus on the raft, no land in sight,
Borne on and on forever on the swells
Beyond the burning houses of the stars,
And nature in its veils of nakedness,
The seven sins and virtues in a dance,
Partners changing, the games of masks and names,
All these a dream within a dreamless sleep,
And death abed our breathless paramour.

iv.

And yet . . . whatever is is surely given,
The syntax of largesse whose timeless verbs,
A fundamental wonder, conjugate
Person and number, tensing moods and modes,
Heavenly etymologies unearthed,
The accidents and essence of a thing,
Kingdom to species, like the water thrush,
Its song descending note by warbled note
Voicing the hillside stream by which it lives,
Both resident and migrant, in accord.
The Psalmist's *Selah* breaking from the strings.

v.

And so with wanting magnanimity
We must be satisfied, yearning to care,
Be cared for, hale, yet nearly out of breath,
Placing our long lost faith in that good day
When noon was of a night no light shone through
Until a twilight dawned midafternoon
And timely hours of sun and moon and star
Would mark a sacred waiting, remembrance
Of what had been as what again would come,
The signs and seasons stations on a way
Where evensong and lauds are sung as one.

Going Home (i-iii)

i.

Out to Pasture

The old workhorse nibbling his winter hay
In pastures near the barn his tilling filled
Nudges and snorts against this stroking hand,
A farmer-poet's whose turned verse once spilled
On pages plowed by pen-nibs like a land
Where wingless Pegasus now whinnies soft,
As twilight darkens in the barn's cold loft,
We've had our day and say.

ii.

A Child's History of Reading

Before you learned to read you'd lay your head
Against my heart, then snuggle up to look
With sleepy eyes at bedtime's storybook
Whose pictures figured forth the words I said.

For years you lingered there among your kind
In Pan's Neverland, Pooh's Hundred Acre Wood,
Edenic places, simple, true, and good
Like Mother Goose's England of the mind.

Then you became a woman and you crossed
Bleak regions far beyond those happy dells—
Lyonesse, Lear's heath, Dante's and Eliot's hells—
Badlands sacred to the chosen and the lost.

Yet one day soon, with your own child to hold,
In those old love-worn storybooks you'll see
That once upon a time will ever be
Till time's unending story has been told.

iii.

After Johnson's Final Prayer

5 December 1784

Highest God, to whom the heart's dark inner rooms
Stand open, from whom no lust or trouble
Ever escapes, no guile conceals one sin;
Who contemplate the universe you rule:
By the Holy Ghost expel from sordid mind
The mortal dregs of earth. Let this be done
So that in us your love may hold its sway,
And bring to sluggish tongues fit eloquence
That every voice may ever speak your praise.
For nations in all ages, as he wished,
With merits earned, Christ freely has atoned,
For each of us, by his own blood alone.

AFTERWORD

Painting with Words: My Life as a Louisiana Poet North and South
A Reading and Commentary by David Middleton

Delivered Before the New Orleans Fine Arts Club on November 9, 2020

North Louisiana:

My life as a poet who paints with words began many years ago in my hometown of Shreveport, Louisiana. My father, David Vernon Middleton, Jr. (1922-1996), was a founding member of the Shreveport Contemporary Art Group, which brought Modernism to northwest Louisiana after the Second World War. One member of the group–Clyde Connell (1901-1998)–has won international recognition with shows in Paris and New York.

As a child, I was privileged to live in this Shreveport art world, and I recall the long visits to Clyde Connell's studio and house first at the State Penal Farm (where her husband was supervisor) and later on Lake Bistineau, the art exhibits at Centenary's Magale Library and Meadows Museum, the Barnwell Art Center by Red River, and the Louisiana State Exhibit Museum; and the many hours at home watching my father work in his studio and shop in watercolors, oils, pen and ink, acrylics, wood, and clay. To me the smell of oil paint is an aroma of the soul, and my love of vivid images in poems comes from that art.

From my father's world of art I also remember most vividly those long Sunday afternoons when members of the Contemporary Art Group were busy hanging a show at the Louisiana State Exhibit Museum while I circled again and again the museum's rounded hall gazing at Curator H.B. Wright's wonderful dioramas of Louisiana life–Indians, oil wells, salt mines, slave cabins, plantations, cane and cotton fields–and especially at that magnificent topographical map of the state railed off and sunken down into the museum's floor. I mused upon and pondered that map not knowing at the time that I was absorbing a symbol of the essential subject of poems I would write a quarter century later.

My father, who died of Parkinson's Disease, once made a sketch of me as a boy straddling the thick low limb of an oak atop a hill outside my grandparents' house in Saline, a village in Bienville Parish where I came to know north Louisiana rural life, its flora and fauna, its weather and geography. That sketch, unfortunately now lost, remains emblematic to me of our shared lives as artists and is the of subject my poem "For an Artist with Parkinson's":

So still beside the window in a chair
Whose wheels you cannot move and barely clutch,
You scan with eyes harsh medicine has blurred
A winter world once rendered by your touch.

Black seedpods and a last few orange leaves
Crackling in dwarf crape myrtles, stark pecans
Mistletoed and bared of leaf and nut, grackles
Cracking berries in the frosted holly groves—
All these you stained in ink, the pot's baked glaze,
Or brought alive in oils—those earthen shades
Made from the very things whose shapes they made.

When you were in your prime I was a child
Held tight in the softened muscles of your hug
Riding on your shoulders while the spring
Grew wild with buttercups and ladybugs.
On summer days, heat pouring from above
Beat strong on your hard arm that hammered down
Long boards to roof a workshop where you wrought—
Absorbed in the timeless habitude of craft—
God's objects set aflame with human love.
And though your gift was modest, still in kind
You knew the joy of Buonarroti's mind.

One day in fall now forty years ago
You took me to a sloping melon field
That crested in an oak whose thickest limb
I straddled as you sketched me from below.
Evasive of your gaze grown so intense
I stared down at the dried and shriveled vines,
Dreaming of greenest rinds in late July
And heard in the still green needles of the pine
Faint windblown strains refining to a quiet
In which a newborn gift delayed by grace
First stirred as you shaded-in my gazing face.

Now you are old and ill beyond all art
Yet just as when you sketched me on the day
My head of curls was wreathed in curling leaves
And I was drawn and chosen we still serve
The Giver of our gifts: for when I draft
Quiet poems upon this table whose thick top,
Split with hard use, you covered up at last
With plastic sheets held taut by roofing nails
My pen moves where you painted, stained, and glazed
Giving for years to beauty and the muse
Those hands a child had thought would never fail.

But in addition to my father and the Shreveport art world there was also Miss Caroline Dormon (1888-1971), Louisiana's famous naturalist, who lived just outside Saline at Briarwood where she grew and studied native Louisiana flowers, observed and wrote about our birds, participated on the state and national levels in conservation projects, and composed and illustrated her great books on Louisiana birds and wildflowers.

Since my maternal grandparents lived in Saline, I grew up knowing "Miss Carrie" but simply as an older woman who lived in a cabin outside of town and made pictures of and wrote books on Louisiana flowers and birds. I did not know that she was world-renowned. (As I'm sure you know, as members of the New Orleans Fine Arts Club, some of Caroline Dorman's works are exhibited at Long Vue House in New Orleans where "Miss Carrie" is honored each April on the annual Louisiana Iris Day.)

"Miss Carrie" encouraged me with my poetry some years later both in person and by letter. I will never forget the remarkable experience of watching at a distance as she called down out of the wildwood birds of many species that alighted on her arms and hands to take the seeds she had placed there. This union in one extraordinary woman of the botanist, the painter, the gardener, the conservationist, and the writer has remained with me as an example of the unity of being for which as a mature poet I have always striven.

My poem on her life and her influence on me is entitled "Calling Down the Birds—in memory of Louisiana naturalist Caroline Dormon (1888-1971)":

1.

You saw them just the way they really were,
Those flowers in your gardens and the wild,
Studied, preserved, in earth and paint and words,
The naturalist and artist of one mind.

The red woodbine and orange-yellow phlox,
Greenbriar, blue larkspur, nodding indigo,
The violet oxalis—rainbow names—
A covenant in pastoral catalogue.

You knew the birds as well, the goldfinch, wren,
The swallow, warbler, sparrow and the food
They loved to eat, calling them from the trees
To peck up at your feet the sprinkled seed.

And you would stay at Briarwood—birthplace, home—
Secluded in a wold's uplifted hills,
Your cabin, grounds, a modest green estate
By wisdom and solicitude maintained.

And there some April dawns a pineland quiet
Would draw you on toward spots in partial shade
Good for Celestials, common once, now rare
In north Louisiana's well-drained clays.

Their sky-blue petals graceful on the stem,
They open in midmorning, shrivel at noon,
Then die before their first and only day

Darkens toward far-off clusters of the stars.

And you remembered how their meadowlands
Once flowered around Old Shreveport to its edge,
Now ringed with plants and neighborhood escapes
Lying like slabs above the dusty bulbs.

2.

I came from Shreveport often as a boy
To visit kin close by you, in Saline,
And I would ask to share your solitude
By following and watching for a day.

You taught me birds you named by sight and song
And let me smell new cuttings taking root,
Species at threat that you would propagate,
Their wildness spared and thriving in your care.

And once, when I brought down those early poems
You read and complimented, being kind,
Sensing how I was trying to say my way
Back home to that same place you never left,

You had me stand apart, yet almost near,
Then called the autumn birds from bough and sky
To come to earth and eat Celestial seeds,
This time from open hands you lifted up

Toward feathers cloudy-black and iris-bright,
A kingdom needing peace, a saving grace,
A mixed flock growing larger by your love,
Still trusting that first promise you had made.

*

South Louisiana:

But even though north Louisiana is my native ground, I have deep roots now in South Louisiana as well. I spent most of the 1970s at LSU in Baton Rouge earning my M.A. and Ph.D. in English and learning how to write traditional metrical verse—as opposed to free verse—under the guidance of my major professor, Dr. Donald E. Stanford, himself a formalist poet and editor of LSU's world famous literary quarterly, *The Southern Review*, founded in 1935 by Cleanth Brooks and Robert Penn Warren. It was during those LSU years that I met my future bride and wife now of forty-four years, Francine Anne Kerne, who is with me today and who served for over thirty years at Nicholls State University in Thibodaux, Louisiana as a librarian. Fran is designated a master craftsman in whitework by the State of Louisiana, and, as I once wrote in a poem, we have shared our lives as artists: "Thereafter, when they wove their words and threads / They were each other's muse and truly wed." (I should add that it was also at LSU that I met one of your members, Dr. Lee Pitre, who invited me to speak today.) Since the 1970s, I have lived in Thibodaux, Louisiana where I was professor of English at Nicholls State University and Poet in Residence until my retirement in 2010. So South Louisiana has long since also been my home.

Two of my painterly poems set in south Louisiana are "Blue Herons" and "Hurricane Baby." "Blue Herons" combines direct observation of these birds with research I did in books on Louisiana birds. If I have done my job properly as a poet, you should not be able to tell the difference in the poem between what I saw and what I read about:

> The morning sun inclines us toward its light
> Spreading above scrub willow and the sedge
> Where swamp gives way at last to marshy ponds
> Of pickerel, fire flag, and arrowhead.
> And there in mangle-brush and roseau cane,
> Black mangrove, matted bulrush, and the dense
> Old water-groves of tupelo and gum
> Or high within the doming cypress-stands
> We see the great blue herons in their nests,
> Each platform with its clutch of pale green eggs.
>
> Hatched out by June in softest natal down,
> The birds become tall stalkers in their prime
> Deliberate in movement through the pools
> Darting at minnows, frogs, and dragonflies.
> Their colonies remain throughout the year
> Though when the northern flocks that breed in cold
> Then gaze toward polar wastes of ice and snow
> Are drawn back south by some still hidden sign
> Our residents call out when they return
> Alighting on the islands and the coast.
>
> We make no noise yet when we start to go
> The herons cry and climb as toward a home,
> In columned drafts between the Gulf and sun,
> Alive in fiery light above the foam.
> Bright heirs of an almost winterless domain,
> They hear our voices rising as they glide
> Higher in time's elation and declare
> That time is but a flyway to the side
> Of one who calls all creatures by their names,
> His timbre their intention on the course.

A shorter south Louisiana poem is entitled "Hurricane Baby." As a north Louisianian, I had never encountered the term "hurricane baby" until I overheard it used by two old men standing in line to restock on liquor at a grocery store in

Thibodaux after electricity had been restored in town following a hurricane. The men agreed that, nine months hence, the birth of "hurricane babies" would cause a spike in the birth rate since—and this was before generators in private homes were as widespread as they are now—when a hurricane strikes and the power goes out and time weighs heavily upon them young couples do (more and more) what comes naturally:

Hurricane Baby

They lie there in the golden afterglow
Of hurricane and twilight and the slow
Powerless hours through which they'll stay so still
Till air moves cool past each wet windowsill.
Outside spent gales adrift in sweet release
Blow mild by flattened cane until they cease
While herons high in cypress preen and sleep,
Their hours those primal hours all beings keep.
And with the clocks, A/C, and TV dead,
No light for books, they have the dark instead
In which he turns to touch, then kiss her there
Lost in a gentle storm of flesh and hair.

My first two full-length collections of verse, *The Burning Fields* (1991) and *Beyond the Chandeleurs* (1999), were both published by LSU Press. Each volume contains many poems set in either North or South Louisiana. So, at the turn of the millennium, I had said all I could think of to say at that time about our state and needed a new subject. Given my background in the art world, I thought I would try writing a poem based on a picture.

I chose a painting by the nineteenth-century French artist Jean-François Millet (1814-1875). Like many young artists, Millet began his career by depicting subjects from Greek and Roman myth or from the Bible and by imitating past masters. (I did the same in my earlier poems.)

In time, Millet found his true subject: the peasants who worked the fields and tended flocks of sheep either in Millet's native Normandy or just outside the small city of Barbizon where Millet settled after a few years of living in Paris. Born in the village of Gruchy, Millet himself came of peasant stock and once said, "I was born a peasant, and a peasant I shall remain."

In his pictures, Millet—without sentimentally overly idealizing them—raises these almost medieval peasants of late pre-industrial France up to a level of dignity, sometimes even tragic dignity, traditionally reserved in literature and the other fine arts for persons of high station—persons such as kings and queens, princes and generals.

Little did I know at the time, but by turning to Millet I was actually returning to the North Louisiana of my youth, a place which at that time still retained much of its own nineteenth century agrarian, pre-industrial way of life. Millet called his pictures "The Epic of the Fields," thus elevating peasant labor to the level of an epic poem by Homer, Virgil, or Milton. My poem on Millet led, quite unexpectedly, to fifty-nine more such sixteen-line poems over a three-year period (2000-2002). I will close my talk this morning by reading two Millet poems.

The first one is entitled "Goose Girl Bathing." A "goose girl" was a young girl who from about age three to puberty had the job of shooing the family geese back and forth between the barnyard and a pond. This was her first job on the farm. It ended when she reached her teens:

Goose Girl Bathing

ca. 1863

Late morning and secluded in the cool
Of May's green banks and boughs, this hidden stream,
A girl perhaps fifteen sheds all her clothes
And rests beside the waters where she'll bathe.

Her geese and ganders paddle in the wet
Where she as yet but dips one ankle in,
Her gangling body rounding out in soft
Womanly contours—thighs, hips, belly, breasts.

She's been the family goose girl thirteen years
And knows her time as such is near its end.
Between the trees of life and innocence
She stares at her reflection's steady change.

Above her, in dense foliage, two white cows
See all that young men soon will vie to see:
Flesh warming toward its noon in rose and blue,
Those filtered sun-shafts rippling in the depths.

*

A decided preference for focusing on art about subjects other than oneself also links Millet and me. In my poem on his picture entitled "Self-Portrait," the painter and the poet become all but one as Millet's France and my North and South Louisiana converge:

Self-Portrait

ca. 1840-41

Such portraits in your works are early, rare,
Just two in fact—that Cherbourg fantasy
Tailored to Ono in-laws, white shirt starched,
A black cravat, cheeks shaved like sheep well shorn

And this arch countering image, full rich beard,
High velvet collar, right eye bright, urbane
And frank, the other warier in dark,

Bohemian and peasant, sundered, one—

Yet neither does you justice, your true face
Disclosed in self-effacingness alone,
A model artist modeling on God
Your kingdom ringed by Ptolemaic stars.

And in these poems I've disappeared in you—
Or is it that you've lost yourself in me?—
Our shapes and phrases so alike composed,
Your Channel in the Gulf, my South in Normandy.

After Millet's death in 1875, Vincent Van Gogh saw, and was overwhelmed by, an exhibition of Millet's pictures and called the world of these pictures "holy ground."

Over many years, Louisiana, both North and South, had become my own "holy ground" and so by writing a book of sixty poems on Millet's pictures—a book published in 2005 by LSU Press—I had closed a great circle and, by going to Millet's France, had actually come back home.

Thank you.

BIOGRAPHICAL NOTE

Born in Shreveport, Louisiana in 1949, David Middleton earned his B.A. in English at Louisiana Tech University in 1971 followed by the M.A. (1973) and Ph.D. (1979) in English, both at Louisiana State University in Baton Rouge.

Until his retirement in June of 2010, Middleton served for thirty-three years as Professor of English, Poet-in-Residence, Distinguished Service Professor, Alcee Fortier Distinguished Professor, and Head of the Department of Languages and Literature at Nicholls State University in Thibodaux, Louisiana. He was made Professor Emeritus of English at Nicholls in January of 2011. In August of 2014, Middleton was named the first Poet in Residence Emeritus at Nicholls.

Middleton's books of verse include *The Burning Fields* (LSU Press, 1991), *As Far As Light Remains* (The Cummington Press [Harry Duncan], 1993), *Beyond the Chandeleurs* (LSU Press, 1999), *The Habitual Peacefulness of Gruchy: Poems After Pictures by Jean-François Millet* (LSU Press, 2005), *The Fiddler of Driskill Hill: Poems* (LSU Press, 2013), and *Outside the Gates of Eden* (Measure Press, 2023).

Middleton has also published several chapbooks of verse including *The Language of the Heart*, (Louisiana Literature Press, 2003), which was cited by *The Advocate* (Baton Rouge) as the best book of verse by a Louisianian for 2003. In March of 2014, *The Fiddler of Driskill Hill* won Second Honorable Mention from the Louisiana Library Association as Best Book of the Year for 2013 by a Louisianian or about Louisiana.

In April of 2006 Middleton won The Allen Tate Award for best verse published in *The Sewanee Review* in 2005. In November of 2006 Middleton received the State of Louisiana Governor's Award for Outstanding Professional Artist of 2006.

Middleton has served for over thirty years as literary executor for Alabama poet and essayist John Martin Finlay (1941-1991). Middleton was the editor, along with Dr. John P. Doucet, of a comprehensive, annotated, two-volume edition of Finlay's poetry and prose: *"Dense Poems & Socratic Light": The Poetry of John Martin Finlay (1941-1991)* and *"With Constant Light": The Collected Essays and Reviews, with Selections from the Diaries, Letters, and Other Prose of John Martin Finlay (1941-1991).* These volumes were published in the summer of 2020 by Wiseblood Books.

Middleton's verse has appeared in the *Abbeville Review, Alabama Literary Review, The Anglican, The Anglican Theological Review, Chronicles: A Magazine of American Culture, The Classical Outlook, Critical Quarterly, Europe, First Things, The Formalist, Louisiana English Journal, Louisiana Literature, The Louisiana Review, The Lyric, Measure: A Review of Formal Poetry, Modern Age, POEM, The Sewanee Review, The Sewanee Theological Review, The South Carolina Review, The Southern Review, Xavier Review,* and elsewhere, including several anthologies.

Middleton has served as poetry editor for *The Classical Outlook, The Anglican Theological Review, The Louisiana English Journal,* and *Modern Age.* Middleton was also for many years an advisory editor at *Measure: A Review of Formal Poetry.*

AUTHOR'S NOTE ON THE COLLECTED POEMS

This volume contains all of the poems—in their original order and only very lightly edited—from my four full-length collections from Louisiana State University Press, my latest full-length collection from Measure Press, and my book-length longer poem *The Dwelling Place*, published by *Alabama Literary Review*. The original acknowledgments, epigraph, and dedication pages—omitted here—can be read in the separate collections.

The section entitled "Selected New, Uncollected, and Previously Unpublished Poems (1973-2023)" contains some, but by no means all, of my mature poems (1973-2023) that appeared only in chapbooks or in journals or that were left unpublished until now simply because they did not have a place in any of my full-length collections—collections whose poems were carefully selected and placed in sequence in order to make the book, so to speak, a poem in and of itself rather than simply the sum of its individual poems. Two groups of poems in the *Outside the Gates of Eden* and the "Selected" sections—the Millet poems and the poems on The War Between the States—can be read as substantial parts of chapbook-length sequences, though neither grouping has yet been published in its entirety and separately as such.

The David Middleton Papers in the Archives of Ellender Memorial Library at Nicholls State University in Thibodaux, Louisiana contains many sorted and labeled literary documents of almost sixty years: poetry notebooks, handwritten and typescript drafts of poems, essays and book reviews (reviews both of my poems and by me as a poetry editor and scholar), letters to and from many poets and other literary figures as well as family members, Middleton-Sudduth family papers and artifacts, continually updated versions of my curriculum vitae, privately printed collections of verse, and other materials. Among these materials is my long autobiography essay on my life as a poet: "The Unsurrendered Ground: On Becoming A Poet in Louisiana" (1992, 2023).

A link to the Catalogue of *The David Middleton Papers* is as follows:
https://nichollsarchives.libraryhost.com/repositories/2/resources/138chives

Any scholar who may be interested in writing about my life and literary work will find in these papers much if not most of what would be needed to write an essay or a book or to compile a yet fuller edition of my poems or edit a book of my essays, reviews, and other prose. Some items either by me or about my life and work can also now be found online.

The best contact person—in addition to Ellender Memorial Library Archivists—is Dr. John P. Doucet, Dean of the College of Sciences and Technology at Nicholls State University. Dr. Doucet is a fellow formalist poet and has served my assistant and co-editor in several literary projects over many years.

David Middleton

ACKNOWLEDGMENTS

In addition to the section entitled Selected New, Uncollected, and Previously Unpublished Poems (1973-2023), *Time Will Tell* brings together poems from the following books and chapbooks:

Books:

The Burning Fields (LSU Press, 1991)
Beyond the Chandeleurs (LSU Press, 1999)
The Habitual Peacefulness of Gruchy: Poems After Pictures by Jean-François Millet (LSU Press, 2005)
The Fiddler of Driskill Hill (LSU Press, 2013)
The Dwelling Place (*Alabama Literary Review*, William Thompson, Editor, 2022)
Outside the Gates of Eden (Measure Press, 2023)

Chapbooks:

Reliquiae (Robert L. Barth, 1983)
Under the Linden Tree (Robert L. Barth, 1985)
As Far As Light Remains (The Cummington Press [Harry Duncan], 1993)
Bonfires on the Levee (Blue Heron Press, 1996)
The Undivided Realm (Robert L. Barth, 2000)
The Language of the Heart (Louisiana Literature Press, 2003)

Special thanks are due to Dr. John P. Doucet–poet, playwright, and Dean of the College of Sciences and Technology at Nicholls State University–for his editorial assistance in the preparation of this volume. I am also grateful to Octavia Sims for skillful and timely scanning of my poems in my previous books, chapbooks, journals, and pre-computer typescript. Thanks as well are due to Lashika Williams who edited the Indexes to this volume. And I am indebted to J. Bruce Fuller, Director of TRP, for his willingness to bring out my collected poems, an honor not all poets are fortunate enough to live to see.

INDEX OF TITLES

INDEX OF FIRST LINES

The Sabine Series in Literature

Series Editor: J. Bruce Fuller

The Sabine Series in Literature highlights work by authors born in or working in Texas and/or Louisiana. There are no thematic restrictions; TRP seeks the best writing possible by authors from this unique region of the American South.

Books in this Series:

No. 001 - Cody Smith - *Gulf*
No. 002 - David Armand - *The Lord's Acre*
No. 003 - Ron Rozelle - *Leaving the Country of Sin*
No. 004 - Collier Brown - *Scrap Bones*
No. 005 - Esteban Rodríguez - *Lotería*
No. 006 - Elizabeth Burk - *Unmoored*
No. 007 - Cliff Hudder - *Sallowsfield*
No. 008 - C. Prudence Arceneaux - *Proprioception*
No. 009 - Cody Smith - *River Hymnal*
No. 010 - David Middleton - *Time Will Tell: Collected Poems*
No. 011 - Ron Rozelle - *The Windows of Heaven* (25th Anniversary Edition)